Houghton
Mifflin
Harcourt

GO MATH!

Volume 1

© Houghton Mifflin Harcourt Publishing Company • Cover Image Credits: (Goosander) ©Erich Kuchling/ Westend61/Corbis; (Covered bridge, New Hampshire) ©eye35/Alamy Images

Made in the United States
Text printed on 100%
recycled paper

Houghton
Mifflin
Harcourt

2017 Edition

Copyright © by Houghton Mifflin Harcourt Publishing Company

Printed in the U.S.A.

ISBN 978-0-544-71056-6

10   0877   24 23 22 21 20 19 18

4500743274   D E F G

Dear Students and Families,

Welcome to **Go Math!**, Grade 2! In this exciting mathematics program, there are hands-on activities to do and real-world problems to solve. Best of all, you will write your ideas and answers right in your book. In **Go Math!**, writing and drawing on the pages helps you think deeply about what you are learning, and you will really understand math!

By the way, all of the pages in your **Go Math!** book are made using recycled paper. We wanted you to know that you can Go Green with **Go Math!**

Sincerely,

The Authors

Made in the United States
Text printed on 100% recycled paper

© Houghton Mifflin Harcourt Publishing Company • Image Credits: (bg) ©Sankar Salvady/Flickr/Getty Images; (t) ©Blaine Harrington III/Alamy Images; (c) ©Don Johnston/All Canada Photos/Getty Images; (b) ©Erich Kuching/Westend61/Corbis

GO MATH!

Authors

Juli K. Dixon, Ph.D.
Professor, Mathematics Education
University of Central Florida
Orlando, Florida

Edward B. Burger, Ph.D.
President, Southwestern University
Georgetown, Texas

Steven J. Leinwand
Principal Research Analyst
American Institutes for
   Research (AIR)
Washington, D.C.

Contributor

Rena Petrello
Professor, Mathematics
Moorpark College
Moorpark, CA

Matthew R. Larson, Ph.D.
K-12 Curriculum Specialist for
   Mathematics
Lincoln Public Schools
Lincoln, Nebraska

Martha E. Sandoval-Martinez
Math Instructor
El Camino College
Torrance, California

English Language Learners Consultant

Elizabeth Jiménez
CEO, GEMAS Consulting
Professional Expert on English
   Learner Education
Bilingual Education and
   Dual Language
Pomona, California

Big Idea

GO DIGITAL

Go online! Your math lessons are interactive. Use *iTools*, Animated Math Models, the Multimedia *eGlossary*, and more.

Chapter 1 Overview

In this chapter, you will explore and discover answers to the following **Essential Questions**:

- How do you use place value to find the values of numbers and describe numbers in different ways?
- How do you know the value of a digit?
- What are some different ways to show a number?
- How do you count by 1s, 5s, 10s, and 100s?

Personal Math Trainer
Online Assessment and Intervention

Chapter 2 Overview

In this chapter, you will explore and discover answers to the following **Essential Questions**:

- How can you use place value to model, write, and compare 3-digit numbers?
- How can you use blocks to show a 3-digit number?
- How can you write a 3-digit number in different ways?
- How can place value help you compare 3-digit numbers?

Practice and Homework

Lesson Check and Spiral Review in every lesson

2 Numbers to 1,000   71

Addition and Subtraction

Big Idea Develop fluency with addition and subtraction within 100. Solve addition and subtraction problems within 1,000.

 Vocabulary Reader | All About Animals. 151

3 Basic Facts and Relationships 159

GO DIGITAL

Go online! Your math lessons are interactive. Use *i*Tools, Animated Math Models, the Multimedia *e*Glossary, and more.

Chapter 3 Overview

In this chapter, you will explore and discover answers to the following **Essential Questions**:

• How can you use patterns and strategies to find sums and differences for basic facts?

• What are some strategies for remembering addition and subtraction facts?

• How are addition and subtraction related?

Personal Math Trainer
Online Assessment and Intervention

Chapter 4 Overview

In this chapter, you will explore and discover answers to the following **Essential Questions**:

- How do you use place value to add 2-digit numbers, and what are some different ways to add 2-digit numbers?

- How do you make an addend a ten to help solve an addition problem?

- How do you record the steps when adding 2-digit numbers?

- What are some ways to add 3 numbers or 4 numbers?

Practice and Homework

Lesson Check and Spiral Review in every lesson

4 2-Digit Addition 233

2-Digit Subtraction 313

Chapter 5 Overview

In this chapter, you will explore and discover answers to the following **Essential Questions**:

- How do you use place value to subtract 2-digit numbers with and without regrouping?
- How can you break apart numbers to help solve a subtraction problem?
- What are the steps you use when you solve 2-digit subtraction problems?
- What are some different ways to model, show, and solve subtraction problems?

3-Digit Addition and Subtraction 387

Chapter 6 Overview

In this chapter, you will explore and discover answers to the following **Essential Questions**:

- What are some strategies for adding and subtracting 3-digit numbers?
- What are the steps when finding the sum in a 3-digit addition problem?
- What are the steps when finding the difference in a 3-digit subtraction problem?
- When do you need to regroup?

Big Idea

Go online! Your math lessons are interactive. Use *i*Tools, Animated Math Models, the Multimedia *e*Glossary, and more.

Chapter 7 Overview

Essential Questions:

- How do you use the values of coins and bills to find the total value of a group of money, and how do you read times shown on analog and digital clocks?

- What are the names and values of the different coins?

- How can you tell the time on a clock by looking at the clock hands?

Chapter 8 Overview

Essential Questions:

- What are some of the methods and tools that can be used to estimate and measure length?

- What tools can be used to measure length and how do you use them?

- What units can be used to measure length and how do they compare with each other?

- How can you estimate the length of an object?

VOLUME 2

Measurement and Data

Big Idea Use standard units of measure and extend conceptual understanding of time, data, and graphs. Develop a conceptual understanding of money.

Chapter 9 Overview

In this chapter, you will explore and discover answers to the following **Essential Questions**:

• What are some of the methods and tools that can be used to estimate and measure length in metric units?

• What tools can be used to measure length in metric units and how do you use them?

• What metric units can be used to measure length and how do they compare with each other?

• If you know the length of one object, how can you estimate the length of another object?

Practice and Homework

Lesson Check and Spiral Review in every lesson

Chapter 10 Overview

In this chapter, you will explore and discover answers to the following **Essential Questions**:

• How do tally charts, picture graphs, and bar graphs help you solve problems?

• How are tally marks used to record data for a survey?

• How is a picture graph made?

• How do you know what the bars in a bar graph stand for?

Big Idea

GO DIGITAL

Go online! Your math lessons are interactive. Use *i*Tools, Animated Math Models, the Multimedia *e*Glossary, and more.

Chapter 11 Overview

In this chapter, you will explore and discover answers to the following **Essential Questions:**

- What are some two-dimensional shapes and three-dimensional shapes, and how can you show equal parts of shapes?

- How can you describe some two-dimensional and three-dimensional shapes?

- How can you describe equal parts of shapes?

Personal Math Trainer
Online Assessment and Intervention

Geometry and Fractions

Big Idea Describe, analyze, and draw two- and three-dimensional shapes. Develop a conceptual understanding of fractions.

 Vocabulary Reader

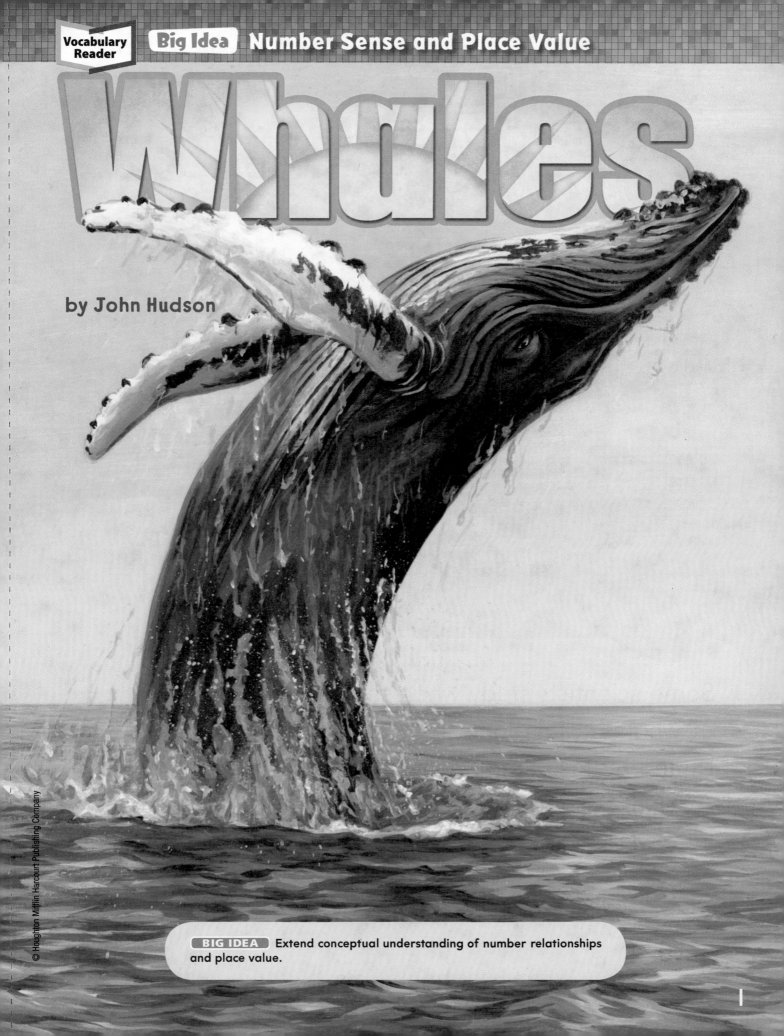

Whales

by John Hudson

BIG IDEA Extend conceptual understanding of number relationships and place value.

Some scientists study whales. Different kinds of whales swim along the west coast of the United States of America.

A scientist sees 8 blue whales.

Blue whales are the largest animals on Earth.

Social Studies

Where is the United States of America on the map?

North America

Alaska

Pacific
Ocean

Canada

Atlantic
Ocean

United States
of America

Mexico

N
W E
S

0   500   1,000 Miles
0   500   1,000 Kilometers

Map Legend
— Border

The scientist also sees 13 humpback whales.

Humpback whales sing underwater.

Did the scientist see more humpback whales or

more blue whales?   more _____ whales

Social Studies

Where is the Pacific Ocean on the map?

Whales also swim along the east coast of Canada and the United States of America. Pilot whales swim behind a leader, or a *pilot*. A scientist sees a group of 29 pilot whales.

Social Studies

Where is Canada on the map?

Pacific
Ocean

Alaska

Canada

Atlantic
Ocean

United States
of America

N

W—O—E

S

Mexico

0   500   1,000 Miles
0   500 1,000 Kilometers

Map Legend
—— Border

Fin whales are fast swimmers. They are the second-largest whales in the world. A scientist sees a group of 27 fin whales. How many tens are in the number 27?

_____ tens

Social Studies

Where is the Atlantic Ocean on the map?

Alaska

Canada

Pacific
Ocean

Atlantic
Ocean

United States
of America

N
W E
S

500   1,000 Miles
0
0   500 1,000 Kilometers

Mexico

Map Legend
—— Border

Humpback whales swim to the warm water near Mexico for the winter. Humpback whales may have as many as 35 throat grooves.

In the number 35, the _____ is in the ones place and the _____ is in the tens place.

Social Studies

Where is Mexico on the map?

Write About the Story

Look at the pictures. Draw and write your own story. Compare two numbers in your story.

Vocabulary Review

more	fewer
tens	greater than
ones	less than

WRITE ▸ Math

_____

_____

_____

_____

_____

7

The Size of Numbers

The table shows how many young whales were seen by scientists.

Young Whales Seen	
Whale	Number of Whales
Humpback	34
Blue	13
Fin	27
Pilot	43

1. Which number of whales has a 4 in the tens place?

   _____

- -

2. How many tens and ones describe the number of young blue whales seen?

   _____ ten _____ ones

- -

3. Compare the number of young humpback whales and the number of young pilot whales seen. Write > or <.

   34 ◯ **43**

- -

4. Compare the number of young fin whales and the number of young blue whales seen. Write > or <.

   27 ◯ **13**

Write a story about a scientist watching sea animals. Use some 2-digit numbers in your story.

8

Number Concepts

At a farmers' market, many different fruits and vegetables are sold.

If there are 2 groups of 10 watermelons on a table, how many watermelons are there?

Show What You Know

Personal Math Trainer
Online Assessment
and Intervention

Model Numbers to 20

Write the number that tells how many.

1.

_____

2.

_____

Use a Hundred Chart to Count

Use the hundred chart.

3. Count from 36 to 47. Which of
the numbers below will you say?
Circle them.

42   31   48   39   37

1	2	3	4	5	6	7	8	9	10
11	12	13	14	15	16	17	18	19	20
21	22	23	24	25	26	27	28	29	30
31	32	33	34	35	36	37	38	39	40
41	42	43	44	45	46	47	48	49	50
51	52	53	54	55	56	57	58	59	60
61	62	63	64	65	66	67	68	69	70
71	72	73	74	75	76	77	78	79	80
81	82	83	84	85	86	87	88	89	90
91	92	93	94	95	96	97	98	99	100

Tens

Write how many tens. Write the number.

4. _____ tens

_____

5. _____ tens

_____

This page checks understanding of important skills needed
for success in Chapter 1.

Review Words

ones
tens
count on
count back

Vocabulary Builder

Visualize It

Fill in the boxes of the graphic organizer.
Write sentences about **ones** and **tens**.

ones → There are 10 ones in 1 ten.

tens →

Understand Vocabulary

1. Start with 1. **Count on** by ones.

   1, ____, ____, ____, ____, ____

2. Start with 8. **Count back** by ones.

   8, ____, ____, ____, ____, ____

 GO DIGITAL • Interactive Student Edition • Multimedia eGlossary

Game

Three in a Row

Materials • 15 ⬤ • 15 ⬤ • ▮▮▮▮▮▮▮▮▮ ▮

Play with a partner.

1. Choose a leaf. Read the number on the leaf. Use ▮▮▮▮▮▮▮▮▮ ▮ to model the number.

2. Your partner checks your model. If your model is correct, put your ⬤ on the leaf.

3. Take turns. Try to get 3 ⬤ in a row.

4. The first player with 3 ⬤ in a row wins.

5	21	13	19	20
25	15	7	8	12
11	9	14	16	24
22	23	17	18	10

Chapter 1 Vocabulary

digit

dígito

15

doubles

dobles

19

even

par

22

is equal to (=)

es igual a

33

odd

impar

44

ones

unidades

45

plus (+)

más

49

ten

decena

61

2 + 2 = 4

0, 1, 2, 3, 4, 5, 6, 7, 8, and 9 are **digits**.

2 plus 1 is equal to 3

2 + 1 = 3

Even numbers show pairs with no left over cubes.

10 ones = 1 ten

Odd numbers show pairs with one cube left over.

10 ones = 1 ten

2 plus 1 is equal to 3

2 + 1 = 3

Going to the Farmers Market

Word Box

digit

doubles

even numbers

is equal to (=)

odd numbers

ones

plus (+)

tens

For 2 to 4 players

Materials

How to Play

1. Put your in the START circle of the same color.

2. To get your out of START, you must roll a 6.
    - If you do not roll a 6, wait until your next turn.
    - If you roll a 6, move your to the circle of that same color on the path.

3. Once you have a on the path, toss the to take a turn. Move your that many.

4. If you land on a space with a question, answer the question. If your answer is correct, move ahead 1 space.

5. To reach FINISH, you need to move your up the path of the same color as the . The first player to reach FINISH wins.

START

Which number is
equal to 12 + 7?

Which digit is in
the ones place in 19?

How can
you tell
when a
number
is even?

How can
you use
doubles
to add 4
and 5?

FINISH

How can
you tell
when a
number
is odd?

Which
digit is in
the tens
place in
45?

What sign shows
that one number is
equal to another?

START

How many ones are in 24?

Game

START

What does plus mean?

Which numbers are even? 32, 25, 15, 6

FINISH

What does + mean?

How can you tell how many ones are in a number?

Which numbers are odd? 13, 34, 22, 47

How can you tell how many tens are in a number?

How can you use doubles to add 9 and 8?

How many tens are in 37?

START

The Write Way

Reflect

Choose one idea. Write about it in the space below.

- Explain two things you know about even numbers and odd numbers.

- Write about all the different ways you can show 25.

- Tell how to count on by different amounts to 1,000.

Name _____

Algebra • Even and Odd Numbers

Essential Question How are even numbers and odd numbers different?

Learning Objective You will determine if a group of objects, up to 20, has an even or odd number of members.

Listen · Real World · Hands On

Use 🔲 to show each number.

FOR THE TEACHER • Read the following problem. Beca has 8 toy cars. Can she put her cars in pairs on a shelf? Have children set pairs of cubes vertically on the ten frames. Continue the activity for the numbers 7 and 10.

Math Talk · Math Processes and Practices ⑥

When you make pairs for 7 and for 10, how are these models different? **Explain.**

Model and Draw

Count out cubes for each number. Make pairs.
Even numbers show pairs with no cubes left over.
Odd numbers show pairs with one cube left over.

5 __odd__   8 __even__   12 _____   15 _____

Share and Show   MATH BOARD

Use cubes. Count out the number of cubes.
Make pairs. Then write **even** or **odd**.

1. 6 _____   2. 3 _____

3. 2 _____   4. 9 _____

5. 4 _____   6. 10 _____

7. 7 _____   8. 13 _____

9. 11 _____   10. 14 _____

Name _____

On Your Own

Shade in the ten frames to show the number.
Circle **even** or **odd**.

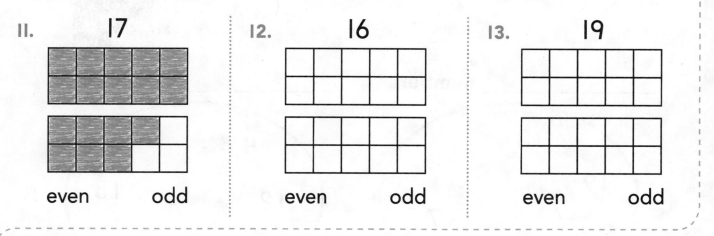

11.   17

even   odd

12.   16

even   odd

13.   19

even   odd

14. There are an even number of boys and an
odd number of girls in Lena's class. How
many boys and girls could be in her class?
Show your work.

_____

_____

_____

15. Math Processes and Practices 3 **Make Arguments**
Which two numbers in the box
are even numbers?

_____ and _____

Explain how you know that they
are even numbers.

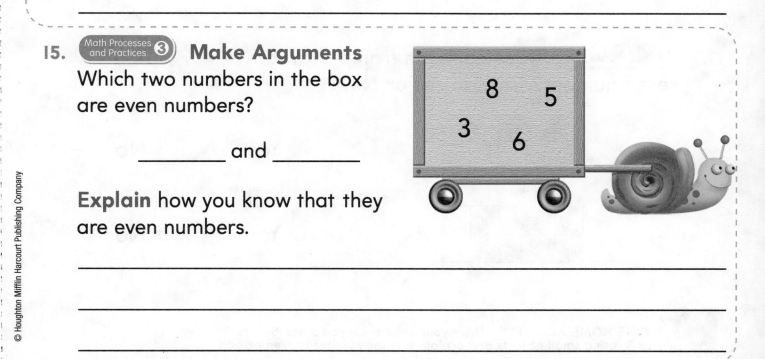

_____

_____

Problem Solving • Applications Real World   WRITE Math

16. **THINK SMARTER** Fill in the blanks to describe the groups of numbers. Write **even** or **odd**.

_____ numbers   _____ numbers

13
19
7

4
12
18

Write each of these numbers inside the correct loop.

5   6   10   11   24   25

17. **THINK SMARTER** Does each ten frame show an even number? Choose Yes or No.

○ Yes   ○ No

○ Yes   ○ No

TAKE HOME ACTIVITY • Have your child show you a number, such as 9, using small objects and explain why the number is even or odd.

Algebra • Even and Odd Numbers

Learning Objective You will determine if a group of objects, up to 20, has an even or odd number of members.

Shade in the ten frames to show the number. Circle even or odd.

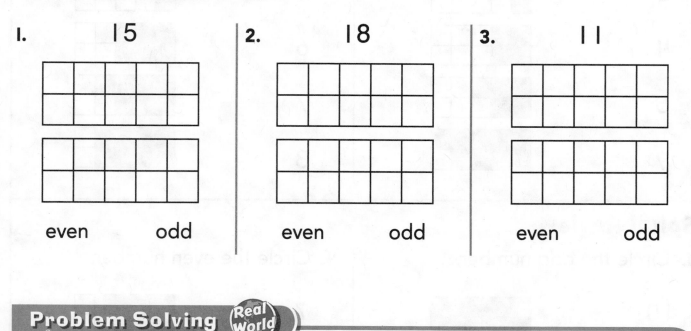

1. 15

even   odd

2. 18

even   odd

3. 11

even   odd

Problem Solving Real World

4. Mr. Dell has an odd number of sheep and an even number of cows on his farm. Circle the choice that could tell about his farm.

9 sheep and 10 cows

10 sheep and 11 cows

8 sheep and 12 cows

5. WRITE Math Write two odd numbers and two even numbers. Explain how you know which numbers are even and which are odd.

Lesson Check

1. Circle the even number.

3

4

5

9

2. Circle the odd number.

2

6

7

8

Spiral Review

3. Circle the odd number.

10

8

3

4

4. Circle the even number.

7

6

5

1

5. Circle the even number.

9

7

5

2

6. Circle the odd number.

1

4

8

10

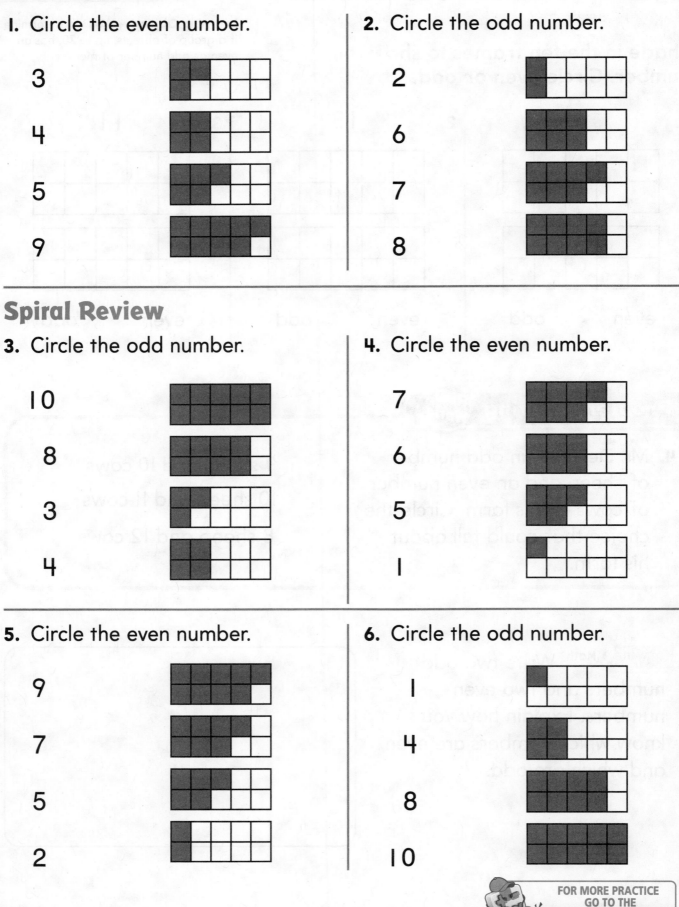

FOR MORE PRACTICE
GO TO THE
Personal Math Trainer

Name _____

Algebra • Represent Even Numbers

Essential Question Why can an even number be shown as the sum of two equal addends?

Learning Objective You will show an even number as the sum of two equal numbers.

Listen and Draw

Make pairs with your cubes. Draw to show the cubes. Then write the numbers you say as you count to find the number of cubes.

_____   _____ cubes

Math Talk Math Processes and Practices ②

Use Reasoning
Explain how you know if a number modeled with cubes is an even number.

FOR THE TEACHER • Give each small group of children a set of 10 to 15 connecting cubes. After children group their cubes into pairs, have them draw a picture of their cubes and write their counting sequence for finding the total number of cubes.

Model and Draw

An even number of cubes can be shown as two equal groups.

You can match each cube in the first group with a cube in the second group.

$$6 = 3 + 3$$

$$10 = 5 + 5$$

Share and Show MATH BOARD

How many cubes are there in all? Complete the addition sentence to show the equal groups.

1. $\underline{4} = \underline{2} + \underline{2}$

2. $\underline{8} = \underline{4} + \underline{4}$

3. $\underline{12} = \underline{8} + \underline{8}$

4. $\underline{14} = \underline{7} + \underline{2}$

On Your Own

Shade in the frames to show two equal groups for each number. Complete the addition sentence to show the groups.

5. 10

$10 = 5 + 5$

6. 16

$10 = 0 + 0$

7. Elena and José have 18 postcards together. They each have the same number of postcards. How many postcards do Elena and José each have?

_____ postcards

THINK SMARTER The number 7 is an odd number. Marc showed 7 with this addition sentence. Use Marc's way to show these odd numbers with addition sentences.

$7 = 3 + 3 + 1$

8. $5 = \underline{} + \underline{} + \underline{}$

9. $11 = \underline{} + \underline{} + \underline{}$

10. $9 = \underline{} + \underline{} + \underline{}$

11. $13 = \underline{} + \underline{} + \underline{}$

Problem Solving • Applications

WRITE Math

Solve. Write or draw to explain.

12. **Math Processes and Practices ②** **Use Reasoning**
Jacob and Lucas each have
the same number of shells.
Together they have 16 shells.
How many shells do
Jacob and Lucas each have?

Jacob: _____ shells

Lucas: _____ shells

Personal Math Trainer

13. **THINK SMARTER +** Choose an even number between
10 and 19. Draw a picture and then write
a sentence to explain why it is an even number.

_____

_____

_____

TAKE HOME ACTIVITY • Have your child explain what he or
she learned in this lesson.

Understand Place Value

Essential Question How do you know the value of a digit?

Learning Objective You will use place value to describe the values of digits in 2-digit numbers.

Listen and Draw

Write the numbers. Then choose a way to show the numbers.

Tens	Ones

Tens	Ones

FOR THE TEACHER • Read the following problem. Have children write the numbers and describe how they chose to represent them. Gabriel collects baseball cards. The number of cards that he has is written with a 2 and a 5. How many cards might he have?

Math Talk Math Processes and Practices ⑥

Explain why the value of 5 is different in the two numbers.

Model and Draw

0, 1, 2, 3, 4, 5, 6, 7, 8, and 9 are **digits**.
In a 2-digit number, you know the value of
a digit by its place.

64

Tens	Ones
6	4

6 tens   4 ones

The digit 6 is in
the tens place. It
tells you there are
6 tens, or 60.

The digit 4 is in
the ones place. It
tells you there are
4 ones, or 4.

Share and Show   MATH BOARD

Circle the value of the red digit.

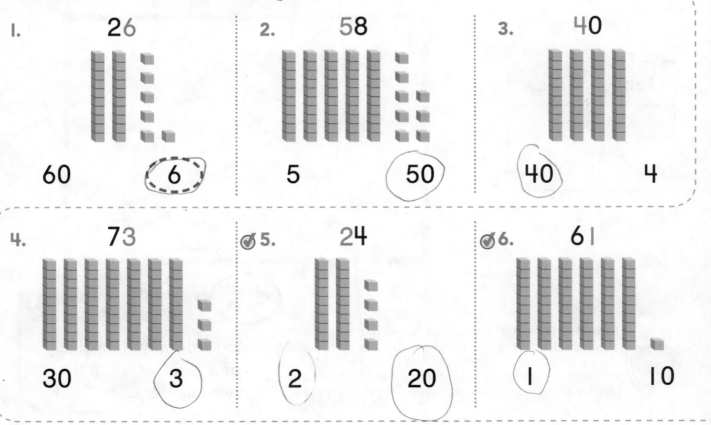

1. 26
60   (6)

2. 58
5   (50)

3. 40
(40)   4

4. 73
30   (3)

5. 24
(2)   (20)

6. 61
(1)   10

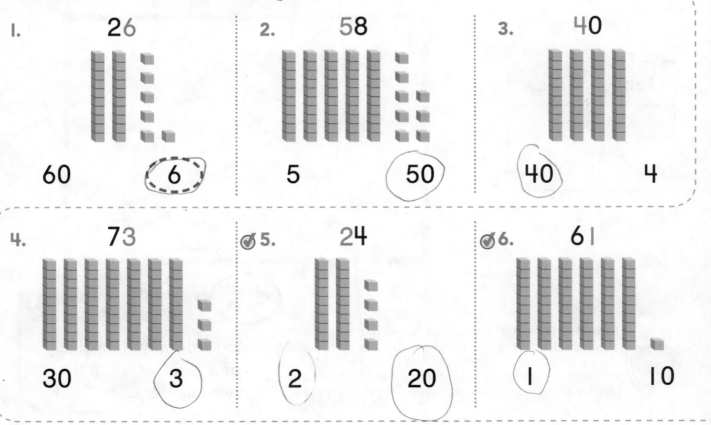

26 twenty-six

© Houghton Mifflin Harcourt Publishing Company

Name _____

On Your Own

Circle the value of the red digit.

7. **5**1

(1)   10

8. **4**9

90   (9)

9. **7**0

(7)   70

10. Phillip bought a puzzle. The number of puzzle pieces has the digit 6 in the ones place and the digit 3 in the tens place. How many puzzle pieces are in Phillip's puzzle?

_____ puzzle pieces

11. Noah baked apple pies. The number of apples he used has the digit 1 in the tens place and an even number less than 5 in the ones place. How many apples could Noah have used to bake apple pies?

_____ apples

12. **THINK SMARTER** Look at the digits of the numbers. Draw quick pictures for the missing blocks.

47

52

Problem Solving • Applications Real World WRITE Math

Write the 2-digit number that matches the clues.

13. My number has 8 tens.

The digit in the ones place is greater than the digit in the tens place.

My number is _____.

14. In my number, the digit in the ones place is double the digit in the tens place.

The sum of the digits is 3.

My number is _____.

15. Math Processes and Practices ❶ **Make Sense of Problems**

In my number, both digits are even numbers.

The digit in the tens place is less than the digit in the ones place.

The sum of the digits is 6.

My number is _____.

16. THINK SMARTER What is the value of the digit 4 in the number 43?

TAKE HOME ACTIVITY • Write the number 56. Have your child tell you which digit is in the tens place, which digit is in the ones place, and the value of each digit.

Name _____

Expanded Form

Essential Question How do you describe a
2-digit number as tens and ones?

Use ▭▭▭▭▭ ▪ or *i*Tools to model each number.

Tens	Ones

Math Talk Math Processes and Practices 6

Explain how you
know how many tens
and ones are in the
number 29.

FOR THE TEACHER • After you read the following
problem, write 38 on the board. Have children
model the number. Emmanuel put 38 stickers on
his paper. How can you model 38 with blocks?
Continue the activity for 83 and 77.

What does 23 mean?

Tens	Ones

The 2 in 23 has a value of 2 tens, or 20.
The 3 in 23 has a value of 3 ones, or 3.

___2___ tens ___3___ ones

___20___ + ___3___

Share and Show MATH BOARD

Draw a quick picture to show the number.
Describe the number in two ways.

1. 37

___3___ tens ___7___ ones

___30___ + ___7___

2. 54

___5___ tens ___4___ ones

___50___ + ___4___

3. 16

___1___ ten ___6___ ones

___10___ + ___6___

4. 60

___6___ tens ___0___ ones

___60___ + ___0___

Name _____

Draw a quick picture to show the number.
Describe the number in two ways.

5. 48

___4___ tens _____ ones

___40___ + ___8___

6. 31

___3___ tens ___1___ one

___30___ + ___1___

7. Riley has some toy dinosaurs.
The number she has is one
less than 50. Describe the
number of toy dinosaurs
in two ways.

_____

_____

Solve. Write or draw to explain.

8. **THINK SMARTER** Eric has 4 bags
of 10 marbles and 6 single
marbles. How many marbles
does Eric have?

_____ marbles

Problem Solving • Applications WRITE Math

Math Processes and Practices 6 Make Connections

Use crayons. Follow the steps.

9. Start at 51 and draw a green line to 43.

10. Draw a blue line from 43 to 34.

11. Draw a red line from 34 to 29.

12. Then draw a yellow line from 29 to 72.

1 ten 5 ones	30 + 2
4 tens 3 ones	20 + 9
10 + 2	3 tens 4 ones
	5 tens 1 one
70 + 2	7 + 2

13. **THINK SMARTER** Draw a picture to show the number 26. Describe the number 26 in two ways.

_____ tens _____ ones

_____ + _____

TAKE HOME ACTIVITY • Ask your child to write 89 as tens plus ones. Then have him or her write 25 as tens plus ones.

Name _____

Different Ways to Write Numbers

Essential Question What are different ways to write a 2-digit number?

Learning Objective You will write 2-digit numbers using words, as tens and ones, as a 2-digit number, and as the sum of the values of the tens and ones digits.

Listen and Draw — Real World

Write the number.
Then write it as tens and ones.

_5_ tens _4_ ones

_30_ + _7_

_10_ + _2_

_2_ tens _9_ ones

FOR THE TEACHER • Read the following problem. Taryn counted 53 books on the table. How many tens and ones are in 53? Continue the activity with the numbers 78, 35, and 40.

Math Talk
Math Processes and Practices ①

Analyze In 44, do both digits have the same value? Explain.

Chapter 1

Model and Draw

A number can be written in different ways.

fifty-nine

5 tens 9 ones

50 + 9

59

ones	teen words	tens
0 zero	11 eleven	10 ten
1 one	12 twelve	20 twenty
2 two	13 thirteen	30 thirty
3 three	14 fourteen	40 forty
4 four	15 fifteen	50 fifty
5 five	16 sixteen	60 sixty
6 six	17 seventeen	70 seventy
7 seven	18 eighteen	80 eighty
8 eight	19 nineteen	90 ninety
9 nine		

Share and Show MATH BOARD

Look at the examples above.
Then write the number another way.

1. thirty-two

    32

2. 20 + 7

    27

3. 63

    6 tens 3 ones

4. ninety-five

    90 + 5

5. 5 tens 1 one

    61

6. seventy-six

    70 + 6

7. twenty-eight

    2 tens 8 ones

8. 8 tens 0 ones

    80

Name _____

Write the number another way.

9. 2 tens 4 ones

$\underline{\qquad 2\quad 4 \qquad}$

10. thirty

$\underline{\quad 3 \quad}$ tens $\underline{\quad 0 \quad}$ ones

11. eighty-five

$\underline{\qquad 8\quad 5 \qquad}$

12. 54

$\underline{\quad 50 \quad} + \underline{\qquad}$

13. Lee has a favorite number. The number has the digit 3 in the ones place and the digit 9 in the tens place. What is another way to write this number?

_____

14. Dan's number has a digit greater than 5 in the ones place and a digit less than 5 in the tens place. What could be Dan's number?

_____

THINK SMARTER Fill in the blanks to make the sentence true.

15. Sixty-seven is the same as _____ tens _____ ones.

16. 4 tens _____ ones is the same as _____ + _____.

17. 20 + _____ is the same as _____.

© Houghton Mifflin Harcourt Publishing Company

TAKE HOME ACTIVITY • Write 20 + 6 on a sheet of paper. Have your child write the 2-digit number. Repeat for 4 tens 9 ones.

Name _____

Personal Math Trainer
Online Assessment
and Intervention

Concepts and Skills

Shade in the ten frames to show the number.
Circle **even** or **odd**.

1. 15

even   odd

2. 18

even   odd

Draw a quick picture to show the number.
Describe the number in two ways.

3. 35

_____ tens _____ ones

_____ + _____

4. 53

_____ tens _____ ones

_____ + _____

5. **THINK SMARTER** Write the number 42 in another way.

_____

PRACTICE
THE
th Trainer

Name _____

Algebra • Different Names for Numbers

Learning Objective You will show the value of a 2-digit number in different ways.

Essential Question How can you show the value of a number in different ways?

Listen and Draw Real World   Hands On

Use to show the number different ways. Record the tens and ones.

_____ tens _____ ones

_____ tens _____ ones

_____ tens _____ ones

Math Talk   Math Processes and Practices ①

Describe how you can use addition to write the number 26.

FOR THE TEACHER • Read the following problem. Syed has 26 rocks. What are some different ways to show 26 with blocks? Have children start with 26 ones blocks. Then have them use base-ten blocks and record the number of tens and ones in each of their models.

© Houghton Mifflin Harcourt Publishing Company

Chapter 1

These are some different ways to show 32.

__3__ tens __2__ ones

__30__ + __2__

__2__ tens __12__ ones

__20__ + __12__

__1__ ten __22__ ones

__10__ + __22__

Share and Show   MATH BOARD

The blocks show the numbers in different ways.
Describe the blocks in two ways.

1. 28

__2__ tens __8__ ones

__20__ + __8__

__1__ ten __18__ ones

__10__ + __18__

__0__ tens __28__ ones

__0__ + __28__

2. 35

__3__ tens __5__ ones

__30__ + __5__

__2__ tens __15__ ones

__20__ + __15__

__0__ tens __35__ ones

__0__ + __35__

Name _____

On Your Own

The blocks show the numbers in different ways.
Describe the blocks in two ways.

3. 43

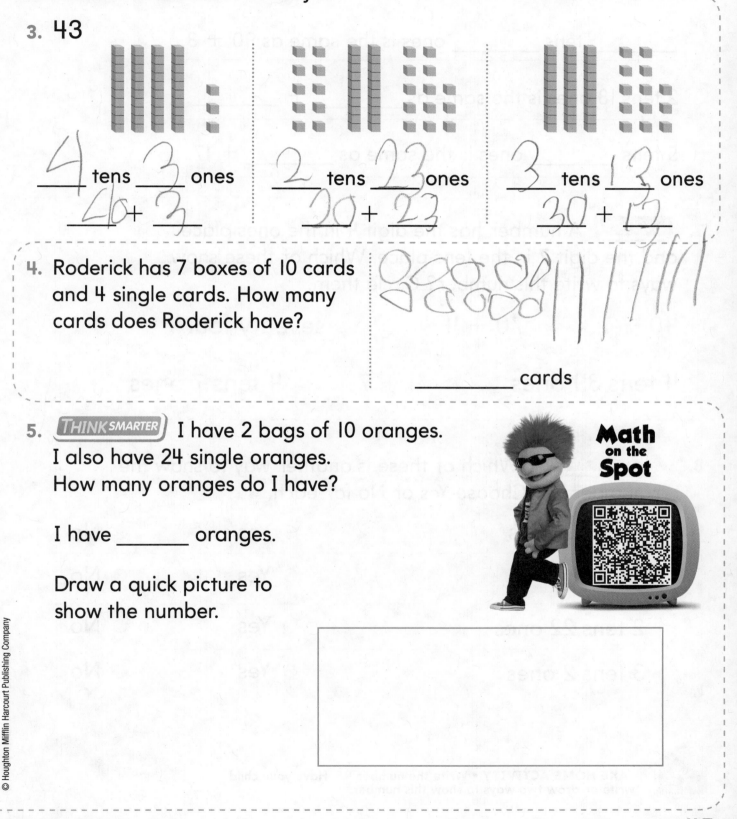

__4__ tens __3__ ones

__40__ + __3__

__2__ tens __23__ ones

__20__ + __23__

__3__ tens __13__ ones

__30__ + __13__

4. Roderick has 7 boxes of 10 cards and 4 single cards. How many cards does Roderick have?

_____ cards

5. **THINK SMARTER** I have 2 bags of 10 oranges. I also have 24 single oranges. How many oranges do I have?

I have _____ oranges.

Draw a quick picture to show the number.

Math on the Spot

© Houghton Mifflin Harcourt Publishing Company

Chapter 1 • Lesson 6

forty-five **45**

Problem Solving • Applications (Real World) WRITE Math

6. (Math Processes and Practices 6) **Make Connections** Fill in the blanks to make each sentence true.

_____ tens _____ ones is the same as 90 + 3.

2 tens 18 ones is the same as _____ + _____.

5 tens _____ ones is the same as _____ + 17.

7. GO DEEPER A number has the digit 4 in the ones place and the digit 7 in the tens place. Which of these show ways to write this number? Circle them.

40 + 7   70 + 4   seventy-four

4 tens 34 ones   4 + 7   4 tens 7 ones

8. THINK SMARTER Which of these is another way to show the number 42? Choose Yes or No for each.

1 ten 42 ones	○ Yes	○ No
30 + 12	○ Yes	○ No
2 tens 22 ones	○ Yes	○ No
3 tens 2 ones	○ Yes	○ No

TAKE HOME ACTIVITY • Write the number 45. Have your child write or draw two ways to show this number.

Name _____

Problem Solving • Tens and Ones

Essential Question How does finding a pattern help you find all the ways to show a number with tens and ones?

Learning Objective You will use the strategy *find a pattern* by making a list to find all the ways to show a number with tens and ones.

Gail needs to buy 32 pencils. She can buy single pencils or boxes of 10 pencils. What are all of the different ways Gail can buy 32 pencils?

Unlock the Problem (Real World)

What do I need to find?

ways Gail can buy
32 pencils

What information do I need to use?

She can buy ___single___ pencils

or ___boxes of 10___ pencils.

Show how to solve the problem.
Draw quick pictures for 32. Complete the chart.

Boxes of 10 pencils	Single pencils
3	2
2	12
1	
0	

HOME CONNECTION • Your child found a pattern in the different combinations of tens and ones. Using a pattern helps to make an organized list.

Chapter 1

Try Another Problem

Find a pattern to solve.

- What do I need to find?
- What information do I need to use?

1. Sara has 36 crayons. She can pack them in boxes of 10 crayons or as single crayons. What are all of the ways Sara can pack the crayons?

Boxes of 10 crayons	Single crayons
3	6

2. Mr. Winter is putting away 48 chairs. He can put away the chairs in stacks of 10 or as single chairs. What are all of the ways Mr. Winter can put away the chairs?

Stacks of 10 chairs	Single chairs
4	8

Math Talk · Math Processes and Practices 7

Look for Structure Describe a pattern you can use to write the number 32.

Share and Show

Find a pattern to solve.

✔ 3. Philip is putting 25 markers into a bag. He can put the markers in the bag as bundles of 10 or as single markers. What are all of the ways Philip can put the markers in the bag?

Bundles of 10 markers	Single markers

✔ 4. Stickers are sold in packs of 10 stickers or as single stickers. Miss Allen wants to buy 33 stickers. What are all of the ways she can buy the stickers?

Packs of 10 stickers	Single stickers

5. **THINK SMARTER** Devin had 32 baseball cards. He gets 7 more cards. He can pack them in boxes of 10 cards or as single cards. What are all of the ways Devin can sort the cards?

Boxes of 10 cards	Single cards

On Your Own

Solve. Write or draw to explain.

6. (Math Processes and Practices **7**) **Look for Structure**

   Lee can pack her toy cars in boxes of 10 cars
   or as single cars. Which of these is a way that
   she can pack her 24 toy cars? Circle your answer.

4 boxes of 10 cars and 2 single cars	1 box of 10 cars and 24 single cars	2 boxes of 10 cars and 4 single cars

Personal Math Trainer

7. **THINK SMARTER +**   Mr. Link needs
   30 cups. He can buy them in
   packs of 10 cups or as single cups.
   What are all of the different
   ways he can buy the cups?
   Find a pattern to solve.

   Choose two of the ways
   from the chart. Explain how
   these two ways show the
   same number of cups.

Packs of 10 cups	Single cups

TAKE HOME ACTIVITY • Have your child explain how
he or she solved one of the exercises in this lesson.

Problem Solving • Tens and Ones

Learning Objective You will use the strategy *find a pattern* by making a list to find all the ways to show a number with tens and ones.

Find a pattern to solve.

1. Ann is grouping 38 rocks. She can put them into groups of 10 rocks or as single rocks. What are the different ways Ann can group the rocks?

Groups of 10 rocks	Single rocks

2. Mr. Grant needs 30 pieces of felt. He can buy them in packs of 10 or as single pieces. What are the different ways Mr. Grant can buy the felt?

Packs of 10 pieces	Single pieces

3. WRITE Math Choose one of the problems above. Describe how you organized the answers.

_____

_____

_____

_____

_____

_____

Lesson Check

1. Mrs. Chang is packing 38 apples. She can pack them in bags of 10 or as single apples. Complete the table to show another way Mrs. Chang can pack the apples.

Bags of 10 apples	Single apples
2	18
1	28
0	38

Spiral Review

2. What is the value of the underlined digit? Write the number.

   5_4_

   _____

3. What number is shown with the blocks? Write the number.

   2 tens 19 ones

   _____

4. Write the number 62 in words.

   _____

5. What number can be written as 8 tens and 6 ones? Write the number.

   _____

FOR MORE PRACTICE
GO TO THE
Personal Math Trainer

Counting Patterns Within 100

Essential Question How do you count by 1s, 5s, and 10s with numbers less than 100?

Learning Objective You will count by 1s, 5s, and 10s with numbers up to at least 100.

Listen and Draw

Look at the hundred chart. Write the missing numbers.

1	2	3	4	5	6	7	8	9	10
11	12	13	14	15	16	17	18	19	20
21	22	23	24	25	26	27	28	29	30
31	32	33	34	35	36	37	38	39	40
41	42	43	44	45	46	47	48	49	50
51	52	53	54	55	56	57	58	59	60
61	62	63	64	65	66	67	68	69	70
71	72	73	74	75	76	77	78	79	80
81	82	83	84	85	86	87	88	89	90
91	92	93	94	95	96	97	98	99	100

Math Talk

Math Processes and Practices ①

Describe some different ways to find the missing numbers in the chart.

FOR THE TEACHER • Have children complete the hundred chart to review counting to 100.

Model and Draw

You can count on by different amounts.
You can start counting with different numbers.

Count by ones.

1, 2, 3, 4, __5__, __6__, __7__, __8__

29, 30, 31, 32, __33__, __34__, __35__, __36__

Count by fives.

5, 10, 15, 20, __25__, __30__, __35__, __40__

50, 55, 60, 65, __70__, __75__, __80__, __85__

Share and Show MATH BOARD

Count by ones.

1. 15, 16, 17, __18__, __19__, __20__, __21__, __22__

Count by fives.

2. 15, 20, 25, __30__, __35__, __40__, __45__, __50__

3. 60, 65, __70__, __75__, __80__, __85__, __90__

Count by tens.

4. 10, 20, __30__, __40__, __50__, __60__, __70__

5. 30, 40, __50__, __60__, __70__, __80__, __90__

Name _____

Count by ones.

6. 77, 78, __79__, __80__, __81__, __82__, __83__

Count by fives.

7. 35, 40, __45__, __50__, __55__, __60__, __65__

Count by tens.

8. 20, 30, __40__, __50__, __60__, __70__, __80__

9. Amber counts by fives to 50.
   How many numbers will she say?

   __55__ numbers

10. THINK SMARTER Dinesh counts by fives to 100.
    Gwen counts by tens to 100.
    Who will say more numbers? Explain.

    _____

    _____

    _____

    _____

    _____

Problem Solving • Applications WRITE Math

Math Processes and Practices ❶ Analyze

11. Andy counts by ones. He starts at 29 and stops at 45. Which of these numbers will he say? Circle them.

31   20
  47   35
40   (46)   39

12. Camila counts by fives. She starts at 5 and stops at 50. Which of these numbers will she say? Circle them.

55   25
        6   40
            18
10   45

13. **THINK SMARTER** Grace starts at the number 40 and counts three different ways. Write to show how Grace counts.

Count by ones. 40, _____, _____, _____, _____, _____, _____

Count by fives. 40, _____, _____, _____, _____, _____, _____

Count by tens. 40, _____, _____, _____, _____, _____, _____

 TAKE HOME ACTIVITY • With your child, practice counting by ones to 100, starting with numbers such as 58 or 62.

Counting Patterns Within 1,000

Essential Question How do you count by 1s, 5s, 10s, and 100s with numbers less than 1,000?

Learning Objective You will count by 1s, 5s, 10s, and 100s with numbers up to at least 1,000.

Listen and Draw

Write the missing numbers in the chart.

401		403	404		406	407	408		410
411				415	416	417	418	419	
421	422	423	424	425		427	428	429	430
	432		434	435	436	437	438		
441	442	443	444		446	447		449	450
		454	455	456	457	458	459	460	
461	462						468	469	470
	472	473	474	475	476	477		479	480
481	482		484	485	486				490
	492	493		495	496	497	498		

Math Talk Math Processes and Practices 7

Look for Structure
What counting patterns could you use to complete the chart?

FOR THE TEACHER • Have children complete the number chart to practice counting with 3-digit numbers.

Model and Draw

Counting can be done in different ways.
Use patterns to count on.

Count by fives.

95, 100, 105, __110__, __115__, _____, _____

140, 145, 150, __155__, _____, _____, _____

Count by tens.

300, 310, 320, _____, _____, _____, _____

470, 480, 490, _____, _____, _____, _____

Share and Show MATH BOARD

Count by fives.

1. 745, 750, 755, _____, _____, _____, _____

Count by tens.

2. 520, 530, 540, _____, _____, _____, _____

3. 600, 610, _____, _____, _____, _____

Count by hundreds.

4. 100, 200, _____, _____, _____, _____, _____

5. 300, 400, _____, _____, _____, _____, _____

On Your Own

Count by fives.

6. 215, 220, 225, _____, _____, _____, _____

7. 905, 910, _____, _____, _____, _____

Count by tens.

8. 730, 740, 750, _____, _____, _____, _____

9. 160, 170, _____, _____, _____, _____, _____

Count by hundreds.

10. 200, 300, _____, _____, _____, _____, _____

11. **THINK SMARTER** Martin starts at 300 and counts by fives to 420. What are the last 6 numbers Martin will say?

_____, _____, _____, _____, _____, _____

12. The book fair has 390 books. They have 5 more boxes with 10 books in each box. Count by tens. How many books are at the book fair.

_____ books

Problem Solving • Applications (Real World) WRITE Math

Math Processes and Practices 7 Look for a Pattern

13. Lisa counts by fives. She starts at 120 and stops at 175. Which of these numbers will she say? Circle them.

170   151   135

155   200   180

14. George counts by tens. He starts at 750 and stops at 830. Which of these numbers will he say? Circle them.

755   690   780

760   795   810

15. THINK SMARTER Carl counts by hundreds. Which of these show ways that Carl could count? Choose Yes or No for each.

100, 110, 120, 130, 140	○ Yes	○ No
100, 200, 300, 400, 500	○ Yes	○ No
500, 600, 700, 800, 900	○ Yes	○ No
300, 305, 310, 315, 320	○ Yes	○ No

 TAKE HOME ACTIVITY • With your child, count by fives from 150 to 200.

Counting Patterns Within 1,000

Learning Objective You will count by 1s, 5s, 10s, and 100s with numbers up to at least 1,000.

Count by fives.

1. 415, 420, _____, _____, _____, _____

2. 675, 680, _____, _____, _____, _____

Count by tens.

3. 210, 220, _____, _____, _____, _____

Count by hundreds.

4. 300, 400, _____, _____, _____, _____

Count back by ones.

5. 953, 952, _____, _____, _____, _____

Problem Solving Real World

6. Lee has a jar of 100 pennies.
   She adds groups of 10 pennies to the jar.
   She adds 5 groups. What numbers does she say?

   _____, _____, _____, _____, _____

7. **WRITE** Math Count by fives
   from 135 to 175. Write these
   numbers and describe the
   pattern.

   _____

   _____

Lesson Check

1. Count by tens.

160, ____, ____, ____, ____

2. Count by hundreds.

400, ____, ____, ____, ____

Spiral Review

3. Count by fives.

245, ____, ____, ____, ____

4. Count back by ones.

71, ____, ____, ____, ____

5. Describe 45 in another way.

____ tens ____ ones

6. Describe 7 tens 9 ones in another way.

_____

FOR MORE PRACTICE
GO TO THE
Personal Math Trainer

Name _____

1. Does the ten frame show an even number? Choose Yes or No.

   ○ Yes   ○ No

   ○ Yes   ○ No

2. Write an even number between 7 and 16. Draw a picture and then write a sentence to explain why it is an even number.

   _____

   _____

3. What is the value of the digit 5 in the number 75?

   _____

4. **GO DEEPER** Ted has an even number of yellow markers and an odd number of green markers. Choose all the groups of markers that could belong to Ted.

   ○ 8 yellow markers and 3 green markers

   ○ 3 yellow markers and 6 green markers

   ○ 4 yellow markers and 2 green markers

   ○ 6 yellow markers and 7 green markers

5. Jeff starts at 190 and counts by tens. What are the next 6 numbers Jeff will say?

   190, _____, _____, _____, _____, _____, _____

6. Megan counts by ones to 10. Lee counts by fives to 20. Who will say more numbers? Explain.

   _____

   _____

   _____

© Houghton Mifflin Harcourt Publishing Company

7. Draw a picture to show the number 43.

Describe the number 43 in two ways.

| 4 3 | tens | 4 3 | ones |

_____ + _____

---

8. Jo lives on Maple Road.
Her address has the digit 2 in
the ones place and the digit
4 in the tens place. What is
Jo's address?

_____ Maple Road

---

9. Do the numbers show counting by fives?
Choose Yes or No.

76, 77, 78, 79, 80	○ Yes	○ No
20, 30, 40, 50, 60	○ Yes	○ No
70, 75, 80, 85, 90	○ Yes	○ No
35, 40, 45, 50, 55	○ Yes	○ No

10. **THINK SMARTER +** Mrs. Payne needs 35 notepads. She can buy them in packs of 10 notepads or as single pads. What are all the different ways Mrs. Payne can buy the notepads? Find a pattern to solve.

Packs of 10 notepads	Single notepads

Choose two of the ways from the chart. Explain how these two ways show the same number of notepads.

11. Ann has a favorite number. It has a digit less than 4 in the tens place. It has a digit greater than 6 in the ones place. Could the number be Ann's number? Choose Yes or No.

30 + 9   ○ Yes   ○ No

sixty-seven   ○ Yes   ○ No

2 tens 8 ones   ○ Yes   ○ No

Write another number that could be Ann's favorite. _____

© Houghton Mifflin Harcourt Publishing Company

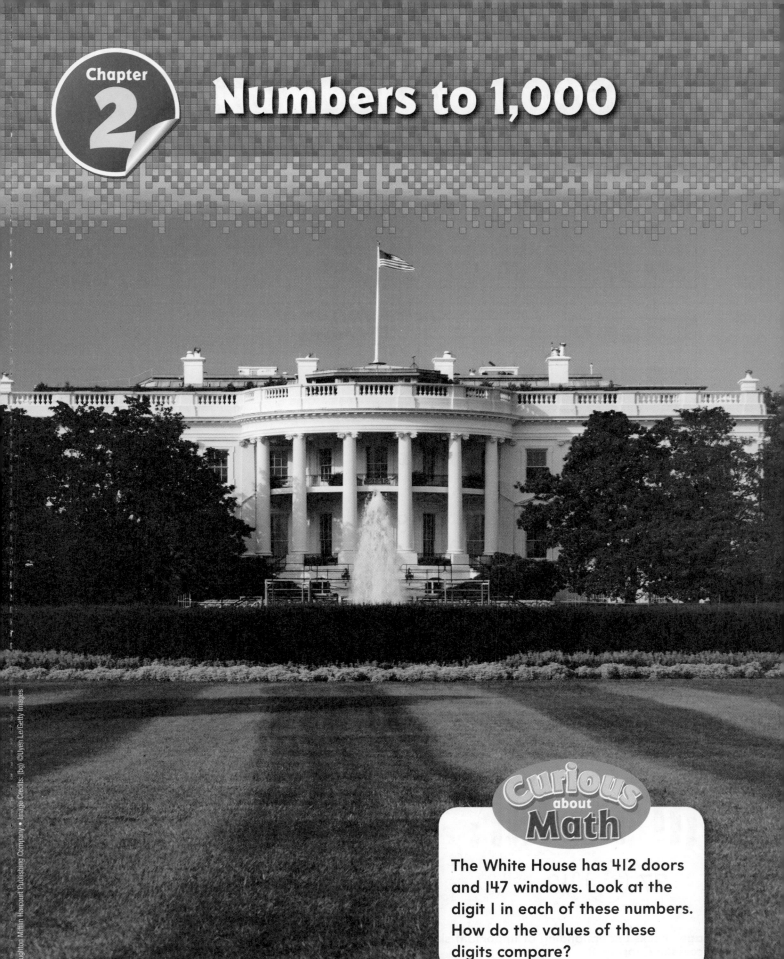

Numbers to 1,000

Curious about Math

The White House has 412 doors and 147 windows. Look at the digit 1 in each of these numbers. How do the values of these digits compare?

© Houghton Mifflin Harcourt Publishing Company • Image Credits: (bg) ©Uyen Le/Getty Images

✓ **Show What You Know**

Personal Math Trainer
Online Assessment
and Intervention

Identify Numbers to 30

Write how many.

1. _____ leaves

2. _____ bugs

Place Value: 2-Digit Numbers

Circle the value of the red digit.

3. 47   40   4

4. 84   4   40

5. 65   6   60

Compare 2-Digit Numbers Using Symbols

Compare. Write >, <, or =.

6. 37 ◯ 42

7. 40 ◯ 33

This page checks understanding of important skills needed for success in Chapter 2.

Vocabulary Builder

Review Words

more
fewer
digits
tens
ones

Visualize It

Fill in the boxes of the graphic organizer.
Write sentences using **fewer** and **more**.

fewer → 9 pens is fewer than 11 pens.

→ [ ]

more → [ ]

→ [ ]

Understand Vocabulary

Use the review words. Complete the sentences.

1. 3 and 9 are _____ in the number 39.

2. 7 is in the _____ place in the number 87.

3. 8 is in the _____ place in the number 87.

GO DIGITAL
• Interactive Student Edition
• Multimedia eGlossary

Game Fish for Digits

Materials

- 12
- 12 ⚪
- 1 🎲

Play with a partner.

1. Name a place for a digit. You can say **tens place** or **ones place**. Toss the 🎲.

2. Match the number on the 🎲 and the place that you named with a fish.

3. Put a ⚫ on that fish. Take turns.

4. Match all the fish. The player with more ⚫ on the board wins.

14

56

12

23

46

25

32

53

65

61

41

34

compare

comparar

8

digit

dígito

15

hundred

centena

31

is equal to (=)

es igual a

33

is greater than (>)

es mayor que (>)

34

is less than (<)

es menor que (<)

35

ten

decena

61

thousand

millar

64

0, 1, 2, 3, 4, 5, 6, 7, 8, and 9 are **digits**.

Use these symbols when you **compare**: >, <, =.

241 > 234

123 < 128

247 = 247

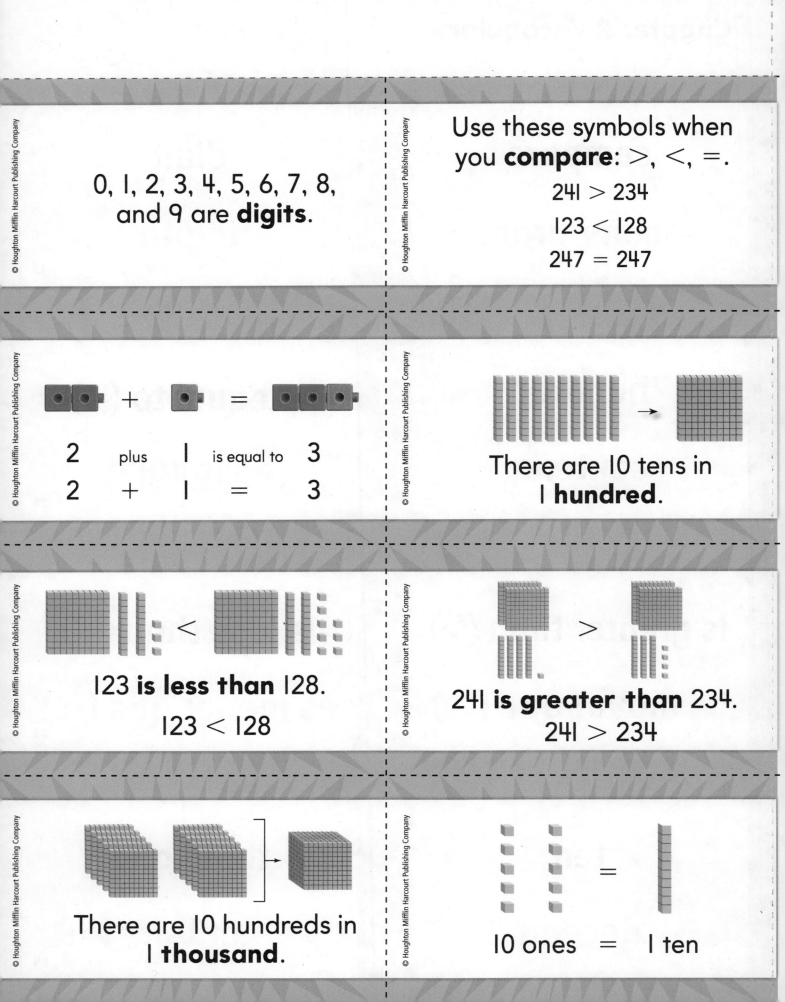

2   plus   1   is equal to   3

2   +   1   =   3

There are 10 tens in 1 **hundred**.

123 **is less than** 128.

123 < 128

241 **is greater than** 234.

241 > 234

There are 10 hundreds in 1 **thousand**.

10 ones   =   1 ten

Guess the Word

For 3 to 4 players

Materials
- timer

How to Play
1. Take turns to play.
2. Choose a math word, but do not say it aloud.
3. Set the timer for 1 minute.
4. Give a one-word clue about your word. Give each player one chance to guess your word.
5. If nobody guesses correctly, repeat Step 4 with a different clue. Repeat until a player guesses the word or time runs out.
6. The first player to guess the word gets 1 point. If the player can use the word in a sentence, he or she gets 1 more point. Then that player gets a turn.
7. The first player to score 5 points wins.

Word Box
compare
digit
hundred
is equal to (=)
is greater than (>)
is less than (<)
ten
thousand

The Write Way

Reflect

Choose one idea. Write about it in the space below.

- Draw and write about all the different ways you can show the number 482. Use a separate piece of paper for your drawing.
- Explain how to compare two numbers.
- Write sentences that include at least two of these terms.

digit   is equal to   hundred   thousand

Group Tens as Hundreds

Essential Question How do you group tens as hundreds?

Learning Objective You will group 10 tens as a hundred.

Listen and Draw

Circle groups of ten. Count the groups of ten.

 FOR THE TEACHER • Read the following problem and have children group ones blocks to solve. Marco has 100 cards. How many groups of 10 cards can he make?

Math Talk Math Processes and Practices ⑥

Describe How many ones are in 3 tens? How many ones are in 7 tens? Explain.

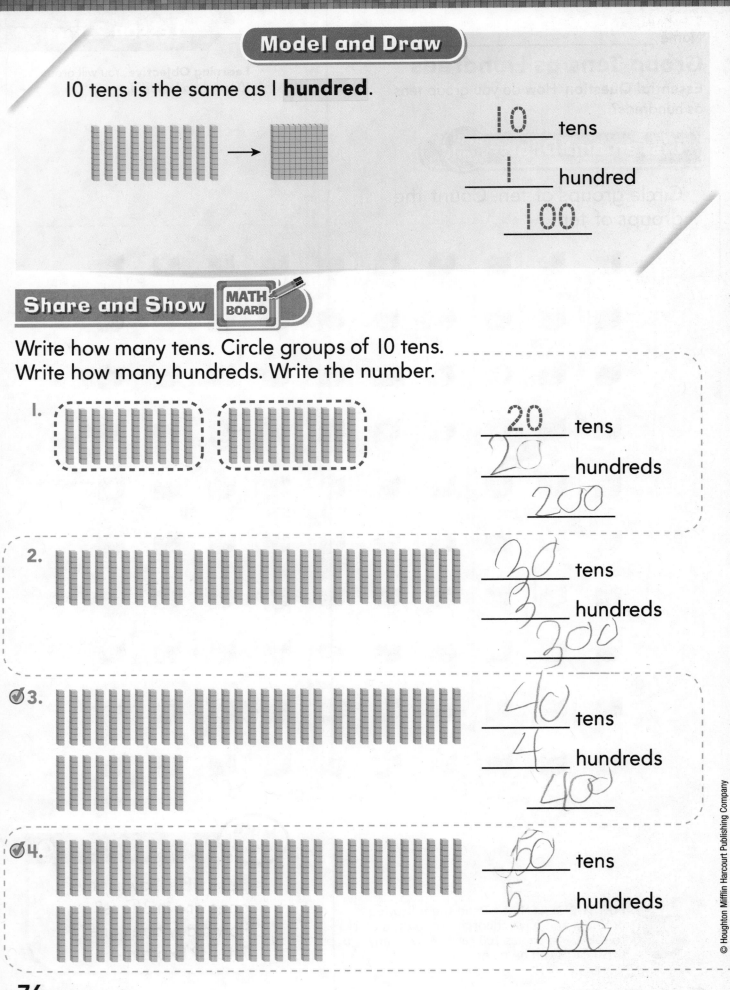

Model and Draw

10 tens is the same as 1 **hundred**.

_10_ tens

_1_ hundred

_100_

Share and Show MATH BOARD

Write how many tens. Circle groups of 10 tens.
Write how many hundreds. Write the number.

1. _20_ tens

_20_ hundreds

_200_

2. _30_ tens

_3_ hundreds

_300_

✓ 3. _40_ tens

_4_ hundreds

_400_

✓ 4. _50_ tens

_5_ hundreds

_500_

On Your Own

Write how many tens. Circle groups of 10 tens.
Write how many hundreds. Write the number.

5.

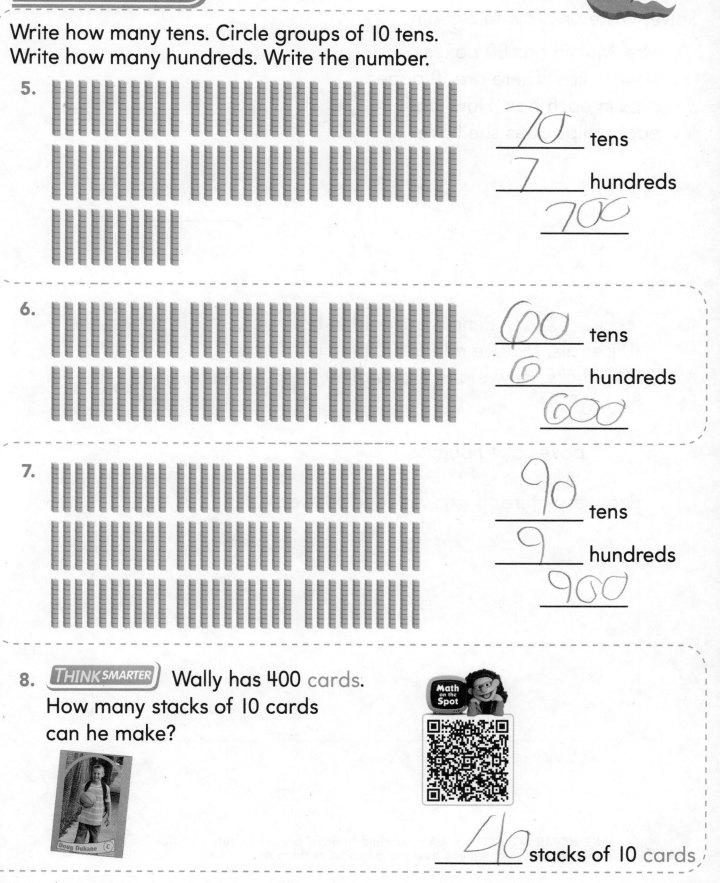

70 tens

7 hundreds

700

6.

60 tens

6 hundreds

600

7.

90 tens

9 hundreds

900

8. **THINK SMARTER** Wally has 400 cards.
How many stacks of 10 cards
can he make?

40 stacks of 10 cards

Problem Solving • Applications Real World   WRITE ▶ Math

Solve. Write or draw to explain.

9. Mrs. Martin has 80 boxes of
paper clips. There are 10 paper
clips in each box. How many
paper clips does she have?

_800_ paper clips

10. **THINK SMARTER** Pencils are sold in boxes of
10 pencils. Mr. Lee needs 100 pencils. He has
40 pencils. How many boxes of 10 pencils should
he buy?

_____ boxes of 10 pencils

Draw a picture to explain your answer.

TAKE HOME ACTIVITY • Ask your child to draw a quick picture
of 20 tens and then tell you how many hundreds there are.

Name _____

Explore 3-Digit Numbers

Essential Question How do you write a 3-digit number for a group of tens?

Learning Objective You will write a 3-digit number that is represented by a group of tens.

Circle groups of blocks to show hundreds.
Count the hundreds.

_____ hundreds

_____ straws

Math Talk Math Processes and Practices ①

Analyze Describe how the number of hundreds would be different if there were 10 more bundles of straws.

FOR THE TEACHER • Read the following problem and have children circle groups of tens blocks to solve. Mrs. Rodriguez has 30 bundles of straws. There are 10 straws in each bundle. How many straws does Mrs. Rodriguez have?

Model and Draw

What number is shown with 11 tens?

___11___ tens

___1___ hundred ___1___ ten

___110___

In the number 110, there is a 1 in the hundreds place and a 1 in the tens place.

Share and Show · MATH BOARD

Circle tens to make 1 hundred. Write the number in different ways.

1. ___12___ tens

    ___1___ hundred ___2___ tens

    ___120___

2. ___13___ tens

    ___1___ hundred ___3___ tens

    ___130___

3. ___10___ tens

    ___1___ hundred ___4___ tens

    ___140___

Name _____

Circle tens to make I hundred. Write the number in different ways.

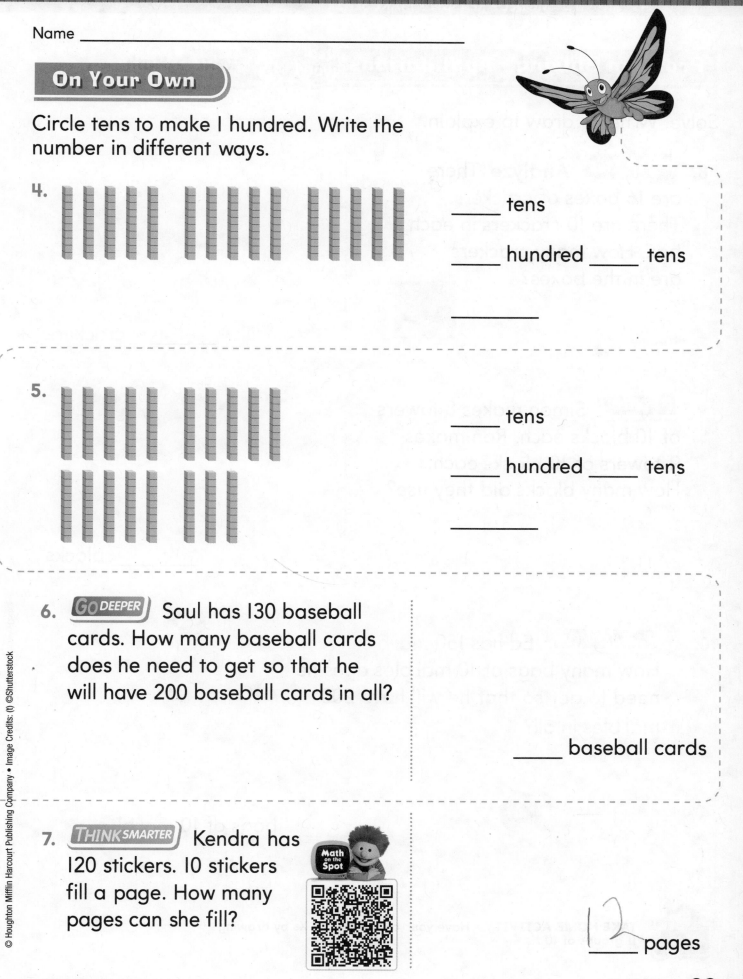

4. _____ tens

_____ hundred _____ tens

_____

5. _____ tens

_____ hundred _____ tens

_____

6. **GO DEEPER** Saul has 130 baseball cards. How many baseball cards does he need to get so that he will have 200 baseball cards in all?

_____ baseball cards

7. **THINK SMARTER** Kendra has 120 stickers. 10 stickers fill a page. How many pages can she fill?

_____ pages

Problem Solving • Applications (Real World)   WRITE Math

Solve. Write or draw to explain.

8. **Math Processes and Practices ❶** **Analyze** There are 16 boxes of crackers. There are 10 crackers in each box. How many crackers are in the boxes?

___160___ crackers

9. **GO DEEPER** Simon makes 8 towers of 10 blocks each. Ron makes 9 towers of 10 blocks each. How many blocks did they use?

___17___ blocks

10. **THINK SMARTER** Ed has 150 marbles. How many bags of 10 marbles does he need to get so that he will have 200 marbles in all?

___50___ bags of 10 marbles

TAKE HOME ACTIVITY • Have your child draw 110 Xs by drawing 11 groups of 10 Xs.

Name _____

Model 3-Digit Numbers

Essential Question How do you show a 3-digit number using blocks?

Learning Objective You will represent a 3-digit number using blocks.

Use ▭▭▭▭▭▭▭. Draw to show what you did.

FOR THE TEACHER • Read the following problem. Jack has 12 tens blocks. How many hundreds and tens does Jack have? Have children show Jack's blocks and then draw quick pictures. Then have children circle 10 tens and solve the problem.

Math Talk Math Processes and Practices ❶

If Jack had 14 tens, how many hundreds and tens would he have? **Explain**

Chapter 2

Model and Draw

In the number 348, the 3 is in the hundreds place, the 4 is in the tens place, and the 8 is in the ones place.

Write how many hundreds, tens, and ones.	__3__ hundreds + __4__ tens + __8__ ones
Show the number 348 using blocks.	
Draw a quick picture.	

Share and Show MATH BOARD

Write how many hundreds, tens, and ones.

Show with ▦ ▭ . Then draw a quick picture.

1. 234

__2__ hundreds + __3__ tens + __4__ ones

2. 156

__1__ hundred + __5__ tens + __6__ ones

Name _____

Write how many hundreds, tens, and ones.

Show with ▦ ⬜ ▭ ▪. Then draw a quick picture.

3. 125

<u>1</u> hundred + <u>2</u> tens + <u>5</u> ones

4. 312

<u>3</u> hundreds + <u>1</u> ten + <u>2</u> ones

5. 245

<u>2</u> hundreds + <u>4</u> tens + <u>5</u> ones

6. 103

<u>1</u> hundred + <u>0</u> tens + <u>3</u> ones

7. THINK SMARTER Lexi needs 144 beads. A large box holds 100 beads. A medium box holds 10 beads. A small box holds 1 bead. Lexi already had 1 large box and 4 small boxes. How many medium boxes of beads does she need?

_____ medium boxes

Problem Solving • Applications ~Real World~   WRITE Math

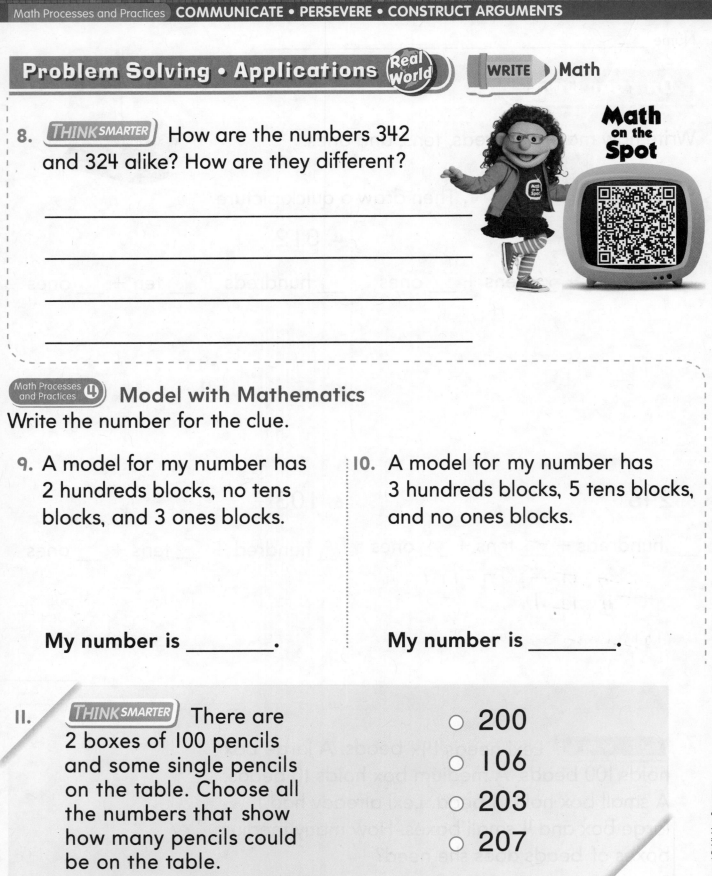

8. **THINK SMARTER** How are the numbers 342 and 324 alike? How are they different?

_____

_____

_____

Math on the Spot

Math Processes and Practices 4   **Model with Mathematics**

Write the number for the clue.

9. A model for my number has 2 hundreds blocks, no tens blocks, and 3 ones blocks.

My number is _____.

10. A model for my number has 3 hundreds blocks, 5 tens blocks, and no ones blocks.

My number is _____.

---

11. **THINK SMARTER** There are 2 boxes of 100 pencils and some single pencils on the table. Choose all the numbers that show how many pencils could be on the table.

○ 200

○ 106

○ 203

○ 207

TAKE HOME ACTIVITY • Write the number 438. Have your child tell you the values of the digits in the number 438.

Name _____

Hundreds, Tens, and Ones

Essential Question How do you write the 3-digit number that is shown by a set of blocks?

Learning Objective You will write the 3-digit number that is represented by a set of blocks.

Write the number of hundreds, tens, and ones.
Then draw a quick picture.

Hundreds	Tens	Ones

Hundreds	Tens	Ones

FOR THE TEACHER • Read the following to children. Sebastion has 243 yellow blocks. How many hundreds, tens, and ones are in this number? Repeat for 423 red blocks.

Math Talk Math Processes and Practices ①

Describe how the two numbers are alike.
Describe how they are different.

Write how many hundreds, tens,
and ones there are in the model.
What are two ways to write this number?

Hundreds	Tens	Ones
2	4	7

247

200 + 40 + 7

Share and Show MATH BOARD

Write how many hundreds, tens, and ones are
in the model. Write the number in two ways.

1.

Hundreds	Tens	Ones
1	6	0

160

100 + 60 + 0

2.

Hundreds	Tens	Ones
2	2	5

225

200 + 20 + 5

3.

Hundreds	Tens	Ones
2	3	9

239

200 + 3 + 9

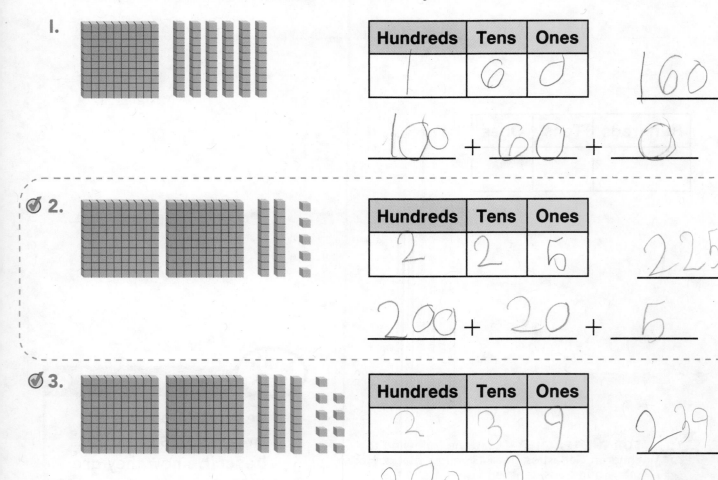

On Your Own

Write how many hundreds, tens, and ones are in the model. Write the number in two ways.

4.

Hundreds	Tens	Ones
3	0	4

304

$300 + 04 + 4$

5.

Hundreds	Tens	Ones
3	7	8

378

$300 + 70 + 8$

6.

Hundreds	Tens	Ones
4	2	6

426

$400 + 20 + 6$

Solve. Write or draw to explain.

7. THINK SMARTER A model for my number has 4 ones blocks, 5 tens blocks, and 7 hundreds blocks. What number am I?

_____

Math on the Spot

Problem Solving • Applications (Real World) | WRITE Math

8. **GO DEEPER** The hundreds digit of my number is greater than the tens digit. The ones digit is less than the tens digit. What could my number be? Write it in two ways.

_____ + _____ + _____

_____

9. **THINK SMARTER** Karen has these bags of marbles. How many marbles does Karen have?

_____ marbles

Explain how you used the picture to find the number of marbles Karen has.

_____

_____

_____

 TAKE HOME ACTIVITY • Say a 3-digit number, such as 546. Have your child draw a quick picture for that number.

Name _____

Hundreds, Tens, and Ones

Learning Objective You will write the 3-digit number that is represented by a set of blocks.

Write how many hundreds, tens, and ones are in the model. Write the number in two ways.

1.

Hundreds	Tens	Ones

_____

_____ + _____ + _____

2.

Hundreds	Tens	Ones

_____

_____ + _____ + _____

Problem Solving (Real World)

3. Write the number that answers the riddle. Use the chart. A model for my number has 6 ones blocks, 2 hundreds blocks, and 3 tens blocks. What number am I?

Hundreds	Tens	Ones

_____

4. **WRITE Math** Write a number that has a zero in the tens place. Draw a quick picture for your number.

Lesson Check

1. Write the number 254 as a sum of hundreds, tens, and ones.

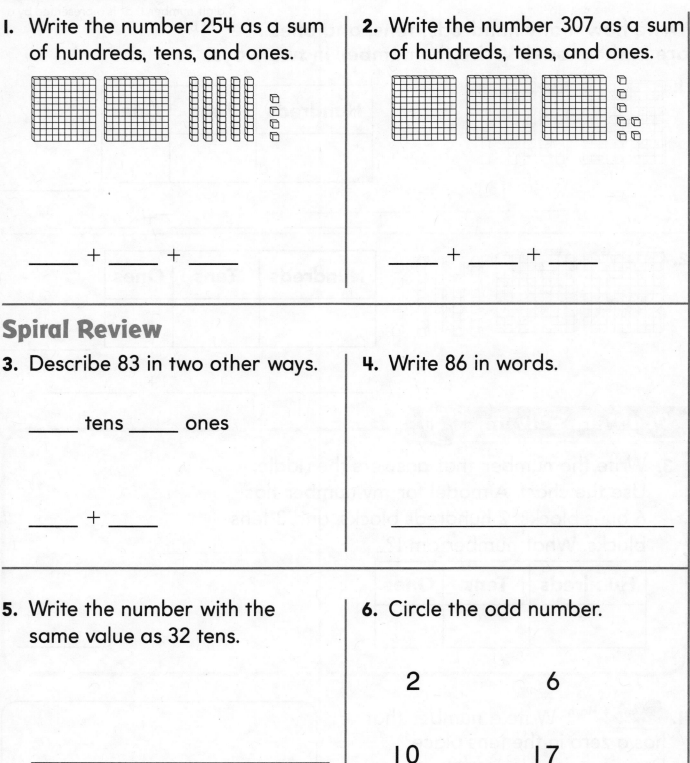

____ + ____ + ____

2. Write the number 307 as a sum of hundreds, tens, and ones.

____ + ____ + ____

Spiral Review

3. Describe 83 in two other ways.

____ tens ____ ones

____ + ____

4. Write 86 in words.

_____

5. Write the number with the same value as 32 tens.

_____

6. Circle the odd number.

2   6

10   17

FOR MORE PRACTICE
GO TO THE
Personal Math Trainer

Name _____

Place Value to 1,000

Essential Question How do you know the values of the digits in numbers?

Learning Objective You will use place value to describe the values of digits in numbers to 1,000.

Listen and Draw (Real World)

Write the numbers. Then draw quick pictures.

_____ sheets of color paper

Hundreds	Tens	Ones

_____ sheets of plain paper

Hundreds	Tens	Ones

Math Talk

Math Processes and Practices ①

Describe how 5 tens is different from 5 hundreds.

FOR THE TEACHER • Read the following. There are 245 sheets of color paper in the closet. There are 458 sheets of plain paper by the table. Have children write each number and draw quick pictures to show the numbers.

The place of a digit in a number tells its value.

 327

The 3 in 327 has a value of 3 hundreds, or 300.

The 2 in 327 has a value of 2 tens, or 20.

The 7 in 327 has a value of 7 ones, or 7.

There are 10 hundreds in 1 **thousand**.

1,000

The 1 is in the thousands place and has a value of 1 thousand.

Share and Show

Circle the value or the meaning of the red digit.

1. 702   2 ones   2 tens   2 hundreds

2. 459   500   50   5

3. 362   3 hundreds   3 tens   3 ones

On Your Own

Circle the value or the meaning of the red digit.

| 4. 54**9** | 400 | 40 | 4 |

| 5. 60**7** | 7 ones | 7 tens | 7 hundreds |

| 6. **1**,000 | 1 one | 1 hundred | 1 thousand |

| 7. **9**14 | 90 | 900 | 9,000 |

8. **THINK SMARTER** The value of the ones digit in George's favorite number is 2. The value of the hundreds digit is 600 and the value of the tens digit is 90. Write George's favorite number.

_____

9. **GO DEEPER** Write the number that matches the clues.

• The value of my hundreds digit is 300.

• The value of my tens digit is 0.

• The value of my ones digit is an even number greater than 7.

The number is _____.

Problem Solving • Applications

WRITE   Math

10. **THINK SMARTER** Ty is making a Venn diagram. Where in the diagram should he write the other numbers?

Numbers with a 5 in the Tens Place   Numbers with a 2 in the Hundreds Place

152

-152-
215
454
257
352
205
250

11. **Math Processes and Practices ③** **Apply** Describe where 752 should be written in the diagram. Explain your answer.

_____

_____

_____

12. **THINK SMARTER +** Fill in the bubble next to all the numbers that have the digit 4 in the tens place.

Personal Math Trainer

○ 764

○ 149

○ 437

○ 342

TAKE HOME ACTIVITY • Ask your child to write 3-digit numbers, such as "a number with 2 hundreds" and "a number with a 9 in the ones place."

Place Value to 1,000

Learning Objective You will use place value to describe the values of digits in numbers to 1,000.

Circle the value or the meaning of the underlined digit.

1. 3<u>3</u>7	3	30	300
2. 46<u>2</u>	200	20	2
3. <u>5</u>72	5	50	500
4. 56<u>7</u>	7 ones	7 tens	7 hundreds
5. <u>4</u>62	4 hundreds	4 ones	4 tens

Problem Solving Real World

6. Write the 3-digit number that answers the riddle.
   - I have the same hundreds digit as ones digit.
   - The value of my tens digit is 50.
   - The value of my ones digit is 4.   The number is _____.

7. **WRITE Math** What is the value of 5 in 756? Write and draw to explain how you know.

_____

_____

Lesson Check

1. What is the value of the underlined digit?

$\underline{3}15$

_____

2. What is the meaning of the underlined digit?

$6\underline{4}8$

_____ tens

Spiral Review

3. What number can be written as $40 + 5$?

_____

4. What number has the same value as 14 tens?

_____

5. Write the number described by 1 ten 16 ones.

_____

6. Circle the even number.

7   16

21   25

FOR MORE PRACTICE GO TO THE Personal Math Trainer

Number Names

Essential Question How do you write 3-digit numbers using words?

Learning Objective You will write 3-digit numbers using words.

Listen and Draw

Write the missing numbers in the chart. Then find and circle the word form of these numbers below.

	12	13		15	16	17	18	19	20
21	22	23	24	25	26	27	28		30
31	32	33	34		36	37	38	39	40
41	42	43	44	45		47	48	49	50
51		53	54	55	56	57	58	59	60

forty-one   ninety-two   fourteen

eleven   thirty-five   forty-six

fifty-three   twenty-nine   fifty-two

Math Talk   Math Processes and Practices 6

Explain Describe how to use words to write the number with a 5 in the tens place and a 7 in the ones place.

HOME CONNECTION • In this activity, your child reviewed the word form of numbers less than 100.

You can use words to write 3-digit numbers.
First, look at the hundreds digit. Then, look at
the tens digit and ones digit together.

245

two hundred forty-five

713

seven hundred thirteen

Share and Show MATH BOARD

Write the number using words.

1. 506

   five hundred six
   _____

2. 189

   _____

⊘3. 328

   _____

Write the number.

4. four hundred fifteen

   _____

5. two hundred ninety-one

   _____

6. six hundred three

   _____

⊘7. eight hundred forty-seven

   _____

On Your Own

Write the number.

8. seven hundred seventeen

_____

9. three hundred ninety

_____

Write the number using words.

10. 568

_____

11. 321

_____

12. **GO DEEPER** My 3-digit number has a 4 in the hundreds place. It has a greater digit in the tens place than in the ones place. The sum of the digits is 6.

What is my number? _____

Write the number using words. _____

13. **THINK SMARTER** Alma counts two hundred sixty-eight leaves. Which is another way to write this number? Circle your answer.

Math on the Spot

$2 + 6 + 8$

$200 + 60 + 8$

$2 + 60 + 8$

Problem Solving • Applications

WRITE Math

Math Processes and Practices ② Connect Symbols and Words

Circle the answer for each problem.

14. Derek counts one hundred ninety cars. Which is another way to write this number?

119

190

910

15. Beth counted three hundred fifty-six straws. Which is another way to write this number?

$3 + 5 + 6$

$30 + 50 + 60$

$300 + 50 + 6$

16. THINK SMARTER There are 537 chairs at the school. Write this number using words.

_____

Show the number in two other ways.

Hundreds	Tens	Ones

_____ + _____ + _____

TAKE HOME ACTIVITY • Ask your child to write the number 940 using words.

Number Names

Learning Objective You will write 3-digit numbers using words.

Write the number.

1. two hundred thirty-two

   _____

2. five hundred forty-four

   _____

3. one hundred fifty-eight

   _____

4. nine hundred fifty

   _____

5. four hundred twenty

   _____

6. six hundred seventy-eight

   _____

Write the number using words.

7. 3 1 7

   _____

Problem Solving Real World

Circle the answer.

8. Six hundred twenty-six children attend Elm Street School. Which is another way to write this number?

   266   626   662

9. **WRITE** Math Write a 3-digit number using the digits 5, 9, and 2. Then write your number using words.

   _____

Lesson Check

1. Write the number 851 in words.

_____

2. Write the number two hundred sixty using numbers.

_____

Spiral Review

3. Write a number with the digit 8 in the tens place.

_____

4. Write the number shown with these blocks.

_____

5. Count by fives.

650, 655,

____, ____, ____

6. Sam has 128 marbles. How many hundreds are in this number?

____ hundred

FOR MORE PRACTICE
GO TO THE
Personal Math Trainer

Name _____

Different Forms of Numbers

Essential Question What are three ways to write a 3-digit number?

Learning Objective You will write a 3-digit number using digits, using words, and as the sum of the values of the hundreds, tens, and ones digits.

Listen and Draw Real World

Write the number. Use the digits to write how many hundreds, tens, and ones.

_____ hundreds _____ tens _____ ones

_____ hundreds _____ tens _____ ones

_____ hundreds _____ tens _____ one

FOR THE TEACHER • Read the following: Evan has 426 marbles. How many hundreds, tens, and ones are in 426? Continue the activity for 204 and 341.

Math Talk Math Processes and Practices 6

How many hundreds are in 368? **Explain.**

Chapter 2

You can use a quick picture to show a number.
You can write a number in different ways.

five hundred thirty-six

__5__ hundreds __3__ tens __6__ ones

__500__ + __30__ + __6__

__536__

Share and Show MATH BOARD

Read the number and draw a quick picture.
Then write the number in different ways.

1. four hundred seven

__4__ hundreds __0__ tens __7__ ones

__400__ + __0__ + __7__

__407__

2. three hundred twenty-five

__3__ hundreds __0__ tens __5__ ones

__300__ + __0__ + __5__

__305__

3. two hundred fifty-three

__2__ hundreds __0__ tens __3__ ones

__200__ + __0__ + __3__

__203__

Name _____

Read the number and draw a quick picture.
Then write the number in different ways.

4. one hundred seventy-two

__1__ hundred __7__ tens __2__ ones

__100__ + __70__ + __2__

__172__

5. three hundred forty-six

__3__ hundreds __4__ tens __6__ ones

__300__ + __40__ + __6__

__346__

6. THINK SMARTER Think of a 3-digit number with a zero
in the ones place. Use words to write that number.

_____

7. THINK SMARTER Ellen used these blocks to show 452.
What is wrong? Cross out blocks and draw
quick pictures for missing blocks.

Math on the Spot

© Houghton Mifflin Harcourt Publishing Company

TAKE HOME ACTIVITY • Ask your child to show
the number 315 in three different ways.

✓ Mid-Chapter Checkpoint

Personal Math Trainer
Online Assessment and Intervention

Concepts and Skills

Circle tens to make 1 hundred. Write the number in different ways.

1.

_13_ tens

_1_ hundred _3_ tens

_13_

Write how many hundreds, tens, and ones are in the model. Write the number in two ways.

2.

Hundreds	Tens	Ones

_____

_____ + _____ + _____

Circle the value or the meaning of the red digit.

3. 528   5   50   500

4. 674   4 ones   4 tens   4 hundreds

5. **THINK SMARTER** Write the number six hundred forty-five in another way.

_____

Name _____

Algebra • Different Ways to Show Numbers

Essential Question How can you use blocks or quick pictures to show the value of a number in different ways?

Learning Objective You will use blocks or quick pictures to show the value of a number in different ways.

Listen and Draw (Real World)

Draw quick pictures to solve.
Write how many tens and ones.

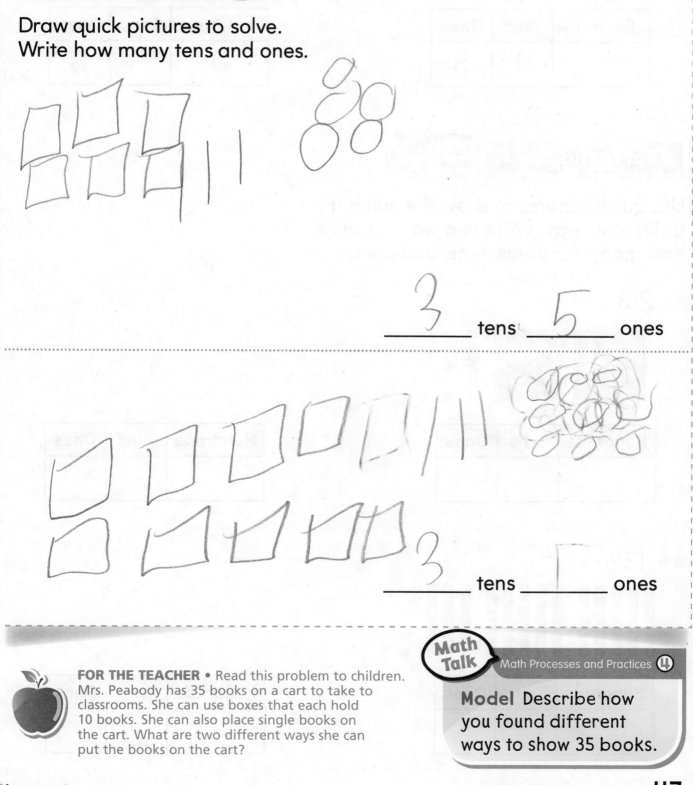

_____3_____ tens _____5_____ ones

_____3_____ tens _____5_____ ones

FOR THE TEACHER • Read this problem to children. Mrs. Peabody has 35 books on a cart to take to classrooms. She can use boxes that each hold 10 books. She can also place single books on the cart. What are two different ways she can put the books on the cart?

Math Talk Math Processes and Practices ④

Model Describe how you found different ways to show 35 books.

Here are two ways to show 148.

Hundreds	Tens	Ones
1	4	8

Hundreds	Tens	Ones
0	14	8

Share and Show MATH BOARD

Use quick pictures to show the number a different way. Write two ways to show how many hundreds, tens, and ones.

☑ 1. 213

Hundreds	Tens	Ones
2	1	3

Hundreds	Tens	Ones
4	6	8

☑ 2. 132

Hundreds	Tens	Ones
1	3	2

Hundreds	Tens	Ones
6	7	10

Name _____

On Your Own

Use quick pictures to show the number a different way. Write two ways to show how many hundreds, tens, and ones.

3. 144

Hundreds	Tens	Ones
1	4	4

Hundreds	Tens	Ones
3	9	5

4. 204

Hundreds	Tens	Ones
1	10	4

Hundreds	Tens	Ones
2	5	8

5. (Math Processes and Practices 3) **Make Arguments**

Sue said that 200 + 20 + 23 is the same as 200 + 30 + 3. Is she correct? Explain.

_____

_____

_____

Problem Solving • Applications Real World   WRITE Math

Marbles are sold in boxes, in bags, or as single marbles. Each box has 10 bags of marbles in it. Each bag has 10 marbles in it.

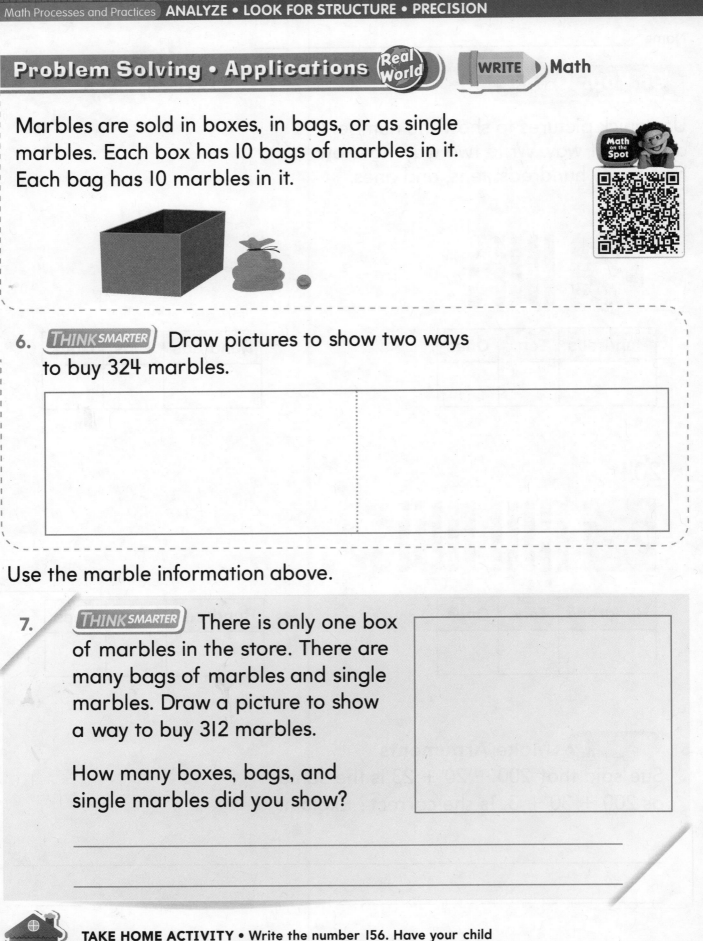

6. THINK SMARTER   Draw pictures to show two ways to buy 324 marbles.

Use the marble information above.

7. THINK SMARTER   There is only one box of marbles in the store. There are many bags of marbles and single marbles. Draw a picture to show a way to buy 312 marbles.

How many boxes, bags, and single marbles did you show?

_____

_____

TAKE HOME ACTIVITY • Write the number 156. Have your child draw quick pictures of two ways to show this number.

Count On and Count Back by 10 and 100

Essential Question How do you use place value to find 10 more, 10 less, 100 more, or 100 less than a 3-digit number?

Learning Objective You will find 10 more, 10 less, 100 more, or 100 less than a 3-digit number.

Listen and Draw *Real World*

Draw quick pictures for the numbers.

Girls

Hundreds	Tens	Ones

Boys

Hundreds	Tens	Ones

FOR THE TEACHER • Tell children that there are 342 girls at Center School. Have children draw quick pictures for 342. Then tell them that there are 352 boys at the school. Have them draw quick pictures for 352.

Math Talk Math Processes and Practices ①

Describe how the two numbers are different.

Model and Draw

You can show 10 less or 10 more than a number by changing the digit in the tens place.

10 less than 264

Hundreds	Tens	Ones
2	5	4

10 more than 264

Hundreds	Tens	Ones
2	7	4

You can show 100 less or 100 more than a number by changing the digit in the hundreds place.

100 less than 264

Hundreds	Tens	Ones
1	6	4

100 more than 264

Hundreds	Tens	Ones
3	6	4

Share and Show MATH BOARD

Write the number.

1. 10 more than 648

_____

2. 100 less than 513

_____

3. 100 more than 329

_____

4. 10 less than 827

_____

Name _____

On Your Own

Write the number.

5. 10 more than 471

_____

6. 10 less than 143

_____

7. 100 more than 555

_____

8. 100 less than 757

_____

9. 100 more than 900

_____

10. 10 less than 689

_____

11. 100 less than 712

_____

12. 10 less than 254

_____

13. **THINK SMARTER** Kyla wrote the riddle below. Fill in the blanks to make the sentence true.

_____ is 10 less than 948 and 10 more than _____.

14. **THINK SMARTER** Rick has 10 more crayons than Lori. Lori has 136 crayons. Tom has 10 fewer crayons than Rick. How many crayons does each child have?

Red

Rick: _____ crayons

Tom: _____ crayons

Lori: _____ crayons

Problem Solving • Applications (Real World) WRITE Math

Math Processes and Practices ① Analyze Relationships

15. Juan's book has 248 pages. This is 10 more pages than there are in Kevin's book. How many pages are in Kevin's book?

_____ pages

16. There are 217 pictures in Tina's book. There are 100 fewer pictures in Mark's book. How many pictures are in Mark's book?

_____ pictures

17. GO DEEPER Use the clues to answer the question.

- Shawn counts 213 cars.
- Maria counts 100 fewer cars than Shawn.
- Jayden counts 10 more cars than Maria.

How many cars does Jayden count?

_____ cars

18. THINK SMARTER Rico has 235 stickers. Gabby has 100 more stickers than Rico. Thomas has 10 fewer stickers than Gabby. Write the number of stickers each child has.

_____   _____   _____
   Rico   Gabby   Thomas

TAKE HOME ACTIVITY • Write the number 596. Have your child name the number that is 100 more than 596.

Name _____

Count On and Count Back by 10 and 100

Learning Objective You will find 10 more, 10 less, 100 more, or 100 less than a 3-digit number.

Write the number.

1. 10 more than 451

_____

2. 10 less than 770

_____

3. 100 more than 367

_____

4. 100 less than 895

_____

5. 10 less than 812

_____

6. 100 more than 543

_____

7. 10 more than 218

_____

8. 100 more than 379

_____

Problem Solving Real World

Solve. Write or draw to explain.

9. Sarah has 128 stickers. Alex has 10 fewer stickers than Sarah. How many stickers does Alex have?

_____ stickers

10. **WRITE** Math Choose any 3-digit number. Describe how to find the number that is 10 more.

_____

Lesson Check

1. Write the number that is 10 less than 526.

_____

2. Write the number that is 100 more than 487.

_____

Spiral Review

3. Write another way to describe 14 tens.

_____ hundred _____ tens

4. What is the value of the underlined digit?

587

_____

5. What number can be written as 30 + 5?

_____

6. What number can be written as 9 tens and 1 one?

_____

FOR MORE PRACTICE
GO TO THE
Personal Math Trainer

Algebra • Number Patterns

Essential Question How does place value help you identify and extend counting patterns?

Learning Objective You will use place value to identify the next numbers in a counting pattern.

Listen and Draw *Real World*

Shade the numbers in the counting pattern.

801	802	803	804	805	806	807	808	809	810
811	812	813	814	815	816	817	818	819	820
821	822	823	824	825	826	827	828	829	830
831	832	833	834	835	836	837	838	839	840
841	842	843	844	845	846	847	848	849	850
851	852	853	854	855	856	857	858	859	860
861	862	863	864	865	866	867	868	869	870
871	872	873	874	875	876	877	878	879	880
881	882	883	884	885	886	887	888	889	890
891	892	893	894	895	896	897	898	899	900

FOR THE TEACHER • Read the following problem and discuss how children can use a counting pattern to solve. At Blossom Bakery, 823 muffins were sold in the morning. In the afternoon, four packages of 10 muffins were sold. How many muffins were sold that day?

Math Talk Math Processes and Practices 7

Look for Structure
What number is next in the counting pattern you see? Explain.

Model and Draw

Look at the digits in the numbers. What two numbers are next in the counting pattern?

114,   214,   314,   414,   ■,   ■

The _____ digit changes by one each time.

The next two numbers are _____ and _____.

Share and Show

Look at the digits to find the next two numbers.

1. 137, 147, 157, 167, ■, ■

   The next two numbers are _____ and _____.

2. 245, 345, 445, 545, ■, ■

   The next two numbers are _____ and _____.

3. 421, 431, 441, 451, ■, ■

   The next two numbers are _____ and _____.

4. 389, 489, 589, 689, ■, ■

   The next two numbers are _____ and _____.

Name _____

On Your Own

Look at the digits to find the next two numbers.

5. 193, 293, 393, 493, ▇, ▇

   The next two numbers are _____ and _____.

6. 484, 494, 504, 514, ▇, ▇

   The next two numbers are _____ and _____.

7. 500, 600, 700, 800, ▇, ▇

   The next two numbers are _____ and _____.

8. 655, 665, 675, 685, ▇, ▇

   The next two numbers are _____ and _____.

9. **THINK SMARTER** Mark read 203 pages.
   Laney read 100 more pages than Mark.
   Gavin read 10 fewer pages than Laney.
   How many pages did Gavin read?

   Math on the Spot

   _____ pages

Problem Solving • Applications (Real World) WRITE Math

Solve.

10. **GO DEEPER** There were 135 buttons in a jar.
After Robin put more buttons into the jar,
there were 175 buttons in the jar. How many
groups of 10 buttons did she put into the jar?

_____ groups of 10 buttons

Explain how you solved the problem.

_____

_____

_____

_____

11. **THINK SMARTER** Write the next number in each
counting pattern.

162, 262, 362, 462, _____

347, 357, 367, 377, _____

609, 619, 629, 639, _____

🏠 **TAKE HOME ACTIVITY** • With your child, take turns writing number
patterns in which you count on by tens or by hundreds.

Name _____

Algebra • Number Patterns

Learning Objective You will use place value to identify the next numbers in a counting pattern.

Look at the digits to find the next two numbers.

1. 232, 242, 252, 262, ⬛, ⬛

   The next two numbers are _____ and _____.

2. 185, 285, 385, 485, ⬛, ⬛

   The next two numbers are _____ and _____.

3. 428, 528, 628, 728, ⬛, ⬛

   The next two numbers are _____ and _____.

4. 654, 664, 674, 684, ⬛, ⬛

   The next two numbers are _____ and _____.

Problem Solving Real World

5. What are the missing numbers in the pattern?

   431, 441, 451, 461, ⬛, 481, 491, ⬛

   The missing numbers are _____ and _____.

6. WRITE Math How can you tell when a pattern shows counting on by tens?

   _____

   _____

Lesson Check

1. What is the next number in this pattern?

453, 463, 473, 483,

_____

2. What is the next number in this pattern?

295, 395, 495, 595,

_____

Spiral Review

3. Write the number seven hundred fifty-one with digits.

_____

4. What is the value of the underlined digit?

1̲95

_____

5. What is another way to write 56?

_____ tens _____ ones

6. Write the number 43 in tens and ones.

_____ tens _____ ones

FOR MORE PRACTICE
GO TO THE
Personal Math Trainer

Problem Solving • Compare Numbers

Essential Question How can you make a model
to solve a problem about comparing numbers?

Learning Objective You will use blocks
and the strategy *make a model* to show
the values of the digits in numbers when
solving problems about comparing
numbers.

Children bought 217 boxes of chocolate milk
and 188 boxes of plain milk. Did they buy
more boxes of chocolate milk or plain milk?

Unlock the Problem (Real World)

What do I need to find?

if the children bought ___more___

boxes of chocolate milk

or plain milk

What information do I need to use?

_____ boxes of chocolate
milk

_____ boxes of plain milk

Show how to solve the problem.
Model the numbers. Draw quick pictures of your models.

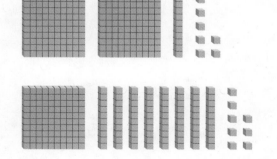

The children bought more boxes of _____ milk.

HOME CONNECTION • Your child used base-ten blocks to represent the
numbers in the problem. These models were used as a tool for comparing
numbers to solve the problem.

Try Another Problem

Model the numbers. Draw quick pictures to show how you solved the problem.

- What do I need to find?
- What information do I need to use?

1. At the zoo, there are 137 birds and 142 reptiles. Are there more birds or more reptiles at the zoo?

   more _____

2. Tom's book has 105 pages.
   Delia's book has 109 pages.
   Whose book has fewer pages? _____ book

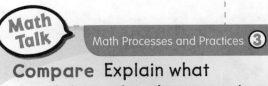

Math Talk

Math Processes and Practices ③

Compare Explain what you did to solve the second problem.

Name _____

Model the numbers. Draw quick pictures
to show how you solved the problem.

3. Mary's puzzle has
164 pieces. Jake's puzzle
has 180 pieces. Whose
puzzle has more pieces?

4. There are 246 people at
the game. There are
251 people at the museum.
At which place are there
fewer people?

_____ puzzle

at the _____

5. There are 131 crayons in a
box. There are 128 crayons in
a bag. Are there more crayons
in the box or in the bag?

6. There are 308 books in
the first room. There are
273 books in the second
room. In which room are
there fewer books?

in the _____

in the _____ room

Problem Solving • Applications Real World WRITE Math

7. **THINK SMARTER** There are 748 children at Dan's school. There are 651 children at Karen's school. There are 763 children at Jason's school. Which school has more than 759 children?

_____ school

8. **Math Processes and Practices ❶** **Analyze** There are 136 crayons in a box. Use the digits 4, 1, and 2 to write a number that is greater than 136.

Green

_____

9. **THINK SMARTER** Becky has 134 stamps. Sara has 129 stamps. Who has more stamps?

_____

Sara buys 10 more stamps. Who has more stamps now?

_____

Draw quick pictures to show the stamps Becky and Sara have now.

🏠 **TAKE HOME ACTIVITY** • Ask your child to explain how he or she solved one of the problems on this page.

Name _____

Problem Solving • Compare Numbers

Learning Objective You will use blocks and the strategy *make a model* to show the values of the digits in numbers when solving problems about comparing numbers.

Model the numbers. Draw quick pictures to show how you solved the problem.

I. Lauryn has 128 marbles. Kristin has 118 marbles. Who has more marbles?

_____

2. Nick has 189 trading cards. Kyle has 198 trading cards. Who has fewer cards?

_____

3. A piano has 36 black keys and 52 white keys. Are there more black keys or white keys on a piano?

_____

4. WRITE Math Draw to show how you can use models to compare 345 and 391.

Chapter 2

one hundred thirty-nine **139**

Lesson Check

1. Gina has 245 stickers. Circle the number less than 245.

285   254

245   239

2. Carl's book has 176 pages. Circle the number greater than 176.

203   174

168   139

Spiral Review

3. Write 63 as a sum of tens and ones.

_____ + _____

4. Write the number 58 in tens and ones.

_____ tens _____ ones

5. Mr. Ford drove 483 miles during his trip. How many hundreds are in this number?

_____

6. Write 20 in words.

_____

FOR MORE PRACTICE
GO TO THE
Personal Math Trainer

Name _____

Algebra • Compare Numbers

Essential Question How do you compare
3-digit numbers?

Learning Objective You will use place
value to compare two 3-digit numbers
using the >, =, and < symbols.

 Listen and Draw

Draw quick pictures to solve the problem.

More _____ were at the park.

Math Talk Math Processes and Practices 6

Explain how you
compared the numbers.

🍎 **FOR THE TEACHER •** Read the following problem
and have children draw quick pictures to compare
the numbers. There were 125 butterflies and
132 birds at the park. Were there more butterflies
or more birds at the park?

Chapter 2

Model and Draw

Use place value to **compare** numbers. Start by looking at the digits in the greatest place value position first.

> **> is greater than**
> **< is less than**
> **= is equal to**

Hundreds	Tens	Ones
4	8	3
5	7	0

4 hundreds < 5 hundreds

483 (<) 570

Hundreds	Tens	Ones
3	5	2
3	4	6

The hundreds are equal.

5 tens > 4 tens

352 (>) 346

Share and Show MATH BOARD

Compare the numbers. Write >, <, or =.

1.

Hundreds	Tens	Ones
2	3	9
1	7	9

239 ( ) 179

2.

Hundreds	Tens	Ones
4	3	5
4	3	7

435 ( ) 437

✓3. 764
     674

764 ( ) 674

✓4. 519
     572

519 ( ) 572

Name _____

On Your Own

Compare the numbers. Write $>$, $<$, or $=$.

5.
378
504

378 $\bigcirc$ 504

6.
821
821

821 $\bigcirc$ 821

7.
560
439

560 $\bigcirc$ 439

8.
934
943

934 $\bigcirc$ 943

THINK SMARTER Write the 3-digit numbers and compare the numbers. Use $>$, $<$, or $=$.

9.
400 + 70 + 5
400 + 70 + 5

_____ $\bigcirc$ _____

10.
700 + 30 + 6
600 + 80 + 7

_____ $\bigcirc$ _____

Math Processes and Practices ② **Use Reasoning** Write a 3-digit number in the box that makes the comparison true.

11. 526 < [   ]

12. 319 > [   ]

13. [   ] > 782

14. [   ] < 131

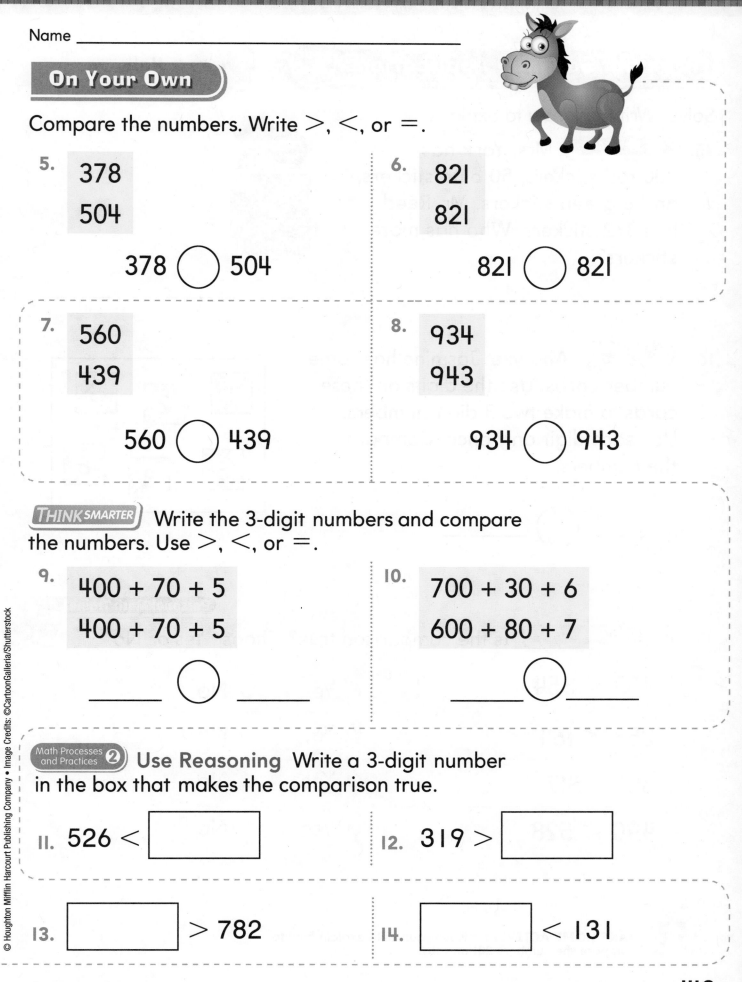

Problem Solving • Applications (Real World) WRITE Math

Solve. Write or draw to explain.

15. **THINK SMARTER** Mrs. York has 300 red stickers, 50 blue stickers, and 8 green stickers. Mr. Reed has 372 stickers. Who has more stickers?

_____

16. **Math Processes and Practices ❶ Analyze** Jasmine has some number cards. Use the digits on these cards to make two 3-digit numbers. Use each digit only once. Compare the numbers.

1   2   5
6   3   8

_____ ◯ _____

Personal Math Trainer

17. **THINK SMARTER +** Is the comparison true? Choose Yes or No.

$453 > 354$	○ Yes	○ No
$253 < 164$	○ Yes	○ No
$391 > 417$	○ Yes	○ No
$490 < 528$	○ Yes	○ No

TAKE HOME ACTIVITY • Have your child explain how to compare the numbers 281 and 157.

Algebra • Compare Numbers

Learning Objective You will use place value to compare two 3-digit numbers using the >, =, and < symbols.

Compare the numbers. Write >, <, or =.

1. 489
   605

   489 $\bigcirc$ 605

2. 719
   719

   719 $\bigcirc$ 719

3. 370
   248

   370 $\bigcirc$ 248

4. 645
   654

   645 $\bigcirc$ 654

5. 205
   250

   205 $\bigcirc$ 250

6. 813
   781

   813 $\bigcirc$ 781

Problem Solving · Real World

Solve. Write or draw to explain.

7. Toby has 178 pennies.
   Bella has 190 pennies.
   Who has more pennies?

   _____ has more pennies.

8. WRITE ⟩ Math Explain how comparing 645 and 738 is different from comparing 645 and 649.

   _____

   _____

Lesson Check

1. Write >, <, or = to compare.

315 ◯ 351

2. Write >, <, or = to compare.

401 ◯ 399

Spiral Review

3. What number has the same value as 50 tens?

_____

4. Write a number with an 8 in the hundreds place.

_____

5. Ned counts by fives. He starts at 80. Which number should he say next?

_____

6. Mr. Dean has an even number of cats and an odd number of dogs. Show how many dogs and cats he might have.

6 cats and _____ dogs

FOR MORE PRACTICE
GO TO THE
Personal Math Trainer

✓ Chapter 2 Review/Test

Personal Math Trainer
Online Assessment and Intervention

1.

Do the choices show a way to represent the blocks? Choose Yes or No.

3 hundreds	○ Yes	○ No
30 ones	○ Yes	○ No
30 hundreds	○ Yes	○ No
30 tens	○ Yes	○ No

2. Robin has 180 stickers. How many pages of 10 stickers does she need so that she will have 200 stickers in all?

_____ pages of stickers

3. Sanjo has 348 marbles. Harry has 100 fewer marbles than Sanjo. Ari has 10 more marbles than Harry. Write the number of marbles each child has.

_____   _____   _____
  Sanjo   Ari   Harry

 Assessment Options
Chapter Test

4. Write the next number in each counting pattern.

214, 314, 414, 514, _____

123, 133, 143, 153, _____

5. **THINK SMARTER +** Is the comparison true? Choose Yes or No.

$787 < 769$	○ Yes	○ No
$405 > 399$	○ Yes	○ No
$396 > 402$	○ Yes	○ No
$128 < 131$	○ Yes	○ No

6. **GO DEEPER** Cody is thinking of the number 627. Write Cody's number in words.

_____

Show Cody's number in two other ways.

Hundreds	Tens	Ones

_____ + _____ + _____

7. Matty needs 200 buttons. Amy
   gives her 13 bags with
   10 buttons in each bag. How many
   buttons does she need now?

   _____ buttons

---

8. There are 4 boxes of 100 sheets of paper and
   some single sheets of paper in the closet.
   Choose all the numbers that show how many
   sheets of paper could be in the closet.

   ○ 348   ○ 324

   ○ 406   ○ 411

---

9. Blocks are sold in boxes, in bags, or as single
   blocks. Each box has 10 bags in it. Each bag
   has 10 blocks in it. Tara needs 216 blocks. Draw
   a picture to show a way to buy 216 blocks.

   How many boxes, bags, and single blocks did
   you show?

   _____

   _____

10. Dan and Hannah collect toy cars.
Dan has 132 cars. Hannah has
138 cars. Who has more cars?　　　　_____

Dan gets 10 more cars. Hannah
gets 3 more cars. Who has more
cars now?　　　　　　　　　　　_____

Draw quick pictures to show how
many cars Dan and Hannah have now.

Dan's Cars	Hannah's Cars

11. Choose all the numbers that have the digit 2
in the tens place.

○ 721

○ 142

○ 425

○ 239

12. Ann has 239 shells. Write the number
in words.

_____

All About Animals

by John Hudson

BIG IDEA Develop fluency with addition and subtraction within 100. Solve addition and subtraction problems within 1,000.

The giraffe is the tallest land animal in the world. Adult giraffes are 13 to 17 feet tall. Newborn giraffes are about 6 feet tall.

A group of 5 giraffes drinks water at a watering hole. A group of 5 giraffes eats leaves from trees. How many giraffes are there in all?

_____ giraffes

How do giraffes care for their young?

The ostrich is the largest bird in the world. Ostriches cannot fly, but they can run fast. Ostrich eggs weigh about 3 pounds each! Several ostriches will lay eggs in a shared nest.

There are 6 eggs in a nest. Then 5 more eggs are put in that nest. How many eggs are in the nest now?

_____ eggs

How do ostriches care for their young?

Kangaroos can move quickly by jumping with their two back legs. When they are moving slowly, they use all four legs.

Western gray kangaroos live in groups called mobs. There are 8 kangaroos in a mob. 4 more kangaroos join the mob. How many kangaroos are in the mob in all?

_____ kangaroos

How do kangaroos care for their young?

Wild boars like to eat roots. They use their tough snouts to dig. Wild boars can be up to 6 feet long.

Wild boars live in groups called sounders. There is one sounder of 14 boars. If 7 of the boars are eating, how many boars are not eating?

_____ boars

How do wild boars care for their young?

Moose are the largest kind of deer. Male moose have antlers that may be 5 to 6 feet wide. Moose can trot and gallop. They are also good swimmers!

A ranger saw 7 moose in the morning and 6 moose in the afternoon. How many moose did the ranger see that day?

_____ moose

How do moose care for their young?

© Houghton Mifflin Harcourt Publishing Company • Image Credits: © Mark Yezbick/Alamy

Write About the Story

Choose one kind of animal. Draw a picture and write your own story about that kind of animal. Use addition in your story.

Vocabulary Review

add   in all

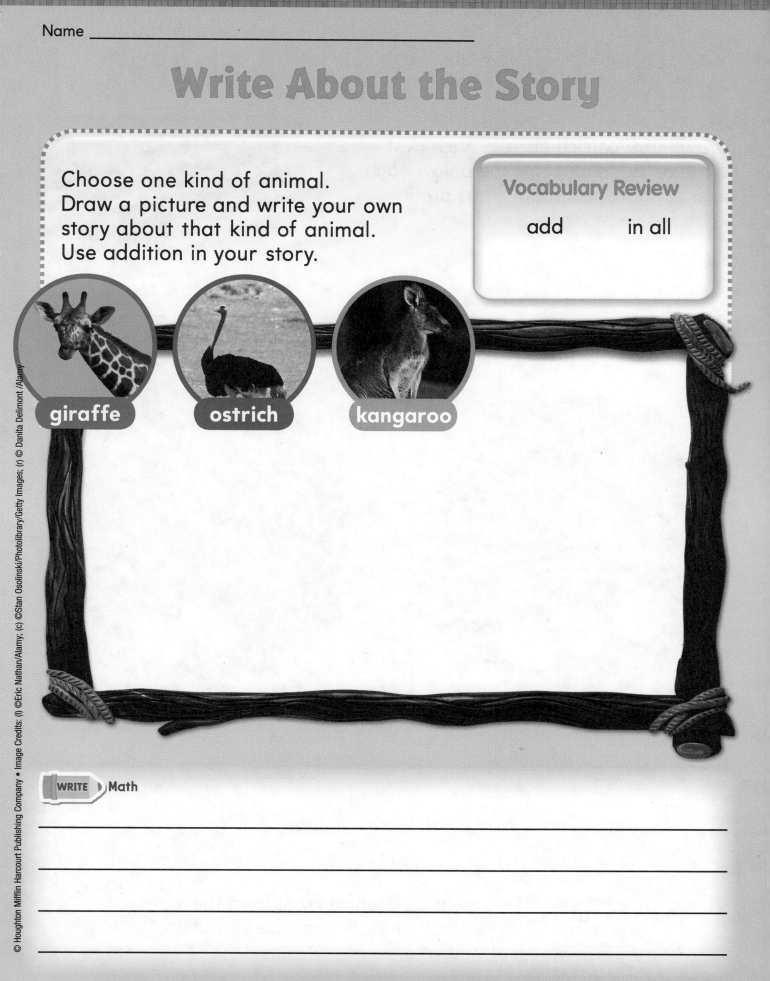

giraffe   ostrich   kangaroo

WRITE Math

_____

_____

_____

_____

How many eggs are there?

Draw more ostrich eggs in each nest.
Write an addition sentence below each
nest to show how many eggs are in
each nest now.

_____

_____

 Choose a different animal from the story.
Write another story that uses addition.

Basic Facts and Relationships

Curious about Math

Parrot fish live near coral reefs in tropical ocean waters. They use their sharp teeth to scrape food off of the coral.

Suppose 10 parrot fish are eating at a coral reef. 3 of the fish swim away. How many fish are still eating?

Name _____

Use Symbols to Add

Use the picture. Use + and = to complete
the addition sentence.

1.

🍎🍎🍎 🍏

3 ◯ 1 ◯ 4

2.

⭐⭐ ⭐⭐⭐

2 ◯ 3 ◯ 5

Sums to 10

Write the sum.

3.	4.	5.	6.	7.
4	5	2	6	9
+3	+0	+7	+2	+1

Doubles and Doubles Plus One

Write the addition sentence.

8.

____ ◯ ____ ◯ ____

9.

____ ◯ ____ ◯ ____

This page checks understanding of important skills needed
for success in Chapter 3.

Vocabulary Builder

© Houghton Mifflin Harcourt Publishing Company

Review Words

addition
subtraction
plus
minus
equals
count on
count back

Visualize It

Sort the review words in the graphic organizer.

Addition Words   **Subtraction** Words

plus

Understand Vocabulary

1. Circle the **addition** sentence. $3 + 6 = 9$ $9 - 6 = 3$

2. Circle the **subtraction** sentence. $8 + 2 = 10$ $10 - 2 = 8$

3. Circle the **count on** fact. $5 - 1 = 4$ $4 + 1 = 5$

4. Circle the **count back** fact. $8 - 2 = 6$ $6 + 2 = 8$

 GO DIGITAL • Interactive Student Edition • Multimedia eGlossary

Game Caterpillar Chase

Materials

- 1 ⬛
- 1 ⬛
- 1 🎲

Play with a partner.

1. Put your cube on START.
2. Toss the 🎲, and move that many spaces.

3. Say the sum or difference. Your partner checks your answer.
4. Take turns. The first person to get to FINISH wins.

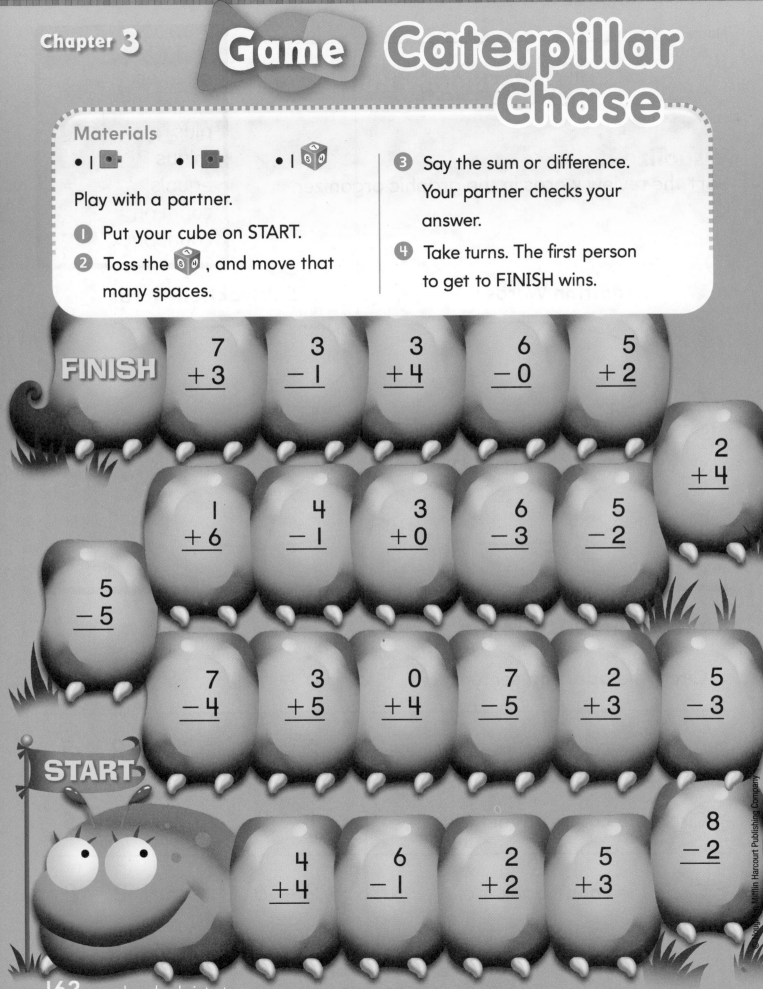

FINISH

$$7 + 3$$ $$3 - 1$$ $$3 + 4$$ $$6 - 0$$ $$5 + 2$$ $$2 + 4$$

$$1 + 6$$ $$4 - 1$$ $$3 + 0$$ $$6 - 3$$ $$5 - 2$$

$$5 - 5$$

$$7 - 4$$ $$3 + 5$$ $$0 + 4$$ $$7 - 5$$ $$2 + 3$$ $$5 - 3$$

START

$$4 + 4$$ $$6 - 1$$ $$2 + 2$$ $$5 + 3$$ $$8 - 2$$

Chapter 3 Vocabulary

addend

sumando

1

difference

diferencia

14

digit

dígito

15

even

par

22

is equal to (=)

es igual a

33

odd

impar

44

sum

suma o total

59

ten

decena

61

$5 - 3 = 2$

difference

$5 + 3 = 8$

addends

Even numbers show pairs with no left over cubes.

0, 1, 2, 3, 4, 5, 6, 7, 8, and 9 are **digits**.

Odd numbers show pairs with one cube left over.

2 plus 1 is equal to 3

$2 + 1 = 3$

10 ones = 1 ten

$4 + 2 = 6$

sum

Game

Going to a Coral Reef

Word Box
addends
difference
digit
even numbers
is equal to (=)
odd numbers
sum
tens

For 2 players

Materials

- 1
- 1
- 1

How to Play

1. Each player chooses a [token] and puts it on START.

2. Toss the [number cube] to take a turn. Move your [token] that many spaces around the track to the right.

3. If you land on these squares:

   White Space Tell the meaning of the math word or use it in a sentence. If you are correct, jump to the next space with that word.

   Green Space Follow the directions on the space. If there are no directions, stay where you are.

4. The first player to reach FINISH wins.

Game

HOW TO PLAY

1. Each player chooses a and puts it on START.
2. Toss the 🎲 to take a turn. Move your ▪️ that many spaces around the track to the right.
3. If you land on these squares:

   White Space Tell the meaning of the math word or use it in a sentence. If you are correct, jump to the next space with that word.

   Green Space Follow the directions on the space. If there are no directions, stay where you are.
4. The first player to reach FINISH wins.

MATERIALS • 1 ▪️ • 1 ▪️ • 1 🎲

FINISH

| sum | odd numbers | even numbers | addends |

| sum | addends | Go back to | difference | tens |

| odd numbers | even numbers | digit | is equal to | |

| digit | numbers | odd numbers | sum | addends |

| is equal to | tens | Go back to | addends | sum |

START

| tens | is equal to | digit | even numbers |

is equal to   Go back to   tens   difference   Go back to

is equal to   digit   even numbers   odd numbers   sum

tens   addends   sum   odd numbers   even numbers

difference   tens   is equal to   digit

odd numbers   even numbers   digit   tens

odd numbers   sum   addends   difference

The Write Way

Reflect

Choose one idea. Write about it in the space below.

- Think about what you did in math class today. Complete this sentence:

  I learned that I _____.

- Write your own story problem that uses addition. Then ask a partner to solve the problem.

- Use the words *addends* and *sum* to explain how to solve this problem:

  7 + 5 = _____.

Name _____

Use Doubles Facts

Essential Question How can you use doubles facts to find sums for near doubles facts?

Learning Objective You will use doubles facts to find sums for other facts.

Listen and Draw (Real World)

Draw a picture to show the problem. Then write an addition sentence for the problem.

_____ toy cars

FOR THE TEACHER • Read this problem and have children draw a picture for the problem. Nathan has 6 toy cars. Alisha gives him 6 more toy cars. How many toy cars does Nathan have now? After children write an addition sentence, have them name other doubles facts that they know.

Math Talk Math Processes and Practices 4

Represent Explain why 4 + 4 = 8 is called a doubles fact.

Model and Draw

You can use doubles facts to find sums for other facts.

$3 + 4 = ?$

$\downarrow$

$3 + 3 + 1 = ?$

$3 + 3 = 6$

$6 + 1 = 7$

So, $3 + 4 = $ _____.

$7 + 6 = ?$

$\downarrow$

$7 + 7 - 1 = ?$

$7 + 7 = 14$

$14 - 1 = 13$

So, $7 + 6 = $ _____.

Share and Show · MATH BOARD

Write a doubles fact you can use to find the sum. Write the sum.

1. $2 + 3 = \underline{5}$

   $\underline{2} + \underline{2} = \underline{4}$

2. $4 + 5 = \underline{9}$

   $\underline{4} + \underline{4} = \underline{8}$

3. $4 + 3 = \underline{7}$

   $\underline{3} + \underline{3} = \underline{6}$

4. $6 + 7 = \underline{13}$

   $\underline{6} + \underline{6} = \underline{12}$

5. $5 + 6 = \underline{11}$

   $\underline{5} + \underline{5} = \underline{10}$

6. $8 + 7 = \underline{15}$

   $\underline{8} + \underline{8} = \underline{16}$

Name _____

Write a doubles fact you can use
to find the sum. Write the sum.

7. $5 + 4 =$ ___9___

___6___ + ___5___ = ___10___

8. $6 + 5 =$ ___11___

___6___ + ___6___ = ___12___

9. $6 + 7 =$ ___13___

___7___ + ___7___ = ___14___

10. $7 + 8 =$ ___15___

___8___ + ___8___ = ___16___

11. $8 + 9 =$ ___17___

___9___ + ___9___ = ___18___

12. $5 + 6 =$ ___11___

___6___ + ___6___ = ___12___

13. $7 + 6 =$ ___13___

___7___ + ___7___ = ___14___

14. $9 + 8 =$ ___17___

___9___ + ___9___ = ___18___

15. **THINK SMARTER** Mr. Norris wrote a doubles fact.
It has a sum greater than 6. The numbers that
he added are each less than 6. What fact
might he have written?

Math on the Spot

_____

Problem Solving • Applications (Real World)   WRITE ▸ Math

Solve. Write or draw to explain.

16. **Math Processes and Practices ①** **Analyze**
Andrea has 8 red buttons and 9 blue buttons. How many buttons does Andrea have?

$\underline{17}$ buttons

17. **GO DEEPER** Henry sees 3 rabbits. Callie sees double that number of rabbits. How many more rabbits does Callie see than Henry?

_____ **more** rabbits

18. **THINK SMARTER** Could you use the doubles fact to find the sum for 4 + 5? Choose Yes or No.

$4 + 4 = 8$	○ Yes	○ No
$5 + 5 = 10$	○ Yes	○ No
$9 + 9 = 18$	○ Yes	○ No

TAKE HOME ACTIVITY • Ask your child to write three different doubles facts with sums less than 17.

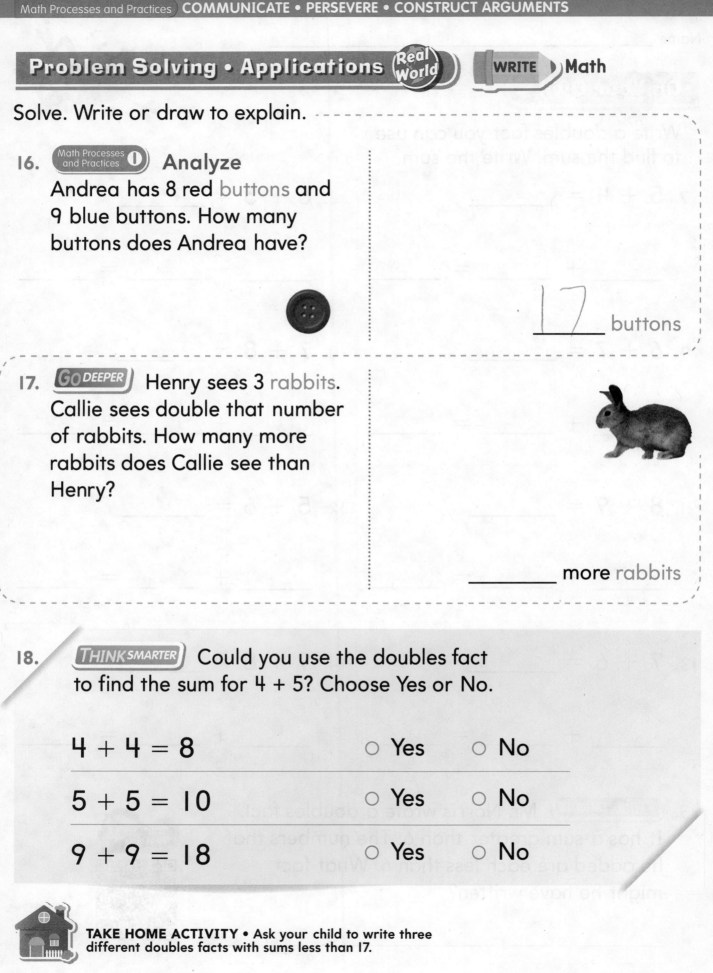

Name _____

Use Doubles Facts

Learning Objective You will use doubles facts to find sums for other facts.

Write a doubles fact you can use to find the sum. Write the sum.

1. 2 + 3 = ____

   ___ + ___ = ___

2. 7 + 6 = ____

   ___ + ___ = ___

3. 3 + 4 = ____

   ___ + ___ = ___

4. 8 + 9 = ____

   ___ + ___ = ___

Problem Solving Real World

Solve. Write or draw to explain.

5. There are 4 ants on a log. Then 5 ants crawl onto the log. How many ants are on the log now?

   _____ ants

6. **WRITE** Math Draw or write to show two ways to use a doubles fact to find 6 + 7.

   _____

   _____

Lesson Check

1. Write a doubles fact you can use to find the sum. Write the sum.

$$4 + 3 = \underline{\hspace{1cm}}$$

$$\underline{\hspace{0.7cm}} + \underline{\hspace{0.7cm}} = \underline{\hspace{0.7cm}}$$

2. Write a doubles fact you can use to find the sum. Write the sum.

$$6 + 7 = \underline{\hspace{1cm}}$$

$$\underline{\hspace{0.7cm}} + \underline{\hspace{0.7cm}} = \underline{\hspace{0.7cm}}$$

Spiral Review

3. There are 451 children in Lia's school. Write a number greater than 451.

$$\underline{\hspace{1cm}}$$

4. What number is shown with these blocks?

$$\underline{\hspace{1cm}}$$

5. Write a number with the digit 8 in the tens place.

$$\underline{\hspace{1cm}}$$

6. Circle the sum that is an even number.

$$2 + 3 = 5$$
$$3 + 4 = 7$$
$$4 + 5 = 9$$
$$6 + 6 = 12$$

FOR MORE PRACTICE
GO TO THE
Personal Math Trainer

Name _____

Practice Addition Facts

Essential Question What are some ways to remember sums?

Learning Objective You will use properties and mental math strategies to add and subtract fluently within 20.

Listen and Draw *Real World*

Draw pictures to show the problems.

_____

_____

FOR THE TEACHER • Read the following two problems. Have children draw a picture and write a number sentence for each. On Monday, Tony saw 3 dogs and 6 cats. How many animals did he see? On Tuesday, Tony saw 6 dogs and 3 cats. How many animals did he see?

Math Talk
Math Processes and Practices ①

Analyze Explain how the two problems are alike. Explain how they are different.

Chapter 3

one hundred sixty-nine **169**

Model and Draw

These are some ways to remember facts.

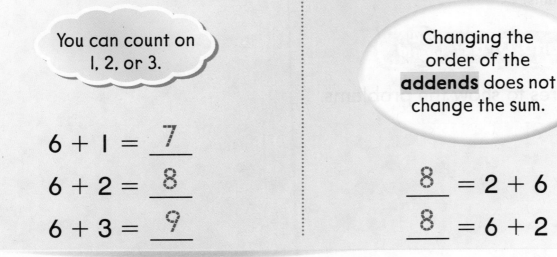

You can count on 1, 2, or 3.

$6 + 1 = \underline{7}$

$6 + 2 = \underline{8}$

$6 + 3 = \underline{9}$

Changing the order of the **addends** does not change the sum.

$\underline{8} = 2 + 6$

$\underline{8} = 6 + 2$

Share and Show

MATH BOARD

Write the sums.

1. $4 + 4 = \underline{8}$

$4 + 5 = \underline{9}$

2. $5 + 0 = \underline{5}$

$2 + 0 = \underline{2}$

3. $3 + 8 = \underline{11}$

$8 + 3 = \underline{11}$

4. $\underline{10} = 5 + 5$

$\underline{9} = 5 + 4$

5. $5 + 7 = \underline{12}$

$7 + 5 = \underline{12}$

6. $\underline{14} = 7 + 7$

$\underline{15} = 7 + 8$

7. $\underline{10} = 3 + 7$

$\underline{10} = 7 + 3$

8. $9 + 3 = \underline{12}$

$3 + 9 = \underline{12}$

9. $\underline{12} = 6 + 6$

$\underline{11} = 6 + 5$

Name _____

Write the sums.

10. $7 + 1 =$ __8__

$1 + 7 =$ __8__

11. __4__ $= 4 + 0$

__9__ $= 9 + 0$

12. $5 + 5 =$ __10__

$5 + 4 =$ __9__

13. $8 + 2 =$ __10__

$2 + 8 =$ __10__

14. $3 + 3 =$ __6__

$3 + 4 =$ __7__

15. $7 + 8 =$ __15__

$8 + 7 =$ __15__

16. __5__ $= 4 + 1$

__5__ $= 1 + 4$

17. $0 + 7 =$ __7__

$0 + 6 =$ __6__

18. $8 + 8 =$ __16__

$8 + 9 =$ __17__

19. $5 + 3 =$ __8__

$3 + 5 =$ __8__

20. __18__ $= 9 + 9$

__17__ $= 9 + 8$

21. $6 + 7 =$ __13__

$7 + 6 =$ __13__

22. **THINK SMARTER** Sam painted 3 pictures. Ellie painted twice as many pictures as Sam. How many pictures did they paint altogether?

Math on the Spot

_____ pictures

Problem Solving • Applications Real World   WRITE Math

Solve. Write or draw to explain.

23. **GO DEEPER** Chloe draws 8 pictures. Reggie draws 1 more picture than Chloe. How many pictures do they draw?

_____ pictures

24. **Math Processes and Practices 1 Analyze** Joanne made 9 clay bowls last week. She made the same number of clay bowls this week. How many clay bowls did she make in two weeks?

_____ clay bowls

Personal Math Trainer

25. **THINK SMARTER +** There are 9 raisins in the bowl. Devon puts 8 more raisins in the bowl. Complete the addition sentence to find how many raisins are in the bowl now.

_____ + _____ = _____

_____ raisins

TAKE HOME ACTIVITY • Ask your child to write several addition facts that he or she knows.

Name _____

Algebra • Make a Ten to Add

Essential Question How is the make a ten strategy used to find sums?

Learning Objective You will use the *make a ten* strategy to find sums.

Listen and Draw *Real World*

Write the fact below the ten frame when you hear the problem that matches the model.

$5 + 5 = 10$

$6 + 4 = 10$

$7 + 3 = 10$

$8 + 2 = 10$

$9 + 1 = 10$

FOR THE TEACHER • Read the following problem. There are 6 large dogs and 4 small dogs. How many dogs are there? Have children find the ten frame that models the problem and write the addition sentence. Repeat by revising the story for each addition fact represented by the other ten frames.

Math Talk Math Processes and Practices ⑦

Look for Structure Describe a pattern you see in these make a ten facts.

Chapter 3

7 + 5 = ?

You need to add 3 to 7 to make a ten. Break apart 5 as 3 and 2.

7 + 5

7 + 3 + 2

10 + 2 = ___12___

So, 7 + 5 = _____.

Share and Show   MATH BOARD

Show how you can make a ten to find the sum.
Write the sum.

1. 8 + 3 = __11__

2

10 + __1__ = __11__

2. 2 + 9 = __11__

10 + __1__ = __11__

3. 8 + 5 = __13__

2

10 + __1__ = __11__

4. 4 + 7 = __11__

10 + ____ = ____

5. 3 + 9 = __12__

10 + __1__ = __11__

6. 7 + 6 = __13__

3

10 + __1__ = __11__

176 one hundred seventy-six

On Your Own

Show how you can make a ten to find the sum.
Write the sum.

7. 4 + 9 = _____

3 1

10 + _____ = _____

8. 9 + 8 = _____

1 7

10 + _____ = _____

9. 8 + 6 = _____

10 + _____ = _____

10. 5 + 9 = _____

10 + _____ = _____

11. 7 + 9 = _____

10 + _____ = _____

12. 8 + 4 = _____

10 + _____ = _____

13. **GO DEEPER** Alex is thinking of a doubles fact. The sum is greater than the sum of 7 + 7 but less than the sum of 8 + 9. What fact is Alex thinking of?

_____ + _____ = _____

14. **THINK SMARTER** There were 5 bees in a hive. How many more bees need to go in the hive for there to be 14 bees?

Math on the Spot

_____ more bees

Problem Solving • Applications (Real World)   WRITE Math

Solve. Write or draw to explain.

15. **Math Processes and Practices ①** **Analyze** There are 9 large bicycles at the store. There are 6 small bicycles at the store. How many bicycles are at the store?

_____ bicycles

16. **GO DEEPER** Max is thinking of a doubles fact. It has a sum that is greater than the sum of 6 + 4 but less than the sum of 8 + 5. What fact is Max thinking of?

_____ + _____ = _____

17. **THINK SMARTER** Natasha had 8 shells. Then she found 5 more shells. Draw to show how to find the number of shells Natasha has now.

How many shells does she have now? _____ shells

🏠 **TAKE HOME ACTIVITY** • Ask your child to name pairs of numbers that have a sum of 10. Then have him or her write the addition sentences.

Name _____

Algebra • Add 3 Addends

Essential Question How do you add three numbers?

Learning Objective You will use addition properties to add three numbers.

Listen and Draw

Write the sum of each pair of addends.

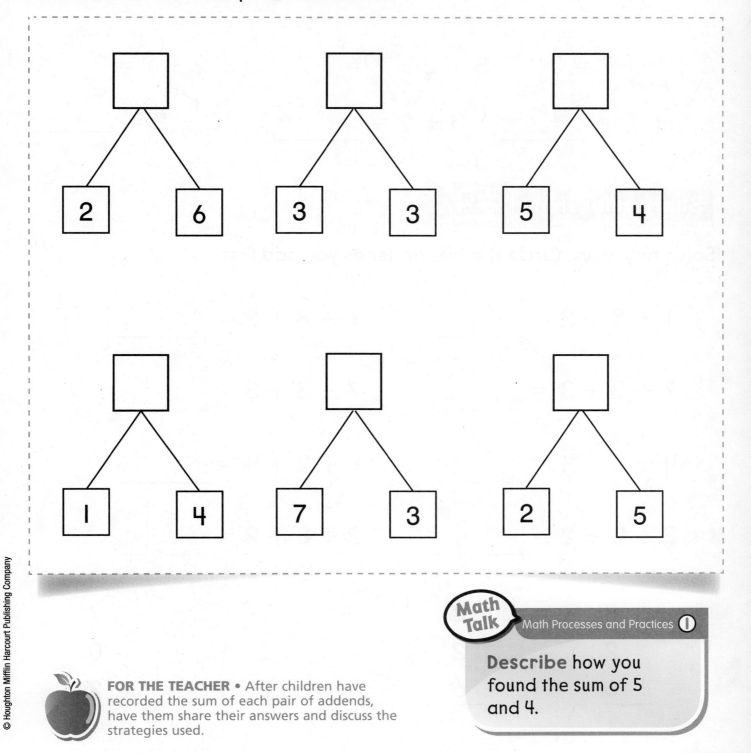

FOR THE TEACHER • After children have recorded the sum of each pair of addends, have them share their answers and discuss the strategies used.

Math Talk Math Processes and Practices ①

Describe how you found the sum of 5 and 4.

Chapter 3

one hundred eighty-one **181**

You can group numbers in different ways to add.

Choose two addends.
Look for facts you know.

Changing the way
the numbers are
grouped does not
change the sum.

$3 + 2 + 7 = ?$

$5 + 7 = \underline{12}$

$3 + 2 + 7 = ?$

$3 + 9 = \underline{\hphantom{00}}$

$3 + 2 + 7 = ?$

$10 + 2 = \underline{\hphantom{000}}$

Share and Show MATH BOARD

Solve two ways. Circle the two addends you add first.

1. $1 + 8 + 2 = \underline{\hphantom{000}}$ $1 + 8 + 2 = \underline{\hphantom{000}}$

2. $7 + 3 + 3 = \underline{\hphantom{000}}$ $7 + 3 + 3 = \underline{\hphantom{000}}$

3. $4 + 2 + 4 = \underline{\hphantom{000}}$ $4 + 2 + 4 = \underline{\hphantom{000}}$

4. $2 + 8 + 2 = \underline{\hphantom{000}}$ $2 + 8 + 2 = \underline{\hphantom{000}}$

5.
$$
\begin{array}{r} 3 \\ 2 \\ + 6 \\ \hline \end{array}
\qquad
\begin{array}{r} 3 \\ 2 \\ + 6 \\ \hline \end{array}
$$

6.
$$
\begin{array}{r} 7 \\ 0 \\ + 2 \\ \hline \end{array}
\qquad
\begin{array}{r} 7 \\ 0 \\ + 2 \\ \hline \end{array}
$$

On Your Own

Solve two ways. Circle the two addends you add first.

7. 4 + 1 + 6 = _____   4 + 1 + 6 = _____

8. 4 + 3 + 3 = _____   4 + 3 + 3 = _____

9. 1 + 5 + 3 = _____   1 + 5 + 3 = _____

10. 6 + 4 + 4 = _____   6 + 4 + 4 = _____

11. 5 + 5 + 5 = _____   5 + 5 + 5 = _____

12. 7 + 0 + 6 = _____   7 + 0 + 6 = _____

13.
```
    5          5
    3          3
  + 4        + 4
  ___        ___
```

14.
```
    4          4
    2          2
  + 5        + 5
  ___        ___
```

Math Processes and Practices 7 Look for Structure

Write the missing addend.

15.
```
    5
    5
  + □
  ___
   14
```

16.
```
    4
    □
  + 4
  ___
   12
```

17.
```
    3
    □
  + 7
  ___
   11
```

18.
```
    5
    3
  + □
  ___
   13
```

Problem Solving • Applications (Real World)   WRITE ▸ Math

Choose a way to solve.
Write or draw to explain.

19. **THINK SMARTER** Nick, Alex, and Sophia eat 15 raisins in all. Nick and Alex each eat 4 raisins. How many raisins does Sophia eat?

_____ raisins

20. **Math Processes and Practices ① Analyze**
There are 5 green grapes and 4 red grapes in a bowl. Eli puts 4 more grapes in the bowl. How many grapes are in the bowl now?

_____ grapes

21. **THINK SMARTER** Mrs. Moore bought 4 small apples, 6 medium apples, and 3 large apples. How many apples did she buy?

_____ apples

TAKE HOME ACTIVITY • Have your child describe two ways to add 3, 6, and 2.

Name _____

Algebra • Add 3 Addends

Learning Objective You will use addition properties to add three numbers.

Solve two ways. Circle the two addends you add first.

1. $2 + 3 + 7 =$ _____ $2 + 3 + 7 =$ _____

2. $5 + 3 + 3 =$ _____ $5 + 3 + 3 =$ _____

3. $4 + 5 + 4 =$ _____ $4 + 5 + 4 =$ _____

4.
$$\begin{array}{r} 5 \\ 4 \\ +\ 5 \\ \hline \end{array} \qquad \begin{array}{r} 5 \\ 4 \\ +\ 5 \\ \hline \end{array}$$

5.
$$\begin{array}{r} 6 \\ 3 \\ +\ 4 \\ \hline \end{array} \qquad \begin{array}{r} 6 \\ 3 \\ +\ 4 \\ \hline \end{array}$$

Problem Solving Real World

Choose a way to solve. Write or draw to explain.

6. Amber has 2 red crayons, 5 blue crayons, and 4 yellow crayons. How many crayons does she have?

_____ crayons

7. **WRITE** Math Write or draw to explain two ways you can find the sum of $3 + 4 + 5$.

_____

Lesson Check

1. What is the sum of
2 + 4 + 6?

_____

2. What is the sum of
5 + 4 + 2?

_____

Spiral Review

3. Write >, <, or = to compare.

688 _____ 648

4. What number can be written
as 4 tens 2 ones?

_____

5. What number has the same
value as 50 tens?

_____

6. What is the next number in
the pattern?

420, 520, 620, 720, _____

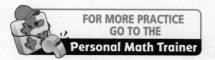

Name _____

Algebra • Relate Addition and Subtraction

Learning Objective You will use an addition fact to find the difference for a related subtraction fact.

Essential Question How are addition and subtraction related?

Listen and Draw Real World

Complete the bar model to show the problem.

_____

_____ soccer balls

15

_____ soccer balls

FOR THE TEACHER • Read the following problems. Have children complete the bar model for each. The soccer team has 8 red balls and 7 yellow balls. How many soccer balls does the team have? The soccer team has 15 balls inside the locker room. The children took the 7 yellow balls outside. How many soccer balls were inside?

Math Talk Math Processes and Practices ⑥

Explain how the bar models for the problems are alike and how they are different.

Chapter 3

one hundred eighty-seven **187**

Model and Draw

You can use addition facts to remember **differences**. Related facts have the same whole and parts.

Think of the addends in an addition fact to find the difference for a related subtraction fact.

6	7

$\underline{13}$

$6 + 7 = \underline{13}$

	7

13

$13 - 7 = \underline{}$

Share and Show MATH BOARD

Write the sum and the difference for the related facts.

1. $5 + 4 = \underline{9}$
   $9 - 4 = \underline{5}$

2. $2 + 7 = \underline{9}$
   $9 - 2 = \underline{7}$

3. $3 + 8 = \underline{11}$
   $11 - 8 = \underline{3}$

4. $5 + 8 = \underline{13}$
   $13 - 5 = \underline{8}$

5. $\underline{9} = 1 + 8$
   $\underline{8} = 9 - 1$

6. $9 + 9 = \underline{18}$
   $18 - 9 = \underline{9}$

7. $\underline{15} = 8 + 7$
   $\underline{7} = 15 - 8$

8. $4 + 7 = \underline{11}$
   $11 - 7 = \underline{4}$

9. $7 + 5 = \underline{12}$
   $12 - 7 = \underline{5}$

© Houghton Mifflin Harcourt Publishing Company

Name _____

On Your Own

Write the sum and the difference for the related facts.

10. $4 + 3 = \underline{7}$

$7 - 3 = \underline{4}$

11. $2 + 6 = \underline{8}$

$8 - 6 = \underline{2}$

12. $6 + 4 = \underline{10}$

$10 - 6 = \underline{4}$

13. $7 + 3 = \underline{10}$

$10 - 7 = \underline{3}$

14. $8 + 6 = \underline{14}$

$14 - 6 = \underline{8}$

15. $\underline{12} = 3 + 9$

$\underline{3} = 12 - 9$

16. $6 + 5 = \underline{11}$

$11 - 5 = \underline{6}$

17. $7 + 7 = \underline{14}$

$14 - 7 = \underline{7}$

18. $9 + 6 = \underline{15}$

$15 - 9 = \underline{6}$

19. $5 + 9 = \underline{14}$

$14 - 9 = \underline{5}$

20. $\underline{12} = 4 + 8$

$\underline{8} = 12 - 4$

21. $9 + 7 = \underline{16}$

$16 - 7 = \underline{9}$

Math Processes and Practices 6) Make Connections

Write a related subtraction fact for each addition fact.

22. $7 + 8 = 15$

$15 - 7 = 8$

23. $5 + 7 = 12$

$12 - 7 = 5$

24. $6 + 7 = 13$

$13 - 6 = 7$

25. $9 + 8 = 17$

$17 - 9 = 8$

Problem Solving • Applications WRITE Math

Solve. Write or draw to explain.

26. Trevor has 7 kites. Pam has 4 kites. How many more kites does Trevor have than Pam?

$7 - 4 = 3$

3

_____ more kites

27. **THINK SMARTER** Mr. Sims has a bag of 7 pears and a bag of 6 pears. His family eats 5 pears. How many pears does he have now?

$7 + 6 = 13$

_____ pears

28. **THINK SMARTER** Elin counts 7 geese in the water and some geese on the shore. There are 16 geese in all. Draw a picture to show the two groups of geese.

Write a number sentence that can help you find how many geese are on the shore.

_____

How many geese are on the shore?   _____ geese

TAKE HOME ACTIVITY • Ask your child to name some subtraction facts that he or she knows well.

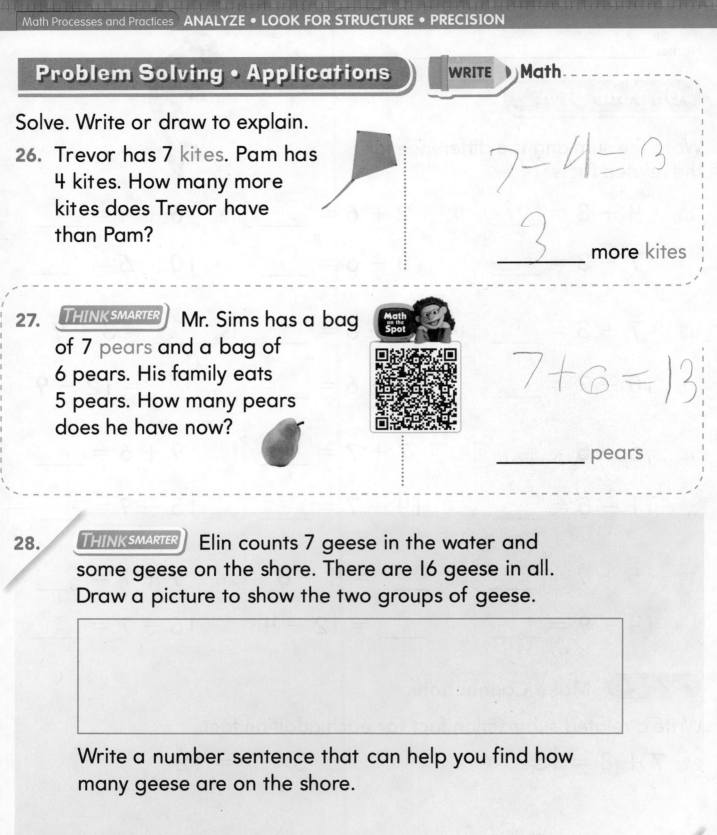

Name _____

Practice Subtraction Facts

Essential Question What are some ways to remember differences?

Learning Objective You will find differences by using a related addition fact or by counting back by 1, 2, or 3.

Listen and Draw *Real World*

Use Gina's model to answer the question.

Gina's Model

_____   _____

_____   _____

FOR THE TEACHER • Tell children that Gina put 4 color tiles inside the circle and then put 3 color tiles outside the circle. Then ask: What addition fact could be written for Gina's model? Repeat with stories for the three facts that are related to this addition fact.

Math Talk
Math Processes and Practices ③

Compare Strategies
Explain how the different facts for Gina's model are related.

Model and Draw

These are some ways to find differences.

You can count back by 1, 2, or 3.

$7 - 2 =$ _____

> Start with 7.
> Say: 6, 5.

$9 - 3 =$ _____

> Start with 9.
> Say: 8, 7, 6.

You can think about a missing addend to subtract.

$8 - 5 = \blacksquare$ $5 + 3 = 8$

So, $8 - 5 =$ _____.

Share and Show MATH BOARD

Write the difference.

1. $6 - 4 = \underline{2}$

2. $10 - 7 = \underline{3}$

3. $\underline{3} = 5 - 2$

4. $14 - 6 = \underline{8}$

5. $\underline{4} = 8 - 4$

6. $11 - 3 = \underline{8}$

7. $\underline{2} = 7 - 5$

8. $10 - 4 = \underline{6}$

9. $5 - 0 = \underline{5}$

10. $13 - 9 = \underline{4}$

11. $9 - 3 = \underline{7}$

12. $\underline{1} = 7 - 6$

13. $12 - 3 = \underline{9}$

14. $6 - 3 = \underline{3}$

15. $9 - 5 = \underline{4}$

16. $10 - 6 = \underline{5}$

17. $\underline{5} = 8 - 3$

18. $13 - 5 = \underline{8}$

Name _____

On Your Own

Write the difference.

19. $11 - 2 = \underline{9}$ 20. $9 - 7 = \underline{2}$ 21. $\underline{3} = 7 - 4$

22. $12 - 5 = \underline{7}$ 23. $8 - 6 = \underline{2}$ 24. $\underline{7} = 7 - 0$

25. $\underline{5} = 10 - 5$ 26. $15 - 8 = \underline{7}$ 27. $13 - 7 = \underline{6}$

28. $10 - 8 = \underline{2}$ 29. $8 - 5 = \underline{3}$ 30. $\underline{3} = 9 - 6$

31. $\underline{5} = 9 - 4$ 32. $11 - 8 = \underline{3}$ 33. $12 - 7 = \underline{5}$

34. **THINK SMARTER**

Write the differences.
Then write the next fact
in the pattern.

$10 - 1 = \underline{9}$ $12 - 9 = \underline{3}$ $18 - 9 = \underline{9}$

$8 - 1 = \underline{7}$ $13 - 9 = \underline{4}$ $17 - 8 = \underline{9}$

$6 - 1 = \underline{5}$ $14 - 9 = \underline{5}$ $16 - 7 = \underline{9}$

$4 - 1 = \underline{3}$ $15 - 9 = \underline{6}$ $15 - 6 = \underline{9}$

_____   _____   _____

TAKE HOME ACTIVITY • With your child, practice
saying subtraction facts from this lesson.

Name _____

✓ Mid-Chapter Checkpoint

Concepts and Skills

Write the sum.

1. $3 + 6 = \underline{9}$

2. $8 + 0 = \underline{8}$

3. $7 + 7 = \underline{14}$

4. $9 + 4 = \underline{13}$

5. $\underline{11} = 5 + 6$

6. $2 + 8 = \underline{10}$

7. $3 + 7 + 2 = \underline{12}$

8. $4 + 4 + 6 = \underline{10}$

Show how you can make a ten to find the sum.
Write the sum.

9. $9 + 7 = \underline{16}$

$10 + \underline{6} = \underline{16}$

10. $6 + 8 = \underline{14}$

$10 + \underline{4} = \underline{14}$

Write the sum and the difference for the related facts.

11. $5 + 4 = \underline{9}$

$9 - 4 = \underline{}$

12. $3 + 9 = \underline{}$

$12 - 9 = \underline{}$

13. $8 + 7 = \underline{}$

$15 - 8 = \underline{}$

14. **THINK SMARTER** Lily has 6 toys cars.
Yong has 5 toy cars. How many
toy cars do they have?

_____ toy cars

Practice Subtraction Facts

Learning Objective You will find differences by using a related addition fact or by counting back by 1, 2, or 3.

Write the difference.

1. $15 - 9 = $ ____	2. $10 - 2 = $ ____	3. ____ $= 13 - 5$
4. $14 - 7 = $ ____	5. $10 - 8 = $ ____	6. $12 - 7 = $ ____
7. ____ $= 10 - 3$	8. $16 - 7 = $ ____	9. $8 - 4 = $ ____
10. $11 - 5 = $ ____	11. $13 - 6 = $ ____	12. ____ $= 12 - 9$
13. $16 - 9 = $ ____	14. ____ $= 11 - 9$	15. $12 - 8 = $ ____

Problem Solving Real World

Solve. Write or draw to explain.

16. Mr. Li has 16 pencils. He gives 9 pencils to some students. How many pencils does Mr. Li have now?

____ pencils

17. **WRITE Math** Write or draw to explain two different ways to find the difference for $12 - 3$.

_____

Lesson Check

1. Write the difference.

$$13 - 6 = \underline{\quad}$$

2. Write the difference.

$$12 - 3 = \underline{\quad}$$

Spiral Review

3. What is the value of the underlined digit?

6$\underline{2}$5

____

4. Count by fives.

405, ____, ____, ____

5. Devin has 39 toy blocks. What is the value of the digit 9 in this number?

____

6. Which number has the same value as 20 tens?

____

FOR MORE PRACTICE
GO TO THE
Personal Math Trainer

Name _____

Use Ten to Subtract

Essential Question How does getting to 10 in subtraction help when finding differences?

Learning Objective You will find a difference on a number line by getting to 10 and then using a tens fact.

Listen and Draw (Real World)

Circle to show the amount you subtract for each problem.

© Houghton Mifflin Harcourt Publishing Company

FOR THE TEACHER • Read the following problem. Deveron has 13 crayons. He gives 3 crayons to Tyler. How many crayons does Deveron have now? Have children circle the part of the blue line segment that shows what is subtracted from the total. Repeat for two more problems.

Math Talk Math Processes and Practices ⑦

Look for Structure Describe a pattern in the three problems and answers.

Chapter 3

You can subtract in steps to use a tens fact.

$14 - 6 = ?$

4   2

Subtract in steps:
$14 - 4 = 10$
$10 - 2 = 8$

- 2   - 4

0 1 2 3 4 5 6 7 8 9 **10** 11 12 13 14 15 16 17 18 19 20

So, $14 - 6 = \underline{8}$.

Share and Show   MATH BOARD

Show the tens fact you used. Write the difference.

0 1 2 3 4 5 6 7 8 9 **10** 11 12 13 14 15 16 17 18 19 20

1. $12 - 5 = \underline{\hphantom{00}}$

2   3

$10 - \underline{\hphantom{00}} = \underline{\hphantom{00}}$

2. $11 - 6 = \underline{\hphantom{00}}$

1   5

$10 - \underline{\hphantom{00}} = \underline{\hphantom{00}}$

3. $15 - 7 = \underline{\hphantom{00}}$

$10 - \underline{\hphantom{00}} = \underline{\hphantom{00}}$

4. $13 - 7 = \underline{\hphantom{00}}$

$10 - \underline{\hphantom{00}} = \underline{\hphantom{00}}$

Name _____

On Your Own

Show the tens fact you used. Write the difference.

0 1 2 3 4 5 6 7 8 9 **10** 11 12 13 14 15 16 17 18 19 20

5. $13 - 5 =$ _____

10 − ____ = ____

6. $15 - 6 =$ _____

10 − ____ = ____

7. $12 - 8 =$ _____

10 − ____ = ____

8. $14 - 8 =$ _____

10 − ____ = ____

9. **GO DEEPER** Chris had 15 stickers. He gave Ann and Suzy each the same number of stickers. Now Chris has 7 stickers. How many stickers did he give to each girl?

_____ stickers

Solve. Write or draw to explain.

10. **THINK SMARTER** Beth has a box of 16 crayons. She gives 3 crayons to Jake and 7 crayons to Wendy. How many crayons does Beth have now?

_____ crayons

Problem Solving • Applications

WRITE Math

GO DEEPER Write number sentences that use both addition and subtraction. Use each choice only once.

~~9 − 2~~

~~3 + 4~~

1 + 4

14 − 6

5 + 4

15 − 6

10 − 5

4 + 4

11.
$$9 - 2 = 3 + 4$$
$$7 = 7$$

12.

_____ = _____

13.

_____ = _____

14.

_____ = _____

15. **THINK SMARTER** Does the number sentence have the same difference as 15 − 7 = ■? Choose Yes or No.

10 − 6 = ■   ○ Yes   ○ No

10 − 2 = ■   ○ Yes   ○ No

10 − 4 = ■   ○ Yes   ○ No

TAKE HOME ACTIVITY • Ask your child to name pairs of numbers that have a difference of 10. Then have him or her write the number sentences.

Name _____

Use Ten to Subtract

Learning Objective You will find a difference on a number line by getting to 10 and then using a tens fact.

**Show the tens fact you used.
Write the difference.**

1. $14 - 6 =$ ____

   $10 -$ ____ $=$ ____

2. $12 - 7 =$ ____

   $10 -$ ____ $=$ ____

3. $13 - 7 =$ ____

   $10 -$ ____ $=$ ____

4. $15 - 8 =$ ____

   $10 -$ ____ $=$ ____

Problem Solving

Solve. Write or draw to explain.

5. Carl read 15 pages on Monday night and 9 pages on Tuesday night. How many more pages did he read on Monday night than on Tuesday night?

   ____ more pages

6. **WRITE** Math Describe how to use a tens fact to find the difference for $15 - 8$.

   _____

Lesson Check

1. Show the tens fact you used.
Write the difference.

$12 - 6 =$ ____

$10 - 4 =$ ____

2. Show the tens fact you used.
Write the difference.

$13 - 8 =$ ____

$10 - 5 =$ ____

Spiral Review

3. Write a related subtraction
fact for $7 + 3 = 10$.

_____

4. Joe has 8 trucks. Carmen has
I more truck than Joe. How
many trucks do they have now?

____ trucks

5. There were 276 people on
an airplane. Write a number
greater than 276.

____

6. Write $>$, $<$, or $=$ to compare.

537 ____ 375

© Houghton Mifflin Harcourt Publishing Company

FOR MORE PRACTICE
GO TO THE
Personal Math Trainer

Name _____

Algebra • Use Drawings to Represent Problems

Essential Question How are bar models used to show addition and subtraction problems?

Learning Objective You will use drawings and number sentences to represent and solve addition and subtraction problems.

Listen and Draw (Real World)

Complete the bar model to show the problem.
Complete the number sentence to solve.

_____ + _____ = _____   _____ pennies

_____ − _____ = _____   _____ pennies

FOR THE TEACHER • Read each problem and have children complete the bar models. Hailey has 5 pennies in her pocket and 7 pennies in her wallet. How many pennies does she have? Blake has 12 pennies in his bank. He gives 5 pennies to his sister. How many pennies does he have now?

(Math Talk) Math Processes and Practices ⑥

Explain how the problems are alike and how they are different.

Model and Draw

You can use bar models to show problems.

Ben eats 14 crackers. Ron eats 6 crackers. How many more crackers does Ben eat than Ron?

| 14 |
| 6 | |

$$14 - 6 = 8$$

_____ more crackers

Suzy had 14 cookies. She gave 6 cookies to Grace. How many cookies does Suzy have now?

| 6 | _____ |
| 14 |

_____

_____ cookies

Share and Show MATH BOARD

Complete the bar model. Then write a number sentence to solve.

1. Mr. James bought 15 plain bagels and 9 raisin bagels. How many more plain bagels than raisin bagels did he buy?

| 15 |
| 9 | |

_____

 _____ more plain bagels

Name _____

Complete the bar model. Then write a number sentence to solve.

2. Cole has 5 books about dogs and 6 books about cats. How many books does Cole have?

5	6

_____

_____ books

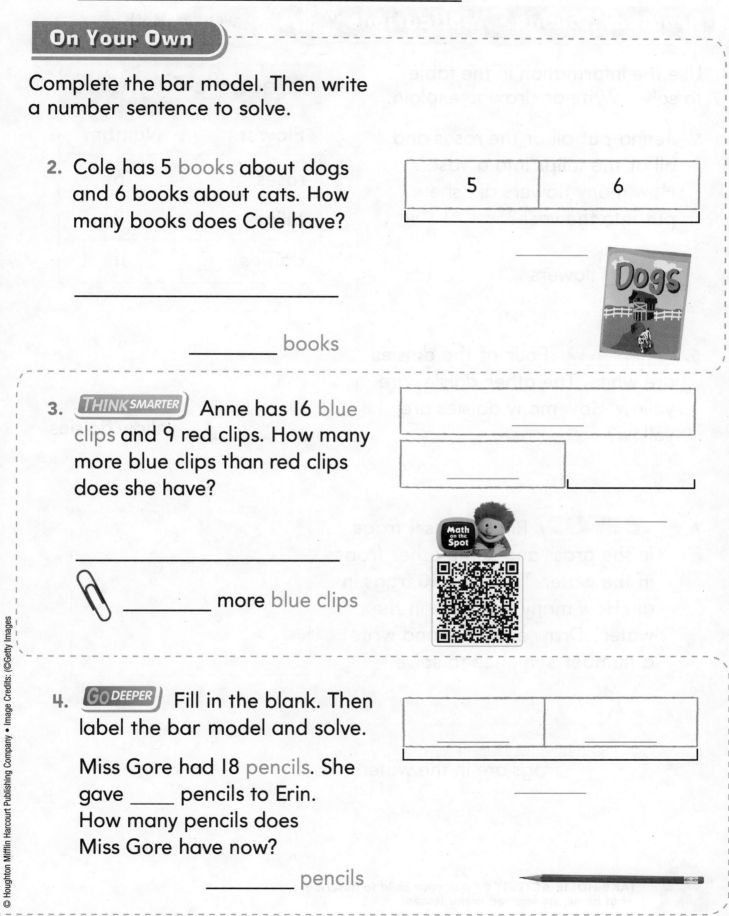

3. **THINK SMARTER** Anne has 16 blue clips and 9 red clips. How many more blue clips than red clips does she have?

_____

_____ more blue clips

4. **GO DEEPER** Fill in the blank. Then label the bar model and solve.

Miss Gore had 18 pencils. She gave ____ pencils to Erin. How many pencils does Miss Gore have now?

_____ pencils

Problem Solving • Applications (Real World)

WRITE Math

Use the information in the table to solve. Write or draw to explain.

Jenna's Flowers	
Flowers	**Number**
roses	6
tulips	8
daisies	11

5. Jenna put all of the roses and all of the tulips into a vase. How many flowers did she put into the vase?

_____ flowers

6. THINK SMARTER Four of the daisies are white. The other daisies are yellow. How many daisies are yellow?

_____ yellow daisies

7. THINK SMARTER Rita counts 4 frogs in the grass and some other frogs in the water. There are 10 frogs in all. How many frogs are in the water? Draw a picture and write a number sentence to solve.

_____

_____ frogs are in the water.

TAKE HOME ACTIVITY • Ask your child to describe what he or she learned in this lesson.

Name _____

Algebra • Use Drawings to Represent Problems

Complete the bar model. Then write a number sentence to solve.

Learning Objective You will use drawings and number sentences to represent and solve addition and subtraction problems.

1. Adam had 12 trucks. He gave 4 trucks to Ed. How many trucks does Adam have now?

_____	4

12

_____

_____ trucks

---

2. Grandma has 14 red roses and 7 pink roses. How many more red roses than pink roses does she have?

14

7	

_____

_____

_____ more red roses

---

3. **Explain how you used the bar model in Exercise 2 to solve the problem**

_____

_____

Lesson Check

1. Complete the bar model. Then solve. Abby has 16 grapes. Jason has 9 grapes. How many more grapes does Abby have than Jason?

_____ more grapes

Spiral Review

2. Write a subtraction fact with the same difference as 16 − 7.

_____

3. What is the difference?

$$18 - 9 = \underline{}$$

4. What is another way to write 300 + 20 + 5?

_____

5. What is the value of the underlined digit?

2̲8

_____

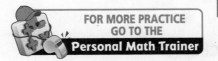

FOR MORE PRACTICE
GO TO THE
Personal Math Trainer

Algebra • Use Equations to Represent Problems

Essential Question How are number sentences used to show addition and subtraction situations?

Learning Objective You will write number sentences with a symbol for the missing number to represent addition and subtraction problems.

Write a story problem that could be solved using this bar model.

	9
_____	

15

_____

_____

_____

_____

_____

FOR THE TEACHER • Discuss with children how this bar model can be used to represent an addition or a subtraction situation.

Math Talk

Math Processes and Practices ②

Would you add or subtract to solve your story problem? **Explain.**

Model and Draw

A number sentence can be used to show a problem.

There were some girls and 4 boys at the park.
There were 9 children in all. How many girls were
at the park?

$$\blacksquare + 4 = 9$$

Think: $5 + 4 = 9$

So, there were __5__ girls at the park.

> The $\blacksquare$ is a placeholder for the missing number.

Share and Show MATH BOARD

Write a number sentence for the problem.
Use a $\blacksquare$ for the missing number. Then solve.

✓ 1. There were 14 ants on the
sidewalk. Then 6 ants went into
the grass. How many ants were
still on the sidewalk?

_____

_____ ants

✓ 2. There were 7 big dogs and
4 little dogs at the park. How
many dogs were at the park?

_____

_____ dogs

Name _____

Write a number sentence for the problem.
Use a ▪ for the missing number. Then solve.

3. A group of children were flying 13 kites. Some kites were put away. Then the children were flying 7 kites. How many kites were put away?

_____

_____ kites

4. There are 18 boys at the field. 9 of the boys are playing soccer. How many boys are not playing soccer?

_____

_____ boys

5. Math Processes and Practices ② **Use Reasoning**
Matthew found 9 acorns. Greg found 6 acorns. How many acorns did the two boys find?

_____

_____ acorns

6. THINKSMARTER There were some ducks in a pond. Four more ducks joined them. Then there were 12 ducks in the pond. How many ducks were in the pond at first?

Math on the Spot

_____ ducks

© Houghton Mifflin Harcourt Publishing Company • Image Credits: (bc) ©Juniors Bildarchiv/Alamy

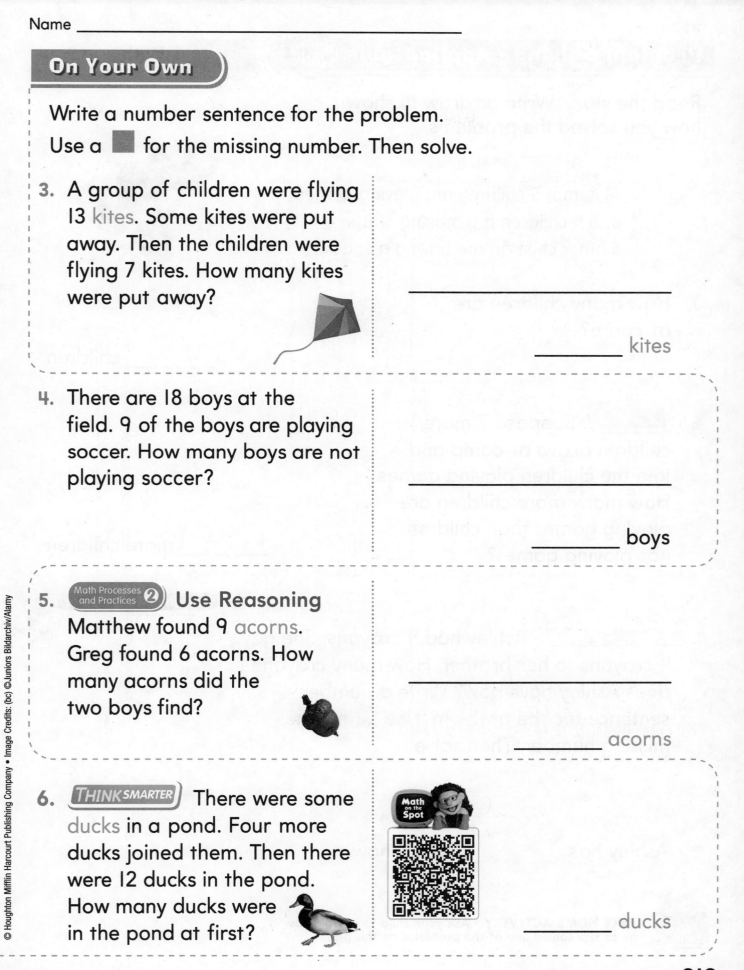

Problem Solving • Applications Real World WRITE Math

Read the story. Write or draw to show how you solved the problems.

> At camp, 5 children are playing games and 4 children are making crafts. 5 other children are having a snack.

7. How many children are at camp?

_____ children

8. GO DEEPER Suppose 7 more children arrive at camp and join the children playing games. How many more children are playing games than children not playing games?

_____ more children

Personal Math Trainer

9. THINK SMARTER + Ashley had 9 crayons. She gave 4 crayons to her brother. How many crayons does Ashley have now? Write a number sentence for the problem. Use ▪ for the missing number. Then solve.

_____

Ashley has _____ crayons now.

TAKE HOME ACTIVITY • Ask your child to explain how he or she solved one of the problems on this page.

Algebra • Use Equations to Represent Problems

Learning Objective You will write number sentences with a symbol for the missing number to represent addition and subtraction problems.

Write a number sentence for the problem.

Use a ▪ for the missing number. Then solve.

1. There were 15 apples in a bowl. Dan used some apples to make a pie. Now there are 7 apples in the bowl. How many apples did Dan use?

_____

____ apples

2. Amy has 16 gift bags. She fills 8 gift bags with whistles. How many gift bags are not filled with whistles?

_____

____ gift bags

Problem Solving Real World

Write or draw to show how you solved the problem.

3. Tony has 7 blue cubes and 6 red cubes. How many cubes does he have?

_____ cubes

4. **WRITE** Math Write a story problem for the addition sentence 7 + ▪ = 9. Solve the story problem.

_____

_____

_____

Lesson Check

1. Fred peeled 9 carrots. Nancy peeled 6 carrots. How many fewer carrots did Nancy peel than Fred?

_____ fewer carrots

2. Omar has 8 marbles. Joy has 7 marbles. How many marbles do they have together?

_____ marbles

Spiral Review

3. What is the sum?

$8 + 8 = $ _____

4. What is the sum?

$5 + 4 + 3 = $ _____

5. What number has the same value as 1 hundred 7 tens?

_____

6. What is another way to write the number 358?

_____ hundreds _____ tens _____ ones

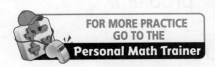

FOR MORE PRACTICE
GO TO THE
Personal Math Trainer

Problem Solving • Equal Groups

Essential Question How can acting it out help when solving a problem about equal groups?

Learning Objective You will use counters, skip counting, and the strategy *act it out* to find the total number of objects arranged in equal groups.

Theo puts his stickers in 5 rows.
There are 3 stickers in each row.
How many stickers does Theo have?

Unlock the Problem Real World

What do I need to find?

how many stickers

Theo has

What information do I need to use?

5 rows of stickers

3 stickers in each row

Show how to solve the problem.

_____ stickers

HOME CONNECTION • Your child used counters to act out the problem. Counters are a concrete tool that helps children act out the problem.

Act out the problem.
Draw to show what you did.

- What do I need to find?
- What information do I need to use?

1. Maria puts all of her postcards in 4 rows. There are 3 postcards in each row. How many postcards does Maria have?

_____ postcards

2. Jamal puts 4 toys in each box. How many toys will he put in 4 boxes?

_____ toys

Math Talk Math Processes and Practices 7

Explain how acting it out and skip counting helped you solve the second problem.

Name _____

Act out the problem.
Draw to show what you did.

✓ 3. Mr. Fulton puts 3 bananas
on each tray. How many
bananas are on 4 trays?

_____ bananas

✓ 4. There are 3 rows of apples.
There are 5 apples in each
row. How many apples are
there?

_____ apples

5. THINK SMARTER There are 4 plates.
Dexter puts 2 grapes on
each plate. Then he puts
2 grapes on each of 6 more
plates. How many grapes in all
does he put on the plates?

Math
on the
Spot

_____ grapes

Problem Solving • Applications

WRITE Math

6. **Math Processes and Practices 6** **Make Connections**

Angela used these counters to act out a problem.

Write a problem about equal groups that Angela could have modeled with these counters.

_____

_____

_____

7. **THINK SMARTER** Max and 4 friends get books from the library. Each person gets 3 books. Draw a picture to show the groups of books.

How many books did they get?

_____ books

TAKE HOME ACTIVITY • Ask your child to explain how he or she solved one of the problems in this lesson.

Problem Solving • Equal Groups

Learning Objective You will use counters, skip counting, and the strategy *act it out* to find the total number of objects arranged in equal groups.

Act out the problem.
Draw to show what you did.

1. Mr. Anderson has 4 plates of cookies. There are 5 cookies on each plate. How many cookies are there?

_____ cookies

2. Ms. Trane puts some stickers in 3 rows. There are 2 stickers in each row. How many stickers does Ms. Trane have?

_____ stickers

3. WRITE Math Draw 3 rows with 2 counters in each row. Write a word problem that can be acted out using these counters.

_____

_____

Lesson Check

1. Jaime puts 3 oranges on each tray. How many oranges does he put on 5 trays?

_____ oranges

2. Maurice has 4 rows of toys with 4 toys in each row. How many toys does he have?

_____ toys

Spiral Review

3. Jack has 12 pencils and 7 pens. How many more pencils than pens does he have?

_____ pencils

4. Laura has 9 apples. Jon has 6 apples. How many apples do they have together?

_____ apples

5. Circle the even number.

1   3   5   8

6. What is the sum?

$7 + 9 = $ _____

FOR MORE PRACTICE
GO TO THE
Personal Math Trainer

Algebra • Repeated Addition

Essential Question How can you write an addition sentence for problems with equal groups?

Learning Objective You will write an addition sentence to represent the total number of objects arranged in equal groups.

Listen and Draw *Real World*

Use counters to model the problem.
Then draw a picture of your model.

FOR THE TEACHER • Read the following problem and have children first model the problem with counters and then draw a picture of their models. Clayton has 3 rows of cards. There are 5 cards in each row. How many cards does Clayton have?

Math Talk Math Processes and Practices ①

Describe how you found the number of counters in your model.

Model and Draw

You can use addition to find the total amount when you have equal groups.

3 rows of 4

Write: ___4___ + ___4___ + ___4___ = _____

_____ in all

Find the number of shapes in each row.
Complete the addition sentence to find the total.

1.

3 rows of _____

___ + ___ + ___ = ___

2.

4 rows of _____

__ + __ + __ + __ = ___

3.

5 rows of _____

___ + ___ + ___ + ___ + ___ = ___

Name _____

On Your Own

Find the number of shapes in each row.
Complete the addition sentence to find the total.

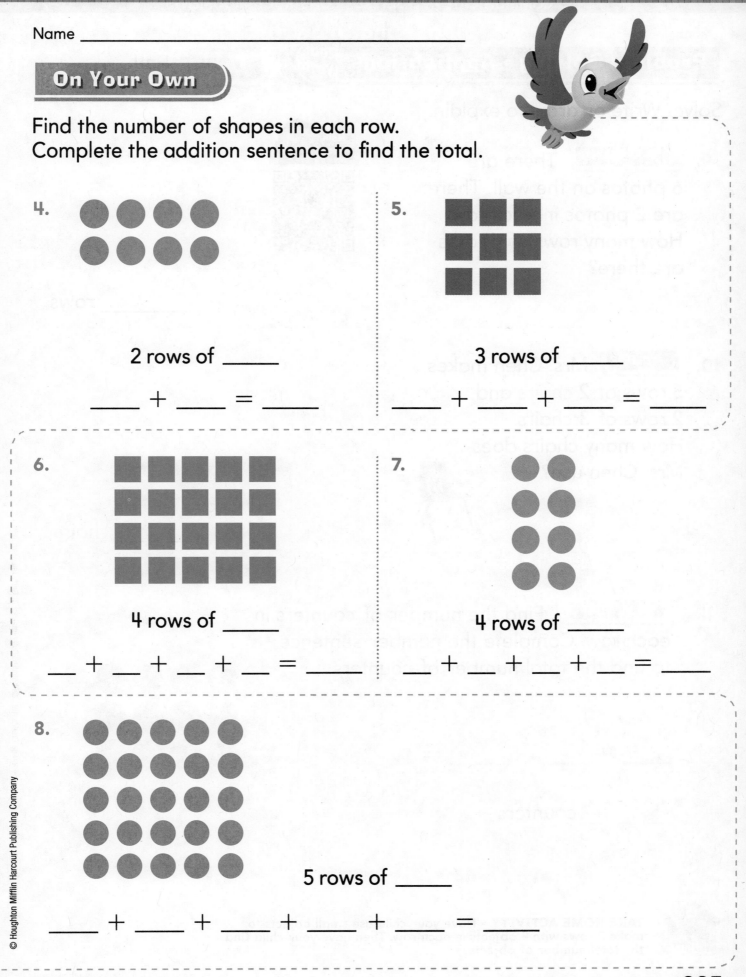

4.

2 rows of _____

_____ + _____ = _____

5.

3 rows of _____

_____ + _____ + _____ = _____

6.

4 rows of _____

_____ + _____ + _____ + _____ = _____

7.

4 rows of _____

_____ + _____ + _____ + _____ = _____

8.

5 rows of _____

_____ + _____ + _____ + _____ + _____ = _____

© Houghton Mifflin Harcourt Publishing Company

Problem Solving • Applications Real World   WRITE Math

Solve. Write or draw to explain.

9. **THINK SMARTER** There are 6 photos on the wall. There are 2 photos in each row. How many rows of photos are there?

_____ rows

10. **GO DEEPER** Mrs. Chen makes 5 rows of 2 chairs and 2 rows of 3 chairs. How many chairs does Mrs. Chen use?

_____ chairs

11. **THINK SMARTER** Find the number of counters in each row. Complete the number sentence to find the total number of counters.

_____ + _____ + _____ = _____

_____ counters

TAKE HOME ACTIVITY • Have your child use small objects to make 2 rows with 4 objects in each row. Then have your child find the total number of objects.

Algebra • Repeated Addition

Find the number of shapes in each row. Complete the addition sentence to find the total.

Learning Objective You will write an addition sentence to represent the total number of objects arranged in equal groups.

1.

3 rows of _____

___ + ___ + ___ = ___

2.

2 rows of _____

___ + ___ = ___

Problem Solving Real World

Solve. Write or draw to explain.

3. A classroom has 3 rows of desks. There are 5 desks in each row. How many desks are there altogether?

_____ desks

4. WRITE Math Explain how to write an addition sentence for a picture of 4 rows with 3 items in each row.

_____

_____

Lesson Check

1. A scrapbook has 4 pages. There are 2 stickers on each page. How many stickers are there?

   _____ stickers

2. Ben makes 5 rows of coins. He puts 3 coins in each row. How many coins are there?

   _____ coins

Spiral Review

3. There are 5 apples and 4 oranges. How many pieces of fruit are there?

   _____ pieces

4. Count by tens.

   40, ____, ____, ____, ____

5. Write the number 260 using words.

   _____

6. Write a fact with the same sum as 7 + 5.

   _____

FOR MORE PRACTICE
GO TO THE
Personal Math Trainer

Name _____

✓ Chapter 3 Review/Test

1. Erin puts 3 small cans, 4 medium cans, and 5 large cans on a shelf. How many cans does she put on the shelf?

   _____ cans

2. Fill in the bubble next to all the doubles facts you could use to find the sum of $3 + 2$?

   ○ $2 + 2$

   ○ $5 + 5$

   ○ $3 + 3$

   ○ $1 + 1$

3. Does the number sentence have the same difference as $14 - 6 = $ ▇ ?
   Choose Yes or No.

$10 - 1 = $ ▇	○ Yes	○ No
$10 - 2 = $ ▇	○ Yes	○ No
$10 - 3 = $ ▇	○ Yes	○ No
$10 - 4 = $ ▇	○ Yes	○ No

4. Mr. Brown sold 5 red backpacks and 8 blue backpacks. Write the number sentence. Show how you can make a ten to find the sum. Write the sum.

5 + 8 = _____

10 + _____ = _____

---

5. Find the number of shapes in each row.

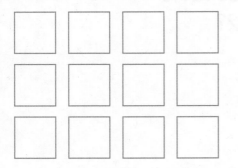

3 rows of _____

Complete the addition sentence to find the total.

_____ + _____ + _____ = _____

---

6. Tanya and 2 friends put rocks on the table. Each person put 2 rocks on the table. Draw a picture to show the groups of rocks.

How many rocks did they put on the table?

_____ rocks

Name _____

7. THINK SMARTER + Lily sees 15 tan puppies and 8 white puppies at the pet store. How many more tan puppies than white puppies does she see? Draw a picture and write a number sentence to solve.

_____

_____ more tan puppies

8. Mark counts 6 ducks in a pond and some ducks on the grass. There are 14 ducks in all. Draw a picture to show the two groups of ducks.

Write a number sentence that can help you find how many ducks are on the grass.

_____ + _____ = _____

How many ducks are on the grass?   _____ ducks

9. There are 8 peaches in a basket. Mrs. Dalton puts 7 more peaches in the basket. Complete the addition sentence to find how many peaches are in the basket now.

_____ + _____ = _____

_____ peaches

10. GO DEEPER Use the numbers on the tiles to write the differences.

Then write the next fact in the pattern.

| 4 | 5 | 6 | 7 |

$12 - 6 =$ _____ $11 - 6 =$ _____

$12 - 7 =$ _____ $12 - 6 =$ _____

$12 - 8 =$ _____ $13 - 6 =$ _____

_____   _____

11. Jose wanted to share 18 strawberries with
his brother equally. Draw a picture to show
how Jose can share the strawberries.

How many strawberries will Jose receive?

_____ strawberries

12. Hank has 13 grapes. He gives 5 grapes to his
sister. How many grapes does Hank have now?
Write a number sentence for the problem.
Use ■ for the missing number. Then solve.

_____

_____ grapes

© Houghton Mifflin Harcourt Publishing Company

2-Digit Addition

The keys of a modern piano are made from wood or plastic. A modern piano has 36 black keys and 52 white keys. How many keys is this in all?

Name _____

✓ Show What You Know

Addition Patterns

Add 2. Complete each addition sentence.

1. $1 + \underline{2} = \underline{3}$

2. $2 + \underline{} = \underline{}$

3. $3 + \underline{} = \underline{}$

4. $4 + \underline{} = \underline{}$

5. $5 + \underline{} = \underline{}$

6. $6 + \underline{} = \underline{}$

Addition Facts

Write the sum.

7. $\begin{array}{r} 7 \\ +3 \\ \hline \end{array}$
8. $\begin{array}{r} 8 \\ +8 \\ \hline \end{array}$
9. $\begin{array}{r} 6 \\ +7 \\ \hline \end{array}$
10. $\begin{array}{r} 4 \\ +4 \\ \hline \end{array}$
11. $\begin{array}{r} 9 \\ +5 \\ \hline \end{array}$
12. $\begin{array}{r} 8 \\ +7 \\ \hline \end{array}$

Tens and Ones

Write how many tens and ones for each number.

13. 43

14. 68

_____ tens _____ ones   _____ tens _____ ones

This page checks understanding of important skills needed
for success in Chapter 4.

Name _____

Review Words

sum
addend
digit
tens
ones

Vocabulary Builder

Visualize It

Use review words to fill in the graphic organizer.

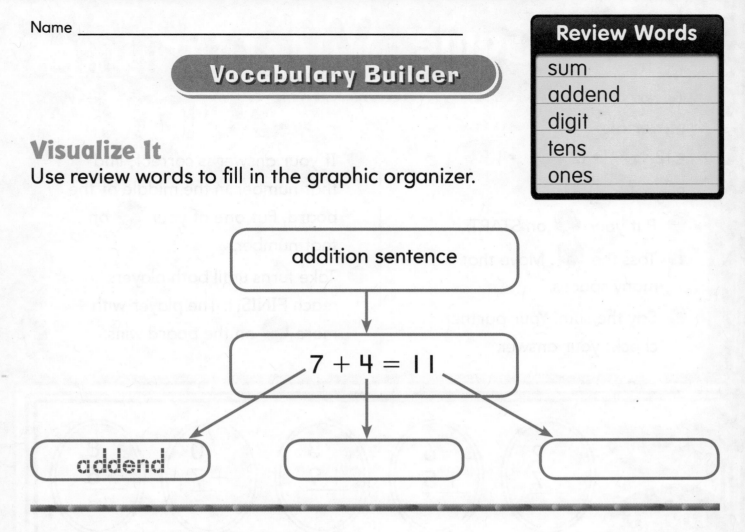

addition sentence

$7 + 4 = 11$

addend

Understand Vocabulary

1. Write a number with the **digit** 3 in the **tens** place.   _____

2. Write a number with the **digit** 5 in the **ones** place.   _____

3. Write a number that has the same **digit** in the **tens** place and in the **ones** place.   _____

4. Write a number with **digits** that have a **sum** of 8.   _____

© Houghton Mifflin Harcourt Publishing Company

Game What is the Sum?

Materials
- 12 ●
- 12 ●
- 1 🎲

Play with a partner.

1. Put your ● on START.
2. Toss the 🎲. Move that many spaces.
3. Say the sum. Your partner checks your answer.
4. If your answer is correct, find that number in the middle of the board. Put one of your ● on that number.
5. Take turns until both players reach FINISH. The player with more ● on the board wins.

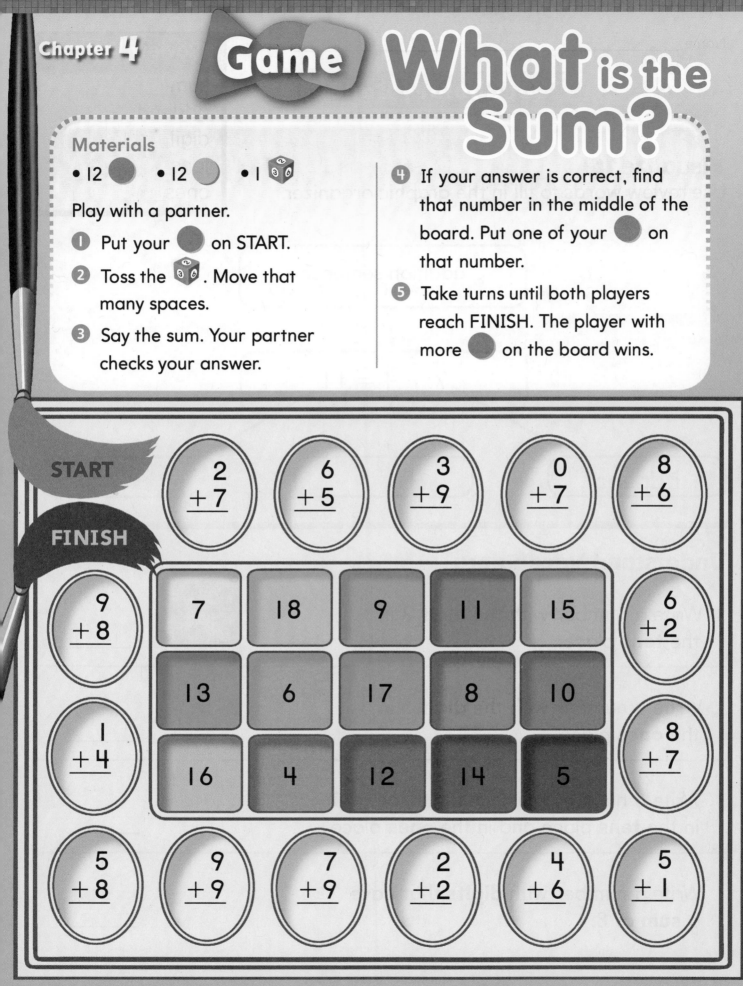

START

$\begin{array}{r}2\\+7\\\hline\end{array}$ $\begin{array}{r}6\\+5\\\hline\end{array}$ $\begin{array}{r}3\\+9\\\hline\end{array}$ $\begin{array}{r}0\\+7\\\hline\end{array}$ $\begin{array}{r}8\\+6\\\hline\end{array}$

FINISH

$\begin{array}{r}9\\+8\\\hline\end{array}$

7	18	9	11	15
13	6	17	8	10
16	4	12	14	5

$\begin{array}{r}6\\+2\\\hline\end{array}$

$\begin{array}{r}1\\+4\\\hline\end{array}$

$\begin{array}{r}8\\+7\\\hline\end{array}$

$\begin{array}{r}5\\+8\\\hline\end{array}$ $\begin{array}{r}9\\+9\\\hline\end{array}$ $\begin{array}{r}7\\+9\\\hline\end{array}$ $\begin{array}{r}2\\+2\\\hline\end{array}$ $\begin{array}{r}4\\+6\\\hline\end{array}$ $\begin{array}{r}5\\+1\\\hline\end{array}$

Chapter 4 Vocabulary

column

columna

7

digit

dígito

15

hundred

centena

31

is equal to (=)

es igual a

33

ones

unidades

45

regroup

reagrupar

56

sum

suma o total

59

ten

decena

61

0, 1, 2, 3, 4, 5, 6, 7, 8, and 9 are **digits**.

column

$$
\begin{array}{r}
3\,|3 \\
3\,|4 \\
+\ 3\,|2 \\
\hline
\end{array}
$$

2	plus	1	is equal to	3
2	+	1	=	3

There are 10 tens in 1 **hundred**.

Tens	Ones

You can trade 10 ones for 1 ten to **regroup**.

10 ones = 1 ten

---

10 ones = 1 ten

4 + 2 = 6

sum

Matchup

Word Box
column
digit
hundred
is equal to (=)
ones
regroup
sum
tens

For 2 to 3 players

Materials
- 1 set of word cards

How to Play
1. Put the cards face-down in rows. Take turns to play.
2. Choose two cards. Turn the cards face-up.
   - If the cards match, keep the pair and take another turn.
   - If the cards do not match, turn them over again.
3. The game is over when all cards have been matched. The players count their pairs. The player with the most pairs wins.

The Write Way

Reflect

Choose one idea. Write about it in the space below.

- Explain how drawing quick pictures helps you add 2-digit numbers.
- Tell about all the different ways you can add 2-digit numbers.
- Write three things you know about regrouping.

Name _____

Break Apart Ones to Add

Essential Question How does breaking apart a number make it easier to add?

Learning Objective You will add two numbers by breaking apart ones to make a ten.

Listen and Draw Real World · Hands On

Use ▭▭▭ ▮. Draw to show what you did.

FOR THE TEACHER • Read the following problem. Have children use blocks to solve. Griffin read 27 books about animals and 6 books about space. How many books did he read?

Math Talk Math Processes and Practices 6

Describe what you did with the blocks.

Model and Draw

Break apart ones to make a ten.
Use this as a way to add.

27 + 8 = ___?___

27 + 8

27 + 3 + 5

30 + 5 = _____

27 + 8 = _____

Share and Show   MATH BOARD

Draw quick pictures. Break apart ones to
make a ten. Then add and write the sum.

1. 15 + 7 = _____

2. 26 + 5 = _____

3. 37 + 8 = _____

4. 28 + 6 = _____

© Houghton Mifflin Harcourt Publishing Company

Name _____

On Your Own

Break apart ones to make a ten.
Then add and write the sum.

5. 23 + 9 = _____

6. 48 + 5 = _____

7. 18 + 5 = _____

8. 33 + 9 = _____

9. 27 + 6 = _____

10. 49 + 4 = _____

11. **GO DEEPER** Alex sets up 32 small
tables and 9 large tables in a room.
Then he sets up 5 more large tables
along a wall. How many tables
does Alex set up?

_____ tables

12. **THINK SMARTER** Bruce sees 29 oak
trees and 4 maple trees at
the park. Then he sees double the
number of pine trees as maple
trees. How many trees does
Bruce see?

Math on the Spot

_____ trees

Problem Solving • Applications (Real World) [WRITE] Math

Solve. Write or draw to explain.

13. **GO DEEPER** Megan has 38 animal pictures, 5 people pictures, and 3 insect pictures. How many pictures does she have?

_____ pictures

14. (Math Processes and Practices 1) **Analyze**

Jamal has a box with 22 toy cars in it. He puts 9 more toy cars into the box. Then he takes 3 toy cars out of the box. How many toy cars are in the box now?

_____ toy cars

15. **THINK SMARTER** Dan has 16 pencils. Quentin gives him 5 more pencils. Choose all the ways you can use to find how many pencils Dan has in all.

- ○ $16 + 5$
- ○ $16 + 4 + 1$
- ○ $16 - 5$

TAKE HOME ACTIVITY • Say a number from 0 to 9. Have your child name a number to add to yours to have a sum of 10.

Name _____

Break Apart Ones to Add

Learning Objective You will add two numbers by breaking apart ones to make a ten.

Break apart ones to make a ten. Then add and write the sum.

1. $62 + 9 =$ ___

2. $27 + 7 =$ ___

3. $28 + 5 =$ ___

4. $17 + 8 =$ ___

5. $57 + 6 =$ ___

6. $23 + 9 =$ ___

7. $39 + 7 =$ ___

8. $26 + 5 =$ ___

9. $13 + 8 =$ ___

10. $18 + 7 =$ ___

Problem Solving Real World

Solve. Write or draw to explain.

11. Jimmy had 18 toy airplanes. His mother bought him 7 more toy airplanes. How many toy airplanes does he have now?

_____ toy airplanes

12. **WRITE** Math Explain how you would find the sum of $46 + 7$.

_____

_____

Lesson Check

1. What is the sum?

$$26 + 7 = \underline{\quad}$$

2. What is the sum?

$$15 + 8 = \underline{\quad}$$

Spiral Review

3. Hannah has 4 blue beads and 8 red beads. How many beads does Hannah have?

$$4 + 8 = \underline{\quad} \text{ beads}$$

4. Rick had 4 stickers. Then he earned 2 more. How many stickers does he have now?

$$4 + 2 = \underline{\quad} \text{ stickers}$$

5. What is the sum?

$$4 + 5 + 4 = \underline{\quad}$$

6. Write 281 using hundreds, tens, and ones.

$$\underline{\quad} \text{ hundreds} \underline{\quad} \text{ tens} \underline{\quad} \text{ one}$$

FOR MORE PRACTICE
GO TO THE
Personal Math Trainer

Use Compensation

Essential Question How can you make an addend a ten to help solve an addition problem?

Learning Objective You will make an addend a tens number to help solve an addition problem.

Listen and Draw (Real World)

Draw quick pictures to show the problems.

Math Talk Math Processes and Practices ①

FOR THE TEACHER • Have children draw quick pictures to solve this problem. Kara has 47 stickers. She buys 20 more stickers. How many stickers does she have now? Repeat for this problem. Tyrone has 30 stickers and buys 52 more stickers. How many stickers does he have now?

Analyze Describe how you found how many stickers Tyrone has.

Model and Draw

Take ones from an addend to make the other addend the next tens number.

Adding can be easier when one of the addends is a tens number.

$$25 + 48 = ?$$

$$\underline{}23 + \underline{}50 = \underline{}$$

Share and Show MATH BOARD

Show how to make one addend the next tens number.
Complete the new addition sentence.

1. $37 + 25 = ?$

   $\underline{40} + \underline{} = \underline{}$

2. $27 + 46 = ?$

   $\underline{} + \underline{} = \underline{}$

3. $14 + 29 = ?$

   $\underline{} + \underline{} = \underline{}$

On Your Own

Show how to make one addend the next tens number.
Complete the new addition sentence.

4. 18 + 13 = ?

_____ + _____ = _____

5. 24 + 18 = ?

_____ + _____ = _____

6. **GO DEEPER** Lee finds 44 shells. Wayne
finds 39 shells. How many shells do
they still need if they want 90 shells
in all?

_____ shells

Solve. Write or draw to explain.

7. **THINK SMARTER** Zach finds
38 sticks. Kelly finds 27 sticks.
How many more sticks do the
two children still need if they
want 70 sticks in all?

_____ **more** sticks

Problem Solving • Applications (Real World) | WRITE) Math

Solve. Write or draw to explain.

8. **Math Processes and Practices 6** **Make Connections**
The chart shows the leaves that Philip collected. He wants a collection of 52 leaves, using only two colors. Which two colors of leaves should he use?

Leaves Collected	
Color	**Number**
green	27
brown	29
yellow	25

_____ and _____

9. **THINK SMARTER** Ava has 39 sheets of white paper. She has 22 sheets of green paper. Draw a picture and write to explain how to find the number of sheets of paper Ava has.

Ava has _____ sheets of paper.

TAKE HOME ACTIVITY • Have your child choose one problem on this page and explain how to solve it in another way.

Use Compensation

Learning Objective You will make an addend a tens number to help solve an addition problem.

Show how to make one addend the next tens number. Complete the new addition sentence.

1. $15 + 37 = ?$ ___ + ___ = ___

2. $22 + 49 = ?$ ___ + ___ = ___

3. $38 + 26 = ?$ ___ + ___ = ___

Problem Solving Real World

Solve. Write or draw to explain.

4. The oak tree at the school was 34 feet tall.
    Then it grew 18 feet taller.
    How tall is the oak tree now?

    _____ feet tall

5. **WRITE** Math Explain why you would make one of the
    addends a tens number when solving an addition problem.

    _____

    _____

Lesson Check

1. What is the sum?

$$18 + 25 = \underline{}$$

2. What is the sum?

$$27 + 24 = \underline{}$$

Spiral Review

3. Circle the even number.

27   14   11   5

4. Andrew sees 4 fish. Kim sees double that number of fish. How many fish does Kim see?

_____ fish

5. Write a related subtraction fact for $7 + 6 = 13$.

_____

6. What is the sum?

$$2 + 8 = \underline{}$$

FOR MORE PRACTICE
GO TO THE
Personal Math Trainer

Name _____

Break Apart Addends as Tens and Ones

Essential Question How do you break apart addends to add tens and then add ones?

Learning Objective You will break apart addends as tens and ones to add within 100.

Listen and Draw

Write the number. Then write the number as tens plus ones.

```
_____ + _____
```

```
_____ + _____
```

```
_____ + _____
```

Math Talk Math Processes and Practices ①

What is the value of the 6 in the number 63? **Explain** how you know.

FOR THE TEACHER • Direct children's attention to the orange box. Have children write 25 inside the large rectangle. Then ask children to write 25 as tens plus ones. Repeat the activity for 36 and 42.

Chapter 4

Model and Draw

Break apart the addends into tens and ones.
Add the tens and add the ones.
Then find the total sum.

$$27 \longrightarrow 20 + 7$$
$$+48 \longrightarrow 40 + 8$$
$$\underline{60} + \underline{15} = \underline{}$$

$$60 + 15$$
$$\diagdown$$
$$10 \quad 5$$
$$70 + 5 = \underline{}$$

Share and Show MATH BOARD

Break apart the addends to find the sum.

1. $35 \longrightarrow \underline{30} + \underline{5}$

$+54 \longrightarrow \underline{50} + \underline{4}$

$\underline{80} + \underline{9} = \underline{89}$

2. $43 \longrightarrow \underline{40} + \underline{3}$

$+29 \longrightarrow \underline{20} + \underline{9}$

$\underline{43} + \underline{29} = \underline{72}$

3. $56 \longrightarrow \underline{50} + \underline{6}$

$+38 \longrightarrow \underline{30} + \underline{8}$

$\underline{38} + \underline{46} = \underline{94}$

On Your Own

Break apart the addends to find the sum.

4. $14 \longrightarrow \underline{10} + \underline{4}$

   $+23 \longrightarrow \underline{20} + \underline{3}$

   _____ + _____ = _____

5. $37 \longrightarrow \underline{} + \underline{}$

   $+45 \longrightarrow \underline{} + \underline{}$

   _____ + _____ = _____

6. **GO DEEPER** Chris read 15 pages of his book. Tony read 4 more pages than Chris. How many pages did Chris and Tony read?

_____ pages

7. **THINK SMARTER** Julie read 18 pages of her book in the morning. She read the same number of pages in the afternoon. How many pages did she read?

_____ pages

Problem Solving • Applications (Real World)

 WRITE **Math**

Write or draw to explain.

8. **Math Processes and Practices ①** **Make Sense of Problems** Len has 35 baseball cards. The rest of his cards are basketball cards. He has 58 cards in all. How many basketball cards does he have?

_____ basketball cards

9. **Math Processes and Practices ①** **Evaluate** Tomás has 17 pencils. He buys 26 more pencils. How many pencils does Tomás have now?

_____ pencils

Personal Math Trainer

10. **THINK SMARTER ✛** Sasha used 38 red stickers and 22 blue stickers. Show how you can break apart the addends to find how many stickers Sasha used.

$$38 \longrightarrow \underline{\quad} + \underline{\quad}$$

$$+22 \longrightarrow \underline{\quad} + \underline{\quad}$$

$$\underline{\quad} + \underline{\quad} = \underline{\quad} \text{ stickers}$$

TAKE HOME ACTIVITY • Write 32 + 48 on a sheet of paper. Have your child break apart the numbers and find the sum.

Name _____

Model Regrouping for Addition

Essential Question When do you regroup in addition?

Learning Objective You will model addition within 100 with regrouping to find sums.

Listen and Draw *Real World* **Hands On**

Use to model the problem.
Draw quick pictures to show what you did.

Tens	Ones

Math Talk

Math Processes and Practices ⑤

Use Tools Describe how you made a ten in your model.

🍎 **FOR THE TEACHER** • Read the following problem. Brandon has 24 books. His friend Mario has 8 books. How many books do they have?

Chapter 4

Add 37 and 25.

Step 1 Look at the ones. Can you make a ten?

Tens	Ones

yes   no

Step 2 If you can make a ten, **regroup**.

Tens	Ones

Trade 10 ones for 1 ten to regroup.

Step 3 Write how many tens and ones. Write the sum.

Tens	Ones

_____ tens _____ ones

_____

Share and Show   MATH BOARD

Draw to show the regrouping. Write how many tens and ones are in the sum. Write the sum.

1. Add 47 and 15.

Tens	Ones

_____ tens _____ ones

_____

☑ 2. Add 48 and 8.

Tens	Ones

_____ tens _____ ones

_____

☑ 3. Add 26 and 38.

Tens	Ones

_____ tens _____ ones

_____

On Your Own

Draw to show if you regroup. Write how many tens and ones are in the sum. Write the sum.

4. Add 79 and 6.

Tens	Ones

_____ tens _____ ones

_____

5. Add 18 and 64.

Tens	Ones

_____ tens _____ ones

_____

6. Add 23 and 39.

Tens	Ones

_____ tens _____ ones

_____

7. Add 54 and 25.

Tens	Ones

_____ tens _____ ones

_____

8. Add 33 and 7.

Tens	Ones

_____ tens _____ ones

_____

9. Add 27 and 68.

Tens	Ones

_____ tens _____ ones

_____

10. THINK SMARTER Kara has 25 toy animals and 12 books. Jorge has 8 more toy animals than Kara has. How many toy animals does Jorge have?

Math on the Spot

_____ toy animals

Problem Solving • Applications (Real World)   WRITE Math

Write or draw to explain.

11. (Math Processes and Practices **①**) **Make Sense of Problems** Mrs. Sanders has two fish tanks. There are 14 fish in the small tank. There are 27 fish in the large tank. How many fish are in the two tanks?

_____ fish

12. THINK SMARTER Charlie climbed 69 steps. Then he climbed 18 more steps. Show two different ways to find how many steps Charlie climbed.

Charlie climbed _____ steps.

TAKE HOME ACTIVITY • Ask your child to write a word problem with 2-digit numbers about adding two groups of stamps.

Model Regrouping for Addition

Draw to show the regrouping. Write how many tens and ones in the sum. Write the sum.

Learning Objective You will model addition within 100 with regrouping to find sums.

1. Add 63 and 9.

Tens	Ones

_____ tens _____ ones

_____

2. Add 25 and 58.

Tens	Ones

_____ tens _____ ones

_____

3. Add 58 and 18.

Tens	Ones

_____ tens _____ ones

_____

4. Add 64 and 26.

Tens	Ones

_____ tens _____ ones

_____

5. Add 17 and 77.

Tens	Ones

_____ tens _____ ones

_____

6. Add 16 and 39.

Tens	Ones

_____ tens _____ ones

_____

Problem Solving *Real World*

Choose a way to solve. Write or draw to explain.

7. Cathy has 43 leaves in her collection. Jane has 38 leaves. How many leaves do the two children have?

_____ leaves

8. **WRITE** Math Suppose you are adding 43 and 28. Will you regroup? Explain.

_____

Lesson Check

1. Add 27 and 48. What is the sum?

_____

Spiral Review

2. What is the sum?

$$7 + 7 = \underline{\quad}$$

3. Circle the odd number.

6   12   21   22

4. What is the sum?

$$39 + 46 = \underline{\quad}$$

5. What is the sum?

$$5 + 3 + 4 = \underline{\quad}$$

FOR MORE PRACTICE
GO TO THE
Personal Math Trainer

Model and Record 2-Digit Addition

Essential Question How do you record 2-digit addition?

Learning Objective You will record sums for models of addition within 100.

Listen and Draw (Real World)

Use ▭▭▭▭ ▭ to model the problem.
Draw quick pictures to show what you did.

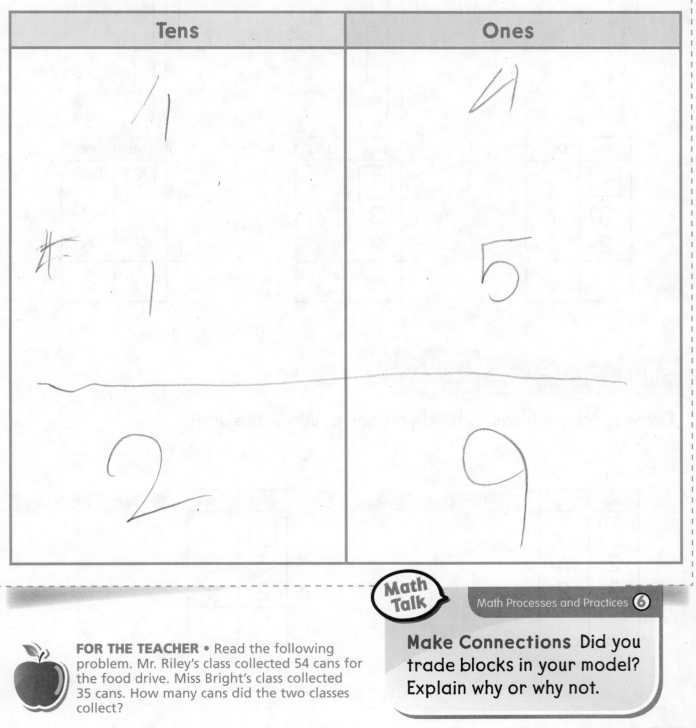

Tens	Ones
1	4
++	
1	5
————	————
2	9

FOR THE TEACHER • Read the following problem. Mr. Riley's class collected 54 cans for the food drive. Miss Bright's class collected 35 cans. How many cans did the two classes collect?

Math Talk Math Processes and Practices ⑥

Make Connections Did you trade blocks in your model? Explain why or why not.

Model and Draw

Trace over the quick pictures in the steps.

Step 1 Model 37 + 26. Are there 10 ones to regroup?

Step 2 Write the regrouped ten. Write how many ones are in the ones place now.

Step 3 How many tens are there? Write how many tens are in the tens place.

Tens	Ones
☐	
3	7
+ 2	6

Tens	Ones
1	
3	7
+ 2	6
	3

Tens	Ones
1	
3	7
+ 2	6
6	3

Share and Show MATH BOARD

Draw quick pictures to help you solve. Write the sum.

1.

Tens	Ones
☐	
2	6
+ 3	2
5	8

Tens	Ones

2.

Tens	Ones
☐	
5	8
+ 2	4

Tens	Ones

On Your Own

Draw quick pictures to help you solve. Write the sum.

3.

Tens	Ones
[1]	
3	4
+	9
4	3

Tens	Ones

4.

Tens	Ones
[1]	
2	7
+ 2	4
5	1

Tens	Ones

5.

Tens	Ones
[ ]	
3	5
+ 2	3
5	8

Tens	Ones

6.

Tens	Ones
[1]	
5	9
+	6
0	5

Tens	Ones

7. **THINK SMARTER** Tim has 36 stickers. Margo has 44 stickers. How many more stickers would they need to have 100 stickers altogether?

_____ more stickers

8. **GO DEEPER** A baker wants to sell 100 muffins. So far the baker has sold 48 corn muffins and 42 bran muffins. How many more muffins does the baker need to sell?

_____ more muffins

Problem Solving • Applications Real World WRITE Math

Write or draw to explain.

9. **Math Processes and Practices ①** **Make Sense of Problems**
Chris and Bianca got 80 points in all in the spelling contest. Each child got more than 20 points. How many points could each child have gotten?

Chris: _____ points

Bianca: _____ points

Personal Math Trainer

10. **THINK SMARTER +** Don built a tower with 24 blocks. He built another tower with 18 blocks. How many blocks did Don use for both towers? Draw quick pictures to solve. Write the sum.

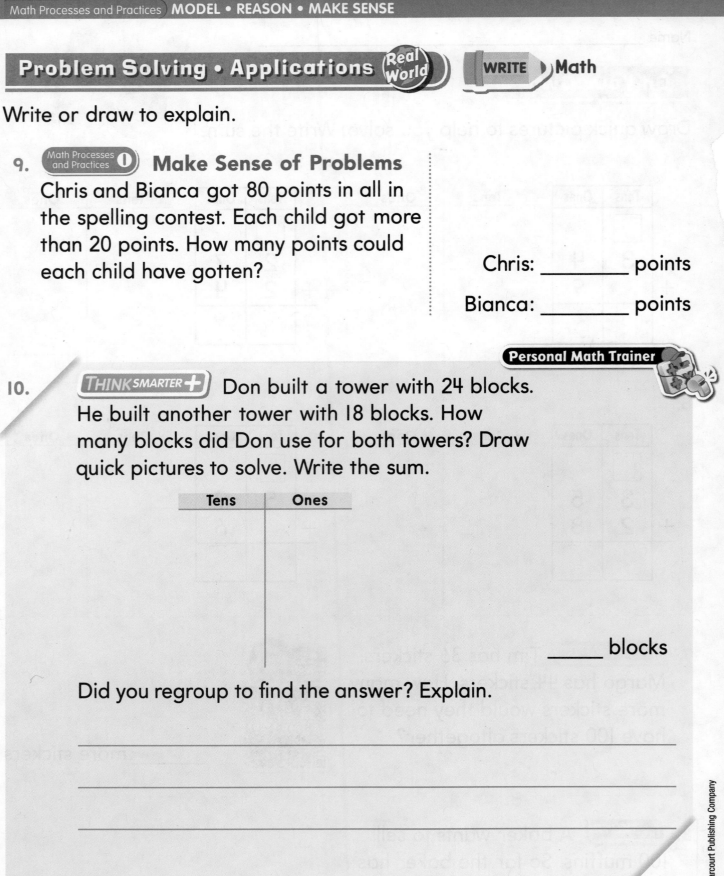

Tens	Ones

_____ blocks

Did you regroup to find the answer? Explain.

_____

_____

_____

TAKE HOME ACTIVITY • Write two 2-digit numbers and ask your child if he or she would regroup to find the sum.

Name _____

2-Digit Addition

Essential Question How do you record the steps when adding 2-digit numbers?

Learning Objective You will record the steps for adding within 100.

Listen and Draw Real World

Draw quick pictures to model each problem.

Tens	Ones

Tens	Ones

Math Talk   Math Processes and Practices ①

Analyze Relationships Explain why regrouping works.

FOR THE TEACHER • Read the following problem and have children draw quick pictures to solve. Jason scored 35 points in one game and 47 points in another game. How many points did Jason score? Repeat the activity with this problem. Patty scored 18 points. Then she scored 21 points. How many points did she score in all?

Chapter 4

Model and Draw

Add 59 and 24.

Step 1 Add the ones.

$9 + 4 = 13$

Tens	Ones
5	9
+ 2	4

Step 2 Regroup.
13 ones is the same as 1 ten 3 ones.

Tens	Ones
1	
5	9
+ 2	4
	3

Step 3 Add the tens.

$1 + 5 + 2 = 8$

Tens	Ones
1	
5	9
+ 2	4
8	3

Share and Show MATH BOARD

Regroup if you need to. Write the sum.

1.

Tens	Ones
1	
4	2
+ 2	9
7	1

2.

Tens	Ones
3	1
+ 1	4
4	5

3.

Tens	Ones
1	
2	7
+ 4	5
7	1

Name _____

Regroup if you need to. Write the sum.

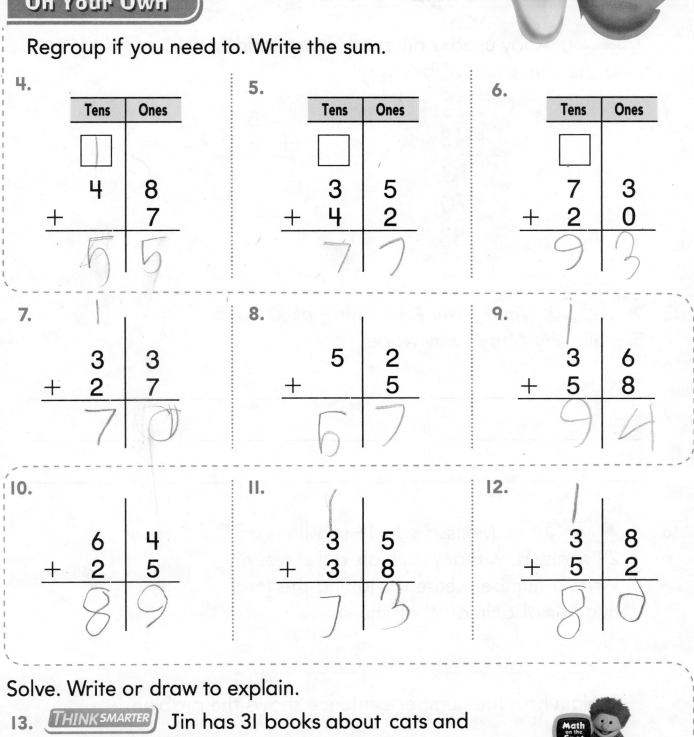

4.

Tens	Ones
☐	
4	8
+	7

5 | 5

5.

Tens	Ones
☐	
3	5
+ 4	2

7 | 7

6.

Tens	Ones
☐	
7	3
+ 2	0

9 | 3

7.

3	3
+ 2	7

7 | 0

8.

5	2
+	5

6 | 7

9.

3	6
+ 5	8

9 | 4

10.

6	4
+ 2	5

8 | 9

11.

3	5
+ 3	8

7 | 3

12.

3	8
+ 5	2

8 | 0

Solve. Write or draw to explain.

13. **THINK SMARTER** Jin has 31 books about cats and 19 books about dogs. He gives 5 books to his sister. How many books does Jin have now?

___40___ books

Problem Solving • Applications (Real World)   WRITE ▶ Math

14. GO DEEPER Abby used a different way to add.
Find the sum using Abby's way.

$$
\begin{array}{r}
35 \\
+\ 48 \\
\hline
13 \\
+\ 70 \\
\hline
83
\end{array}
$$

$$
\begin{array}{r}
5\ 7 \\
+\ 2\ 9 \\
\hline

\end{array}
$$

15. Math Processes and Practices ③ **Verify the Reasoning of Others**
Explain why Abby's way works.

_____

_____

_____

16. THINK SMARTER Melissa saw 14 sea lions and
29 seals. How many animals did she see?
Write a number sentence to find the total
number of animals that she saw.

_____

Explain how the number sentence shows the problem.

_____

_____

🏠 **TAKE HOME ACTIVITY** • Ask your child to show you two ways
to add 45 and 38.

Name _____

Practice 2-Digit Addition

Essential Question How do you record the steps when adding 2-digit numbers?

Learning Objective You will practice 2-digit addition with and without regrouping.

Listen and Draw Real World

Choose one way to solve the problem.
Draw or write to show what you did.

Math Talk Math Processes and Practices 6

Explain why you chose your way of solving the problem.

FOR THE TEACHER • Read the following problem. There were 45 boys and 53 girls who ran in the race. How many children ran in the race?

Chapter 4

two hundred seventy-three **273**

Model and Draw

Mrs. Meyers sold 47 snacks before the game. Then she sold 85 snacks during the game. How many snacks did she sell?

| Step 1 | Add the ones. | Step 2 | Add the tens. | Step 3 | 13 tens can be regrouped as 1 hundred 3 tens. Write the hundreds digit and the tens digit in the sum. |

Step 1 Add the ones.

$7 + 5 = 12$

Regroup 12 ones as 1 ten 2 ones.

```
  1
  4 7
+ 8 5
────────
    2
```

Step 2 Add the tens.

$1 + 4 + 8 = 13$

```
  1
  4 7
+ 8 5
────────
    2
```

Step 3 13 tens can be regrouped as 1 hundred 3 tens. Write the hundreds digit and the tens digit in the sum.

```
  1
  4 7
+ 8 5
────────
1 3 2
```

Share and Show MATH BOARD

Write the sum.

1.
```
  3 8
+ 9 4
──────
```

2.
```
  4 5
+ 5 2
──────
```

3.
```
  8 3
+ 7 6
──────
```

4.
```
  5 6
+ 3 5
──────
```

5.
```
  6 3
+ 5 1
──────
```

6.
```
  7 4
+ 4 9
──────
```

On Your Own

Write the sum.

7.
```
   5 2
+  3 7
_____
```

8.
```
   8 8
+  2 1
_____
```

9.
```
   7 4
+  6 7
_____
```

10.
```
   9 3
+  5 4
_____
```

11.
```
   9 2
+  7 8
_____
```

12.
```
   5 6
+  1 6
_____
```

13.
```
   3 1
+  4 5
_____
```

14.
```
   4 3
+  7 2
_____
```

15. **THINK SMARTER** Without finding the sums, circle the pairs of addends for which the sum will be greater than 100.

Explain how you decided which pairs to circle.

73
18

54
71

47
62

36
59

Math on the Spot

_____

_____

_____

_____

TAKE HOME ACTIVITY • Tell your child two 2-digit numbers. Have him or her write the numbers and find the sum.

Name _____

✓ Mid-Chapter Checkpoint

Personal Math Trainer
Online Assessment
and Intervention

Concepts and Skills

Break apart ones to make a ten.
Then add and write the sum.

1. 37 + 8 = _____

2. 55 + 7 = _____

Break apart the addends to find the sum.

3.   27 ⟶ _____ + _____

  + 36 ⟶ _____ + _____

          _____ + _____ = _____

Write the sum.

4.
```
   2 8
+  5 7
-------
```

5.
```
   6 7
+  3 1
-------
```

6.
```
   7 1
+  1 9
-------
```

7. **THINK SMARTER** Julia collected 25 cans to recycle. Dan collected 14 cans. How many cans did they collect?

_____ cans

Practice 2-Digit Addition

Learning Objective You will practice
2-digit addition with and without
regrouping.

Write the sum.

1.
$$58 + 17$$

2.
$$44 + 86$$

3.
$$36 + 13$$

4.
$$49 + 72$$

5.
$$58 + 87$$

6.
$$32 + 59$$

Problem Solving Real World

Solve. Write or draw to explain.

7. There are 45 books on the shelf.
There are 37 books on the table.
How many books are on the shelf
and the table?

_____ books

8. WRITE Math Describe how you regroup when you find the
sum of 64 + 43.

_____

_____

Lesson Check

1. What is the sum?

$$\begin{array}{r} 56 \\ + 35 \\ \hline \end{array}$$

2. What is the sum?

$$\begin{array}{r} 74 \\ + 15 \\ \hline \end{array}$$

Spiral Review

3. What is the value of the underlined digit?

5̲26

_____

4. Mr. Stevens wants to put 17 books on the shelf. He put 8 books on the shelf. How many more books does he need to put on the shelf?

$17 - 8 = $ _____ books

5. What is the difference?

$11 - 6 = $ _____

6. Write 83 as a sum of tens and ones.

_____ + _____

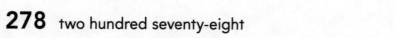

FOR MORE PRACTICE
GO TO THE
Personal Math Trainer

Rewrite 2-Digit Addition

Essential Question What are two different ways to write addition problems?

Learning Objective You will rewrite addition problems within 100 in a different way.

Listen and Draw Real World

Write the numbers for each addition problem.

$+$ _____

$+$ _____

$+$ _____

$+$ _____

Math Talk Math Processes and Practices 7

Look for Structure Explain why it is important to line up the digits of these addends in columns.

FOR THE TEACHER • Read the following problem and have children write the addends in vertical format. Juan's family drove 32 miles to his grandmother's house. Then they drove 14 miles to his aunt's house. How many miles did they drive? Repeat for three more problems.

© Houghton Mifflin Harcourt Publishing Company

Add. 28 + 45 = ?

Step 1 For 28, write the tens digit in the tens column.

Write the ones digit in the ones column.

Repeat for 45.

```
  2  8
+ 4  5
```

Step 2 Add the ones.

Regroup if you need to.

Add the tens.

```
  2  8
+ 4  5
```

Share and Show MATH BOARD

Rewrite the addition problem. Then add.

1. 25 + 8

+ _____

2. 37 + 10

+ _____

3. 25 + 45

+ _____

4. 38 + 29

+ _____

5. 20 + 45

+ _____

6. 63 + 9

+ _____

7. 15 + 36

+ _____

8. 74 + 18

+ _____

On Your Own

Rewrite the addition problem. Then add.

9. $27 + 54$

___ + ___

10. $34 + 30$

___ + ___

11. $26 + 17$

___ + ___

12. $48 + 38$

___ + ___

13. $50 + 32$

___ + ___

14. $61 + 38$

___ + ___

15. $37 + 43$

___ + ___

16. $79 + 17$

___ + ___

17. $45 + 40$

___ + ___

18. $21 + 52$

___ + ___

19. $17 + 76$

___ + ___

20. $68 + 29$

___ + ___

21. **THINK SMARTER** For which of the problems above could you find the sum without rewriting it? Explain.

_____

_____

_____

Problem Solving • Applications WRITE Math

Use the table.
Write or draw to
show how you
solved the problem.

Points Scored This Season	
Player	**Number of Points**
Anna	26
Lou	37
Becky	23
Kevin	19

22. **Math Processes and Practices ①** **Analyze Relationships**
Which two players scored 56 points
in all? Add to check your answer.

_____ and_____

23. **THINK SMARTER** Shawn says he can find the sum
of 20 + 63 without rewriting it. Explain how
to find the sum using mental math.

_____

_____

_____

_____

TAKE HOME ACTIVITY • Have your child write and
solve another problem, using the table above.

Rewrite 2-Digit Addition

Learning Objective You will rewrite addition problems within 100 in a different way.

Rewrite the numbers. Then add.

1. $27 + 19$

   $+$ _____

2. $36 + 23$

   $+$ _____

3. $31 + 29$

   $+$ _____

4. $48 + 23$

   $+$ _____

5. $53 + 12$

   $+$ _____

6. $69 + 13$

   $+$ _____

7. $24 + 38$

   $+$ _____

8. $46 + 37$

   $+$ _____

Problem Solving · Real World

Use the table. Show how you solved the problem.

9. How many pages did Sasha and Kara read together?

   _____ pages

Pages Read This Week	
Child	**Number of Pages**
Sasha	62
Kara	29
Juan	50

10. **WRITE · Math** Explain what can happen if you line up the digits incorrectly when you rewrite addition problems.

    _____
    _____
    _____
    _____

Lesson Check

1. What is the sum of 39 + 17?

$$+$$

2. What is the sum of 28 + 16?

$$+$$

Spiral Review

3. What number is another way to write 60 + 4?

_____

4. The classroom has 4 desks in each row. There are 5 rows. How many desks are there in the classroom?

_____ desks

5. A squirrel collected 17 acorns. Then the squirrel collected 31 acorns. How many acorns did the squirrel collect?

_____ acorns

6. What number can be written as 3 hundreds 7 tens 5 ones?

_____

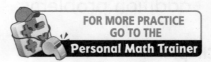

FOR MORE PRACTICE
GO TO THE
Personal Math Trainer

Problem Solving • Addition

Essential Question How can drawing a diagram help when solving addition problems?

Learning Objective You will use the strategy *draw a diagram* by making bar models to solve addition problems within 100.

Kendra had 13 crayons. Her dad gave her some more crayons. Then she had 19 crayons. How many crayons did Kendra's dad give her?

🔑 Unlock the Problem

What do I need to find?

how many crayons
_____
Kendra's dad gave her

What information do I need to use?

She had _____ crayons.
After he gave her some
more crayons, she had
_____ crayons.

Show how to solve the problem.

13	_____

19

There are 19 crayons in all.

13 + ▓ = 19

_____ crayons

HOME CONNECTION • Your child used a bar model and a number sentence to represent the problem. These help show what the missing amount is in order to solve the problem.

Label the bar model. Write a number sentence with a for the missing number. Solve.

- What do I need to find?
- What information do I need to use?

1. Mr. Kane has 24 red pens. He buys 19 blue pens. How many pens does he have now?

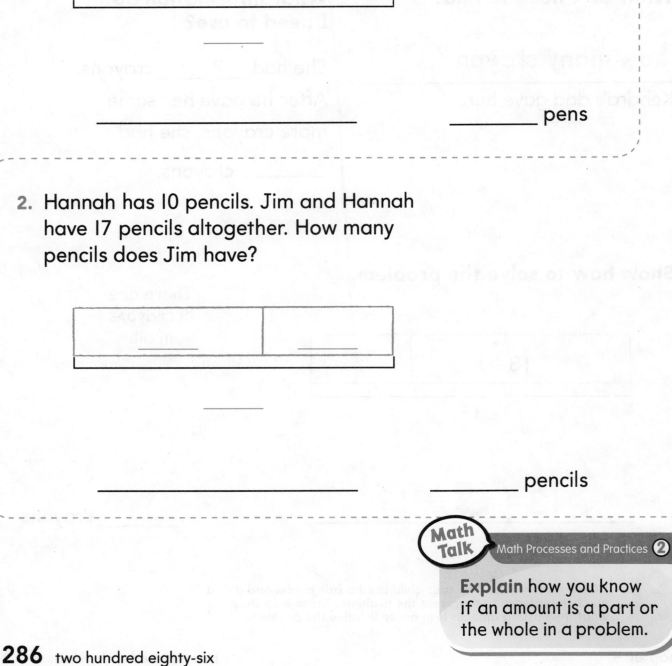

_____   _____ pens

2. Hannah has 10 pencils. Jim and Hannah have 17 pencils altogether. How many pencils does Jim have?

_____   _____ pencils

Math Talk Math Processes and Practices ②

Explain how you know if an amount is a part or the whole in a problem.

Name _____

Label the bar model. Write a number sentence
with a ▮ for the missing number. Solve.

3. Aimee and Matthew
catch 17 crickets in all.
Aimee catches 9 crickets.
How many crickets does
Matthew catch?

_____ crickets

_____

_____

4. Percy counts 16 grasshoppers
at the park. He counts
15 grasshoppers at home.
How many grasshoppers
does Percy count?

_____ grasshoppers

_____

5. **THINK SMARTER** There are three
groups of owls. There are
17 owls in each of the first
two groups. There are
47 owls in all. How many
owls are in the third group?

_____ owls

On Your Own · WRITE ▶ Math

Write or draw to explain.

6. There are 37 paper clips in the box and 24 paper clips on the table. How many paper clips are there in all?

_____ paper clips

7. Math Processes and Practices ① **Make Sense of Problems**
Jeff has 19 postcards and 2 pens. He buys 20 more postcards. How many postcards does he have now?

_____ postcards

8. GO DEEPER There are a total of 41 chickens on the farm. There are 13 chickens in each of the 2 cages in the barn. The rest of the chickens are outside. How many chickens are outside?

_____ chickens

9. THINK SMARTER There are 23 books in a box. There are 29 books on a shelf. How many books are there?

_____ books

TAKE HOME ACTIVITY • Ask your child to explain how to solve one of the problems above.

Problem Solving • Addition

Learning Objective You will use the strategy *draw a diagram* by making bar models to solve addition problems within 100.

Label the bar model. Write a number sentence with a ▪ for the missing number. Solve.

1. Jacob counts 37 ants on the sidewalk and 11 ants on the grass. How many ants does Jacob count?

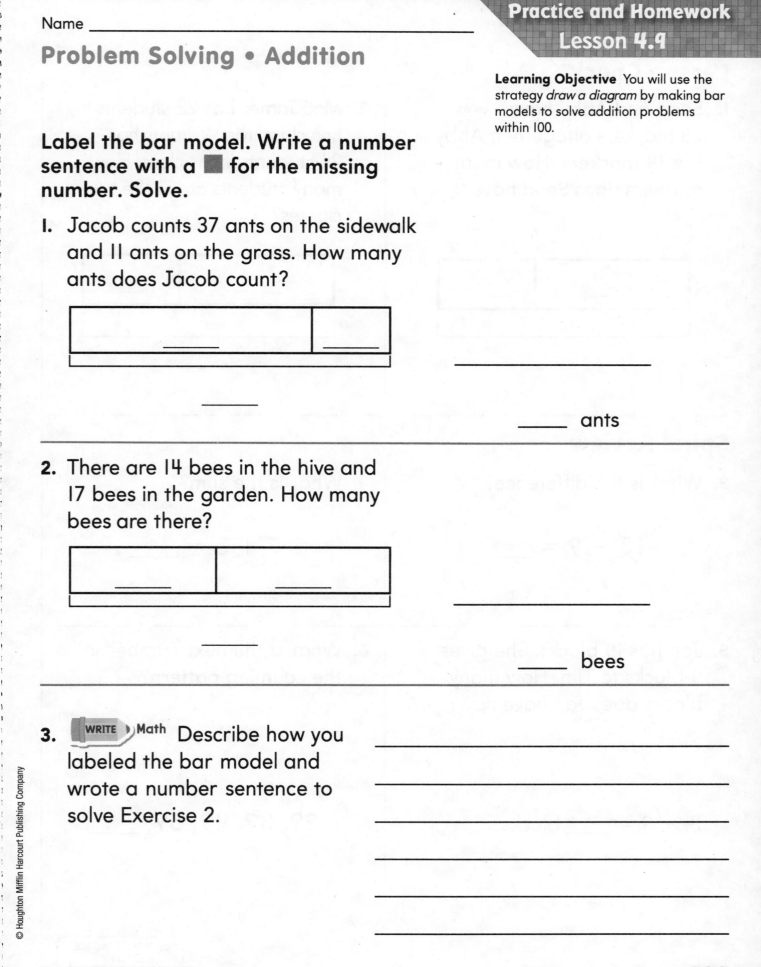

_____

_____ ants

2. There are 14 bees in the hive and 17 bees in the garden. How many bees are there?

_____

_____ bees

3. **WRITE**) Math   Describe how you labeled the bar model and wrote a number sentence to solve Exercise 2.

_____

_____

_____

_____

_____

Lesson Check

1. Sean and Abby have 23 markers altogether. Abby has 14 markers. How many markers does Sean have?

___	___

___

2. Mrs. James has 22 students in her class. Mr. Williams has 24 students in his class. How many students are in the two classes?

___

Spiral Review

3. What is the difference?

$$15 - 9 = \underline{\quad}$$

4. What is the sum?

$$7 + 5 = \underline{\quad}$$

5. Jan has 14 blocks. She gives 9 blocks to Tim. How many blocks does Jan have now?

$$14 - 9 = \underline{\quad} \text{ blocks}$$

6. What is the next number in the counting pattern?

29, 39, 49, 59, ___

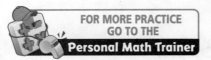

FOR MORE PRACTICE
GO TO THE
Personal Math Trainer

Algebra • Write Equations to Represent Addition

Essential Question How do you write a number sentence to represent a problem?

Learning Objective You will show an addition problem by writing a number sentence with a symbol for the missing number.

Listen and Draw Real World

Draw to show how you found the answer.

FOR THE TEACHER • Read the following problem and have children choose their own methods for solving. There are 15 children on the bus. Then 9 more children get on the bus. How many children are on the bus now?

Math Talk Math Processes and Practices 5

Communicate Explain how you found the number of children on the bus.

Model and Draw

You can write a number sentence to show a problem.

Sandy has 16 pencils. Nancy has 13 pencils. How many pencils do the two girls have?

$$16 + 13 = \blacksquare$$

THINK:
$$
\begin{array}{r}
16 \text{ pencils} \\
+ \ 13 \text{ pencils} \\
\hline
29 \text{ pencils}
\end{array}
$$

The two girls have _____ pencils.

Share and Show MATH BOARD

Write a number sentence for the problem.
Use a ■ for the missing number. Then solve.

☑ 1. Carl sees 25 melons at the store. 15 are small and the rest are large. How many melons are large?

_____

_____ melons

☑ 2. 83 people went to a movie on Thursday. 53 of them were children and the rest were adults. How many adults were at the movie?

_____

_____ adults

On Your Own

Write a number sentence for the problem.
Use a ▇ for the missing number. Then solve.

3. Jake had some stamps. Then
he bought 20 more stamps.
Now he has 56 stamps. How
many stamps did Jake have
to start?

_____   _____ stamps

4. **THINK SMARTER** Braden's class went to the
park. They saw 26 oak trees and
14 maple trees. They also saw 13 cardinals
and 35 blue jays. Compare the number of
trees and the number of birds that
the class saw.

_____ ◯ _____

5. **Math Processes and Practices 6** **Explain** Amy needs about
70 paper clips. Without adding,
circle 2 boxes that would be close
to the amount that she needs.

| 70 clips | 81 clips | 54 clips |
| 19 clips | 35 clips | 32 clips |

Explain how you made your choices.

_____

_____

_____

Problem Solving • Applications (Real World) WRITE Math

6. (Math Processes and Practices ①) **Make Sense of Problems**

Mr. Walton baked 24 loaves of bread last week. He baked 28 loaves of bread this week. How many loaves of bread did he bake in the two weeks?

_____ loaves of bread

7. THINK SMARTER Denise saw these bags of oranges at the store.

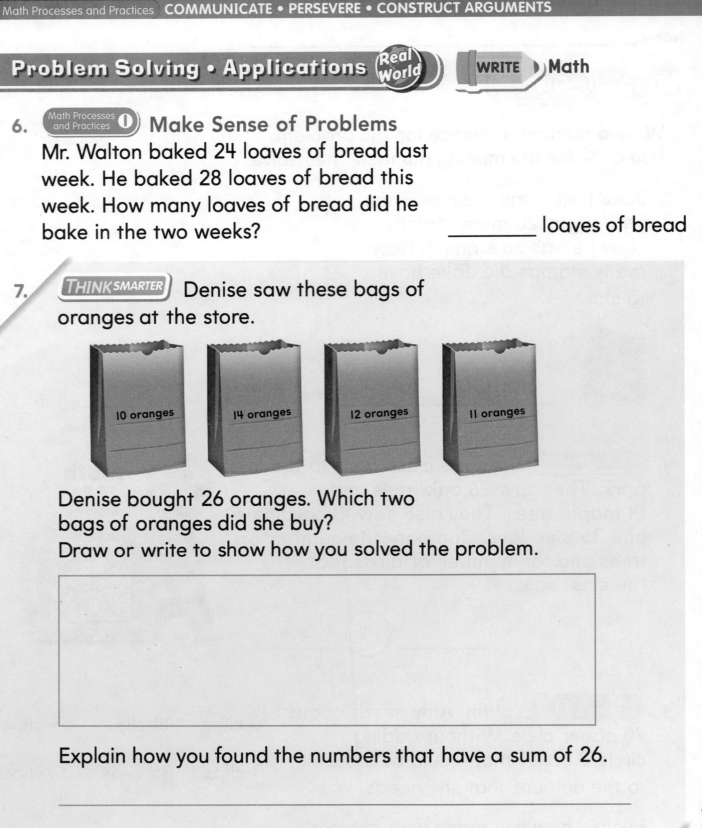

10 oranges   14 oranges   12 oranges   11 oranges

Denise bought 26 oranges. Which two bags of oranges did she buy?

Draw or write to show how you solved the problem.

Explain how you found the numbers that have a sum of 26.

_____

_____

_____

🏠 **TAKE HOME ACTIVITY** • Have your child explain how he or she writes a number sentence to stand for a problem.

Algebra • Write Equations to Represent Addition

Learning Objective You will show an addition problem by writing a number sentence with a symbol for the missing number.

Write a number sentence for the problem. Use a ■ for the missing number. Then solve.

1. Emily and her friends went to the park. They saw 15 robins and 9 blue jays. How many birds did they see?

_____ _____ birds

2. Joe has 13 fish in one tank. He has 8 fish in another tank. How many fish does Joe have?

_____ _____ fish

Problem Solving (Real World)

Solve.

3. There are 21 children in Kathleen's class. 12 of the children are girls. How many children in her class are boys?

_____ boys

4. **WRITE** Math Explain how you decided what number sentence to write for Exercise 1.

_____

_____

_____

_____

Lesson Check

1. Clare has 14 blocks. Jasmine has 6 blocks. How many blocks do they have?

$$14 + 6 = \underline{\hspace{1cm}} \text{ blocks}$$

2. Matt finds 16 acorns at the park. Trevor finds 18 acorns. How many acorns do they find?

$$16 + 18 = \underline{\hspace{1cm}} \text{ acorns}$$

Spiral Review

3. Leanne counted 19 ants. Gregory counted 6 ants. How many more ants did Leanne count than Gregory?

$$19 - 6 = \underline{\hspace{1cm}} \text{ ants}$$

4. What is the sum?

$$4 + 3 + 6 = \underline{\hspace{1cm}}$$

5. Ms. Santos puts seashells into 4 rows. She puts 6 seashells in each row. How many seashells are there altogether?

____ seashells

6. Circle the even number.

9   14   17   21

FOR MORE PRACTICE
GO TO THE
Personal Math Trainer

Name _____

Algebra • Find Sums for 3 Addends

Essential Question What are some ways to add 3 numbers?

Learning Objective You will add three 2-digit numbers within 1,000.

Listen and Draw Real World

Draw to show each problem.

Math Talk Math Processes and Practices ①

Which numbers did you add first in the first problem? **Explain** why.

 FOR THE TEACHER • Read the following problem and have children draw to show it. Mr. Kim bought 5 blue balloons, 4 red balloons, and 5 yellow balloons. How many balloons did Mr. Kim buy? Repeat for another problem.

Chapter 4

Model and Draw

There are different ways to add three numbers.

How can you add 23, 41, and 17?

Think of different ways to choose digits in the ones **column** to add first.

Add from top to bottom. First add the top two digits in the ones column, then add the next digit. Then add the tens.

You can make a ten first. Then add the other ones digit. Then add the tens.

$$
\begin{array}{r}
2\;\textcircled{3} \\
4\;1 \\
+\;1\;\textcircled{7} \\
\hline
\end{array}
$$

$3 + 7 = 10$
$10 + 1 = 11$

$$
\begin{array}{r}
2\;\textcircled{3} \\
4\;\textcircled{1} \\
+\;1\;7 \\
\hline
\end{array}
$$

$3 + 1 = 4$
$4 + 7 = 11$

Share and Show   MATH BOARD

Add.

1.
$$
\begin{array}{r}
33 \\
34 \\
+\;32 \\
\hline
\end{array}
$$

2.
$$
\begin{array}{r}
47 \\
21 \\
+\;\;7 \\
\hline
\end{array}
$$

3.
$$
\begin{array}{r}
65 \\
13 \\
+\;15 \\
\hline
\end{array}
$$

4.
$$
\begin{array}{r}
58 \\
27 \\
+\;22 \\
\hline
\end{array}
$$

5.
$$
\begin{array}{r}
12 \\
22 \\
+\;36 \\
\hline
\end{array}
$$

6.
$$
\begin{array}{r}
10 \\
42 \\
+\;36 \\
\hline
\end{array}
$$

✓7.
$$
\begin{array}{r}
31 \\
21 \\
+\;16 \\
\hline
\end{array}
$$

✓8.
$$
\begin{array}{r}
30 \\
29 \\
+\;48 \\
\hline
\end{array}
$$

Name _____

On Your Own

Add.

9.
```
  22
  27
+ 18
```

10.
```
  26
  31
+ 19
```

11.
```
  24
  11
+ 53
```

12.
```
  33
  43
+  4
```

13.
```
  40
  17
+ 32
```

14.
```
  25
  25
+ 25
```

15.
```
  19
  65
+ 24
```

16.
```
  73
   4
+ 16
```

17. **GO DEEPER** Mrs. Carson is making food for a party. She makes 20 ham sandwiches, 34 turkey sandwiches, and 38 tuna salad sandwiches. How many sandwiches does she make for the party?

_____ sandwiches

18. **THINK SMARTER** Sophia had 44 marbles. She bought 24 more marbles. Then John gave her 35 marbles. How many marbles does Sophia have now?

_____ marbles

Problem Solving • Applications   Real World   WRITE Math

Solve. Write or draw to explain.

19. **Math Processes and Practices ①** **Evaluate** Mrs. Shaw has 23 red notebooks, 15 blue notebooks, and 27 green notebooks. How many notebooks does she have?

_____ notebooks

20. **Math Processes and Practices ④** **Model Mathematics**
Write a story problem that could be solved using this number sentence.

$$12 + 28 + \blacksquare = 53$$

_____

_____

_____

_____

21. **THINK SMARTER** Mr. Samson gave his students 31 yellow pencils, 27 red pencils, and 25 blue pencils. How many pencils did he give to his students?

_____ pencils

TAKE HOME ACTIVITY • Ask your child to show you two ways to add 17, 13, and 24.

Algebra • Find Sums for 3 Addends

Learning Objective You will add three 2-digit numbers within 1,000.

Add.

1.
```
  2 3
  2 0
+ 2 5
```

2.
```
  1 5
  2 2
+ 3 8
```

3.
```
  1 3
  5 2
+ 3 4
```

4.
```
  2 7
  4 0
+ 1 9
```

5.
```
  3 1
  4 5
+ 2 4
```

6.
```
  3 4
  1 1
+ 2 8
```

7.
```
  4 2
  3 6
+ 1 1
```

8.
```
  1 8
  2 2
+ 3 4
```

9.
```
  5 3
  1 9
+ 2 5
```

Problem Solving (Real World)

Solve. Write or draw to explain.

10. Liam has 24 yellow pencils, 15 red pencils, and 9 blue pencils. How many pencils does he have altogether?

_____ pencils

11. WRITE Math Describe how you would find the sum of 24, 36, and 13.

_____

_____

Lesson Check

1. What is the sum?

$$
\begin{array}{r}
22 \\
31 \\
+\ 16 \\
\hline
\end{array}
$$

2. What is the sum?

$$
\begin{array}{r}
17 \\
26 \\
+\ 30 \\
\hline
\end{array}
$$

Spiral Review

3. What number is 10 more than 127?

_____

4. Mr. Howard's phone has 4 rows of buttons. There are 3 buttons in each row. How many buttons are on Mr. Howard's phone?

_____ buttons

5. Bob tosses 8 horseshoes. Liz tosses 9 horseshoes. How many horseshoes do they toss?

$8 + 9 =$ _____ horseshoes

6. What number can be written 3 hundreds 1 ten 5 ones?

_____

FOR MORE PRACTICE
GO TO THE
Personal Math Trainer

Name _____

Algebra • Find Sums for 4 Addends

Essential Question What are some ways to add 4 numbers?

Learning Objective You will add four 2-digit numbers within 1,000.

Listen and Draw Real World

Show how you solved each problem.

FOR THE TEACHER • Read this problem and have children choose a way to solve it. Shelly counts 16 ants in her ant farm. Pedro counts 22 ants in his farm. Tara counts 14 ants in her farm. How many ants do the 3 children count? Repeat for another problem.

Math Talk

Math Processes and Practices 6

Describe how you found the answer to the first problem.

Model and Draw

You can add digits in a column in more than one way. Add the ones first. Then add the tens.

Find a sum that you know. Then add to it.

```
  3 1
  1 4
  2 7
+ 2 4
```

THINK: 8 + 1 = 9, then add on 7 more. The sum of the ones is 16 ones.

Add pairs of digits first. Then add these sums.

```
  3 1
  1 4
  2 7
+ 2 4
```

THINK: 5 + 11 = 16, so there are 16 ones in all.

Share and Show MATH BOARD

Add.

1.
```
  23
  11
  22
+ 31
```

2.
```
  30
  15
   3
+ 25
```

3.
```
  13
  26
  54
+ 12
```

4.
```
  27
   2
  23
+ 13
```

5.
```
  45
  14
  35
+ 51
```

6.
```
  32
  21
  15
+ 30
```

Name _____

On Your Own

Add.

7.
```
  36
  12
  21
+ 26
```

8.
```
  14
  23
  20
+ 11
```

9.
```
  22
  13
  15
+ 27
```

10.
```
  45
  12
  41
+ 22
```

11.
```
  59
  31
  51
+ 73
```

12.
```
  34
  10
  31
+ 22
```

13. **GO DEEPER** Some friends need 100 bows for a project. Sara brings 12 bows, Angela brings 50 bows, and Nora brings 34 bows. How many more bows do they need?

_____ more bows

Solve. Write or draw to explain.

14. **THINK SMARTER** Laney added four numbers which have a total of 128. She spilled some juice over one number. What is that number?

$22 + 43 + + 30 = 128$

_____

Math on the Spot

© Houghton Mifflin Harcourt Publishing Company

Problem Solving • Applications

WRITE Math

Use the table.
Write or draw to show how
you solved the problems.

Shells Collected at the Beach	
Child	Number of Shells
Katie	34
Paul	15
Noah	26
Laura	21

15. **Math Processes and Practices ①** **Evaluate** How many shells did the four children collect at the beach?

_____ shells

16. **GO DEEPER** Which two children collected more shells at the beach, Katie and Paul, or Noah and Laura?

_____

17. **THINK SMARTER** There were 24 red beads, 31 blue beads, and 8 green beads in a jar. Then Emma put 16 beads into the jar. Write a number sentence to show the number of beads in the jar.

_____

TAKE HOME ACTIVITY • Have your child explain what he or she learned in this lesson.

Algebra • Find Sums for 4 Addends

Learning Objective You will add four 2-digit numbers within 1,000.

Add.

1.
```
  1 8
  3 2
  2 3
+   3
```

2.
```
  4 5
  3 1
  2 9
+ 7 2
```

3.
```
  2 4
  6 2
  7 0
+ 3 3
```

4.
```
  8 3
  3 2
  6 1
+ 2 2
```

5.
```
  3 7
  1 5
  3 1
+ 1 2
```

6.
```
  2 1
  1 3
  9 6
+ 1 8
```

Problem Solving Real World

Solve. Show how you solved the problem.

7. Kinza jogs 16 minutes on Monday, 13 minutes on Tuesday, 9 minutes on Wednesday, and 20 minutes on Thursday. What is the total number of minutes she jogged?

_____ minutes

8. **WRITE** Math Describe two different strategies you could use to add 16 + 35 + 24 + 14.

_____

Lesson Check

1. What is the sum?

```
    1 2
    3 3
    5 6
+   3 2
```

2. What is the sum?

```
    4 1
    7 4
    4 3
+   2 0
```

Spiral Review

3. Laura had 6 daisies. Then she found 7 more daisies. How many daisies does she have now?

6 + 7 = _____ daisies

4. What is the sum?

```
    5 2
+   2 7
```

5. Alan has 25 trading cards. He buys 8 more. How many cards does he have now?

25 + 8 = _____ cards

6. Jen saw 13 guinea pigs and 18 gerbils at the pet store. How many pets did she see?

13 + 18 = _____ pets

FOR MORE PRACTICE
GO TO THE
Personal Math Trainer

✓ Chapter 4 Review/Test

Personal Math Trainer
Online Assessment and Intervention

I. Beth baked 24 carrot muffins. She baked 18 apple muffins. How many muffins did Beth bake?

Label the bar model. Write a number sentence with a ■ for the missing number. Solve.

_____ _____ muffins

---

2. Carlos has 23 red keys, 36 blue keys, and 44 green keys. How many keys does he have? Circle your answer.

Carlos has
| 67 |
| 80 |
| 103 |
keys.

---

3. Mike sees 17 blue cars and 25 green cars. Choose all the ways you can use to find how many cars he sees. Then solve.

   ○ 17
   + 25

   ○ 25
   − 17

   ○ 25
   + 17

   ○ 17
   + 17

Mike sees _____ cars.

Describe how you solved the problem.

_____

_____

4. Jerry has 53 pencils in one drawer. He has 27 pencils in another drawer.

Draw a picture or write to explain how to find the number of pencils in both drawers.

Jerry has _____ pencils.

5. THINK SMARTER ✚ Lauren sees 14 birds. Her friend sees 7 birds. How many birds do Lauren and her friend see? Draw quick pictures to solve. Write the sum.

Tens	Ones

_____ birds

Did you regroup to find the answer? Explain.

_____

_____

6. Matt says he can find the sum of 45 + 50 without rewriting it. Explain how you can solve this problem using mental math.

_____

_____

7. Ling sees the three signs at the theater.

| **Section A** | **Section B** | **Section C** |
| 35 seats | 43 seats | 17 seats |

Which two sections have 78 seats?

Explain how you made your choices.

_____

_____

_____

8. Leah put 21 white marbles, 31 black marbles, and 7 blue marbles in a bag. Then her sister added 19 yellow marbles.

Write a number sentence to show the number of marbles in the bag.

_____

_____

9. Nicole made a necklace. She used 13 red beads and 26 blue beads. Show how you can break apart the addends to find how many beads Nicole used.

13 ⟶ _____ + _____

+ 26 ⟶ _____ + _____
_____

_____ + _____ = _____

10. **GO DEEPER** Without finding the sums, does the pair of addends have a sum greater than 100? Choose Yes or No.

$51 + 92$	○ Yes	○ No
$42 + 27$	○ Yes	○ No
$82 + 33$	○ Yes	○ No
$62 + 14$	○ Yes	○ No

Explain how you decided which pairs have a sum greater than 100.

_____

_____

_____

11. Leslie finds 24 paper clips in her desk. She finds 8 more paper clips in her pencil box. Choose all the ways you can use to find how many paper clips Leslie has in all.

○ $24 + 8$

○ $24 - 8$

○ $24 + 6 + 2$

12. Mr. O'Brien visited a lighthouse. He climbed 26 stairs. Then he climbed 64 more stairs to the top. How many stairs did he climb at the lighthouse?

_____ stairs

2-Digit Subtraction

Curious about Math

There are hundreds of different kinds of dragonflies. If 52 dragonflies are in a garden and 10 fly away, how many dragonflies are left? How many are left if 10 more fly away?

✓ **Show What You Know**

Personal Math Trainer
Online Assessment
and Intervention

Subtraction Patterns

Subtract 2. Complete each subtraction sentence.

1. $7 - \underline{2} = \underline{5}$

2. $6 - \underline{} = \underline{}$

3. $5 - \underline{} = \underline{}$

4. $4 - \underline{} = \underline{}$

5. $3 - \underline{} = \underline{}$

6. $2 - \underline{} = \underline{}$

Subtraction Facts

Write the difference.

7. $\begin{array}{r} 8 \\ -5 \\ \hline \end{array}$ 8. $\begin{array}{r} 14 \\ -6 \\ \hline \end{array}$ 9. $\begin{array}{r} 9 \\ -6 \\ \hline \end{array}$ 10. $\begin{array}{r} 16 \\ -7 \\ \hline \end{array}$ 11. $\begin{array}{r} 12 \\ -6 \\ \hline \end{array}$ 12. $\begin{array}{r} 10 \\ -8 \\ \hline \end{array}$

Tens and Ones

Write how many tens and ones are in each model.

13. 54

14. 45

_____ tens _____ ones   _____ tens _____ ones

This page checks understanding of important
skills needed for success in Chapter 5.

Name _____

Vocabulary Builder

Review Words

difference
regroup
tens
ones
digit

Visualize It
Fill in the boxes of the graphic organizer.

difference

Describe it.

_____

_____

Examples

$10 - 4 = 6$

_____

_____

Not Examples

$4 + 6 = 10$

_____

_____

Understand Vocabulary
Draw a line to complete the sentence.

1. A **digit** can be •   • as 2 **tens**.

2. You can **regroup** •   • 0, 1, 2, 3, 4, 5, 6, 7, 8, or 9.

3. 20 **ones** are the same •   • to trade 10 ones for 1 ten.

• **Interactive Student Edition**
• **Multimedia eGlossary**

Game Subtraction Search

Materials
- 3 sets of number cards 4–9
- 18 ●

Play with a partner.

1. Shuffle all the cards. Place them face down in one stack.

2. Take one card. Find a square with a subtraction problem with this number as the difference. Your partner checks your answer.

3. If you are correct, place a ● on that square. If there is no match, skip your turn.

4. Take turns. The first player to have ● on all the squares wins.

Player 1		
12 − 5	9 − 2	10 − 5
16 − 7	13 − 7	17 − 9
7 − 3	11 − 5	18 − 9

Player 2		
8 − 3	15 − 7	11 − 6
17 − 8	9 − 3	16 − 8
13 − 9	6 − 2	14 − 7

addend

sumando

1

column

columna

7

difference

diferencia

14

digit

dígito

15

is equal to (=)

es igual a

33

ones

unidades

45

regroup

reagrupar

56

ten

decena

61

column

$$\begin{array}{r} 3\boxed{3} \\ 3\boxed{4} \\ + 3\boxed{2} \\ \hline \end{array}$$

$5 + 3 = 8$

addends

0, 1, 2, 3, 4, 5, 6, 7, 8, and 9 are **digits**.

$5 - 3 = 2$

difference

10 ones = 1 ten

2   plus   1   is equal to   3

$2 + 1 = 3$

10 ones = 1 ten

Tens   Ones

You can trade 10 ones for 1 ten to **regroup**.

© Houghton Mifflin Harcourt Publishing Company

Bingo

For 3 to 6 players

Materials
- 1 set of word cards
- 1 bingo board for each player
- game markers

How to Play

1. The caller chooses a word card and reads the word. Then the caller puts the word card in a second pile.
2. Players put a marker on the word each time they find it on their bingo boards.
3. Repeat steps 1 and 2 until a player marks 5 boxes in a line going down, across, or on a slant and calls "Bingo."
4. Check the answers. Have the player who said "Bingo" read the words aloud while the caller checks the word cards in the second pile.

Word Box
addend
column
difference
digit
is equal to (=)
ones
regroup
ten

The Write Way

Reflect

Choose one idea. Write about it in the space below.

- Explain how drawing quick pictures helps you subtract 2-digit numbers.
- Tell about all the different ways you can subtract 2-digit numbers.
- Write about a time that you helped explain something to a classmate. What was your classmate having trouble with? How did you help him or her?

Algebra • Break Apart Ones to Subtract

Name _____

Learning Objective You will break apart ones to make subtracting easier.

Essential Question How does breaking apart a number make subtracting easier?

Listen and Draw

Write two addends for each sum.

Math Talk Math Processes and Practices 6

Describe how you chose addends for each sum.

🍎 **FOR THE TEACHER •** After children have recorded addends for each sum, have a class discussion about the different facts that children represented on their papers.

Chapter 5

three hundred seventeen **317**

Model and Draw

Break apart ones. Subtract in two steps.

$63 - 7 = \blacksquare$

3   4

> Start at 63. Subtract 3 to get to 60. Then subtract 4 more.

So, $63 - 7 =$ _____.

Share and Show MATH BOARD

Break apart ones to subtract. Write the difference.

1. $55 - 8 =$ _____

   5   3

2. $42 - 5 =$ _____

   2   3

3. $41 - 9 =$ _____

4. $53 - 6 =$ _____

5. $44 - 7 =$ _____

6. $52 - 8 =$ _____

Name _____

Break apart ones to subtract. Write the difference.

60 61 62 63 64 65 66 67 68 69 **70** 71 72 73 74 75 76 77 78 79 **80** 81 82 83 84 85 86 87 88 89 **90**

7. 75 − 7 = _____

8. 86 − 8 = _____

9. 82 − 5 = _____

10. 83 − 7 = _____

11. 72 − 7 = _____

12. 76 − 9 = _____

13. 85 − 8 = _____

14. 71 − 6 = _____

15. **THINK SMARTER** Cheryl brought 27 bagels for the bake sale. Mike brought 24 bagels. They sold all but 9 of them. How many bagels did they sell?

_____ bagels

16. **Math Processes and Practices ①** **Analyze** Lexi has 8 fewer crayons than Ken. Ken has 45 crayons. How many crayons does Lexi have?

_____ crayons

Problem Solving • Applications Real World   WRITE Math

Write or draw to explain.

17. Cheryl built a toy train with 27 train cars. Then she added 18 more train cars. How many train cars are on the toy train now?

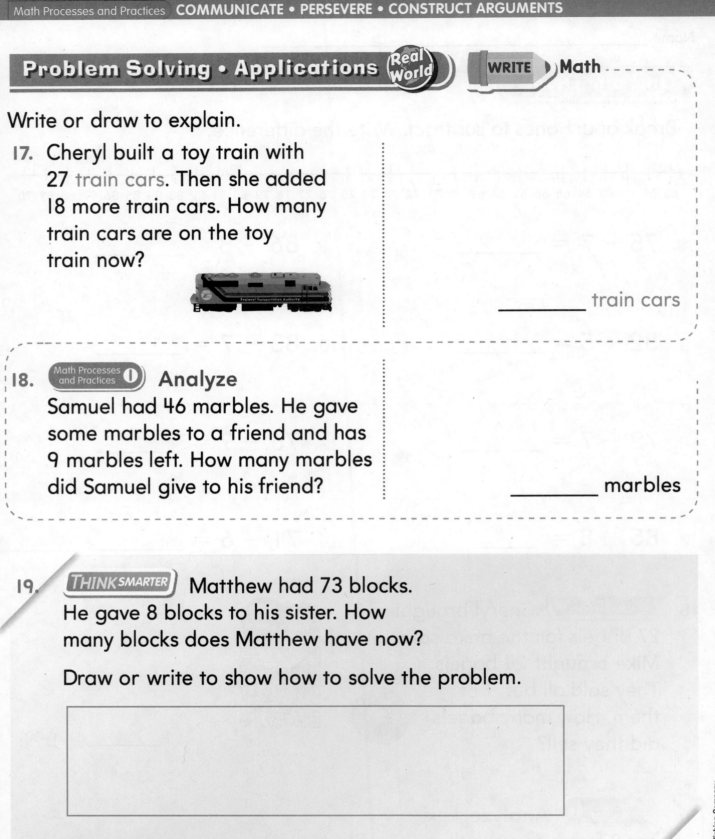

_____ train cars

18. Math Processes and Practices ❶ **Analyze**
Samuel had 46 marbles. He gave some marbles to a friend and has 9 marbles left. How many marbles did Samuel give to his friend?

_____ marbles

19. THINK SMARTER   Matthew had 73 blocks. He gave 8 blocks to his sister. How many blocks does Matthew have now?

Draw or write to show how to solve the problem.

Matthew has _____ blocks now.

 TAKE HOME ACTIVITY • Ask your child to describe how to find 34 − 6.

Name _____

Practice and Homework
Lesson 5.1

Algebra • Break Apart Ones to Subtract

Learning Objective You will break apart ones to make subtracting easier.

Break apart ones to subtract.
Write the difference.

20 21 22 23 24 25 26 27 28 29 **30** 31 32 33 34 35 36 37 38 39 **40** 41 42 43 44 45 46 47 48 49 **50**

1. $36 - 7 =$ _____

2. $35 - 8 =$ _____

3. $37 - 9 =$ _____

4. $41 - 6 =$ _____

5. $44 - 5 =$ _____

6. $33 - 7 =$ _____

7. $32 - 4 =$ _____

8. $31 - 6 =$ _____

Problem Solving • Real World

Choose a way to solve. Write or draw to explain.

9. Beth had 44 marbles. She gave
9 marbles to her brother.
How many marbles does
Beth have now?

_____ marbles

10. WRITE ▸ Math Draw a number line and
show how to find the difference for
$24 - 6$ using the break apart method
in this lesson.

Lesson Check

1. What is the difference?

40 41 42 43 44 45 46 47 48 49 **50** 51 52 53 54 55 56 57 58 59 **60** 61 62 63 64 65 66 67 68 69 **70**

$$58 - 9 = \underline{}$$

Spiral Review

2. What is the difference?

$$14 - 6 = \underline{}$$

3. What is the sum?

$$3 + 6 + 2 = \underline{}$$

4. What is the sum?

$$64 + 7 = \underline{}$$

5. What is the sum?

$$56 + 18 = \underline{}$$

FOR MORE PRACTICE
GO TO THE
Personal Math Trainer

Name _____

Algebra • Break Apart Numbers to Subtract

Learning Objective You will break apart a 2-digit number to subtract it from a 2-digit number.

Essential Question How does breaking apart a number make subtracting easier?

Listen and Draw (Real World)

Draw jumps on the number line to show how to break apart the number to subtract.

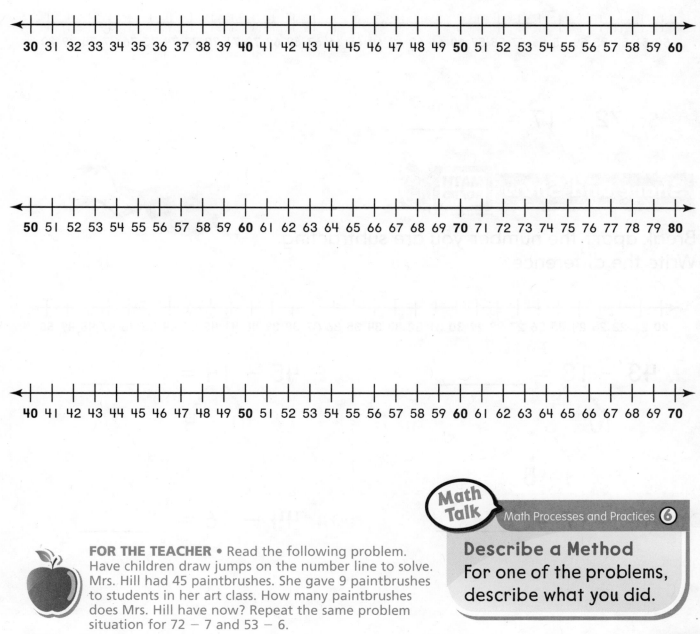

30 31 32 33 34 35 36 37 38 39 **40** 41 42 43 44 45 46 47 48 49 **50** 51 52 53 54 55 56 57 58 59 **60**

50 51 52 53 54 55 56 57 58 59 **60** 61 62 63 64 65 66 67 68 69 **70** 71 72 73 74 75 76 77 78 79 **80**

40 41 42 43 44 45 46 47 48 49 **50** 51 52 53 54 55 56 57 58 59 **60** 61 62 63 64 65 66 67 68 69 **70**

FOR THE TEACHER • Read the following problem. Have children draw jumps on the number line to solve. Mrs. Hill had 45 paintbrushes. She gave 9 paintbrushes to students in her art class. How many paintbrushes does Mrs. Hill have now? Repeat the same problem situation for 72 − 7 and 53 − 6.

Math Talk Math Processes and Practices ⑥

Describe a Method For one of the problems, describe what you did.

Chapter 5

three hundred twenty-three **323**

Break apart the number you are subtracting into tens and ones.

Subtract 10.
Next, subtract 2 to get to 60.
Then subtract 5 more.

$$72 - 17 = \blacksquare$$

10   7

2   5

$$10 + 2 + 5 = 17$$

−5   −2   −10

50 51 52 53 54 55 56 57 58 59 **60** 61 62 63 64 65 66 67 68 69 **70** 71 72 73 74 75 76 77 78 79 **80**

So, $72 - 17 =$ _____.

Share and Show   MATH BOARD

Break apart the number you are subtracting.
Write the difference.

20 21 22 23 24 25 26 27 28 29 **30** 31 32 33 34 35 36 37 38 39 **40** 41 42 43 44 45 46 47 48 49 **50**

1. $43 - 18 =$ _____

10   8

3   5

2. $45 - 14 =$ _____

10   4

3. $46 - 17 =$ _____

4. $44 - 16 =$ _____

On Your Own

Break apart the number you are subtracting.
Write the difference.

```
←—+——+——+——+——+——+——+——+——+——+——+——+——+——+——+——+——+——+——+——+——+——+——+——+——+——+——+——+——+——+→
  40 41 42 43 44 45 46 47 48 49 50 51 52 53 54 55 56 57 58 59 60 61 62 63 64 65 66 67 68 69 70
```

5. $57 - 15 =$ _____

6. $63 - 17 =$ _____

7. $68 - 19 =$ _____

8. $61 - 18 =$ _____

9. **THINK SMARTER** Jane has 53 toys in a box. She takes some toys out. Now there are 36 toys in the box. How many toys did Jane take out of the box?

Math on the Spot

_____ toys

10. **GO DEEPER** Look at Tom's steps to solve a problem. Solve this problem in the same way.

$42 - 15 = ?$

Tom
$35 - 18 = ?$
$35 - 10 = 25$
$25 - 5 = 20$
$20 - 3 = (17)$

Problem Solving • Applications (Real World)   WRITE Math

11. 38 people are in the library. Then 33 more people go into the library. How many people are in the library now?

_____ people

12. **Math Processes and Practices ❶** **Analyze** Alex has 24 toys in a chest. He takes some toys out of the chest. Then there are 16 toys in the chest. How many toys did he take out of the chest?

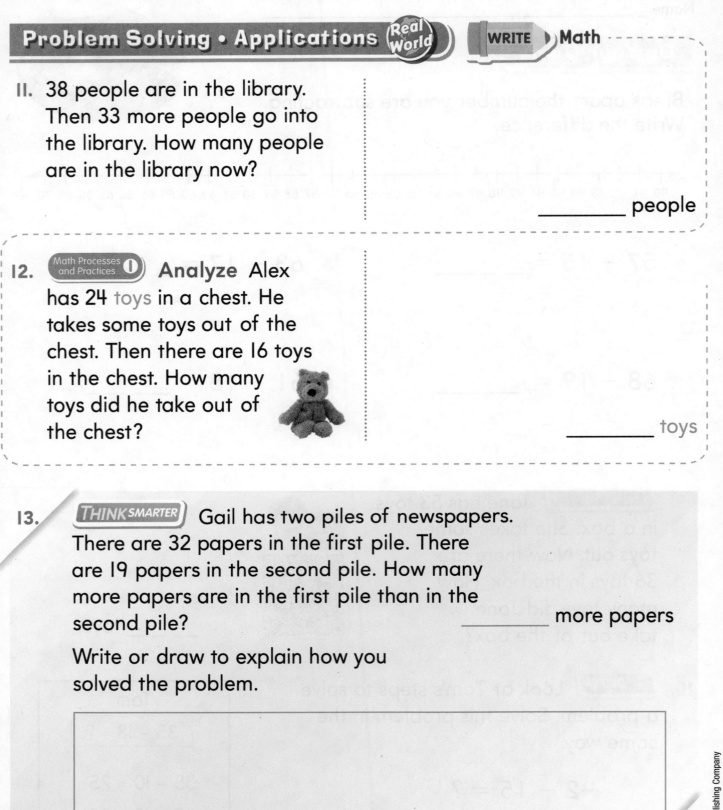

_____ toys

13. **THINK SMARTER** Gail has two piles of newspapers. There are 32 papers in the first pile. There are 19 papers in the second pile. How many more papers are in the first pile than in the second pile?

_____ more papers

Write or draw to explain how you solved the problem.

 TAKE HOME ACTIVITY • Ask your child to write a subtraction story that uses 2-digit numbers.

© Houghton Mifflin Harcourt Publishing Company

Algebra • Break Apart Numbers to Subtract

Learning Objective You will break apart a 2-digit number to subtract it from a 2-digit number.

Break apart the number you are subtracting. Write the difference.

```
←┼─┼─┼─┼─┼─┼─┼─┼─┼─┼─┼─┼─┼─┼─┼─┼─┼─┼─┼─┼─┼─┼─┼─┼─┼─┼─┼─┼─┼─┼→
 60 61 62 63 64 65 66 67 68 69 70 71 72 73 74 75 76 77 78 79 80 81 82 83 84 85 86 87 88 89 90
```

1. 81 − 14 = _____

2. 84 − 16 = _____

3. 77 − 14 = _____

4. 83 − 19 = _____

5. 81 − 17 = _____

6. 88 − 13 = _____

7. 84 − 19 = _____

8. 86 − 18 = _____

Problem Solving (Real World)

Solve. Write or draw to explain.

9. Mr. Pearce bought 43 plants. He gave 14 plants to his sister. How many plants does Mr. Pearce have now?

_____ plants

10. **WRITE Math** Draw a number line and show how to find the difference for 36 − 17 using the break apart method in this lesson.

Lesson Check

I. What is the difference?

40 41 42 43 44 45 46 47 48 49 **50** 51 52 53 54 55 56 57 58 59 **60** 61 62 63 64 65 66 67 68 69 **70**

$$63 - 19 = \underline{\hspace{1cm}}$$

Spiral Review

2. What is the sum?

$$\begin{array}{r} 14 \\ + 23 \\ \hline \end{array}$$

3. What is the sum?

$$8 + 7 = \underline{\hspace{1cm}}$$

4. Write a related subtraction fact for $6 + 8 = 14$.

_____

5. John has 7 kites. Annie has 4 kites. How many kites do they have altogether?

____ kites

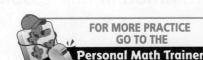

FOR MORE PRACTICE
GO TO THE
Personal Math Trainer

Name _____

Model Regrouping for Subtraction

Essential Question When do you regroup in subtraction?

Learning Objective You will model subtraction within 100 with regrouping.

Listen and Draw Real World · Hands On

Use ▭▭▭▭ ▫ to model the problem.
Draw quick pictures to show your model.

Tens	Ones

Math Talk — Math Processes and Practices 6

Describe why you traded a tens block for 10 ones blocks.

FOR THE TEACHER • Read the following problem. Michelle counted 21 butterflies in her garden. Then 7 butterflies flew away. How many butterflies were still in the garden?

Chapter 5

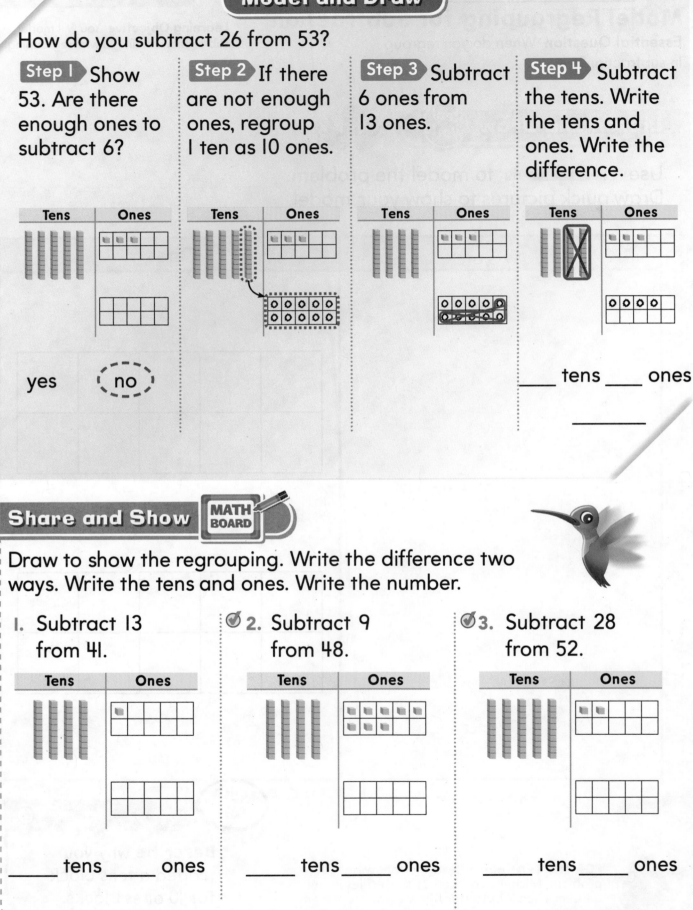

Model and Draw

How do you subtract 26 from 53?

Step 1 Show 53. Are there enough ones to subtract 6?

Tens	Ones

yes ~~no~~

Step 2 If there are not enough ones, regroup 1 ten as 10 ones.

Tens	Ones

Step 3 Subtract 6 ones from 13 ones.

Tens	Ones

Step 4 Subtract the tens. Write the tens and ones. Write the difference.

Tens	Ones

____ tens ____ ones

_____

Share and Show MATH BOARD

Draw to show the regrouping. Write the difference two ways. Write the tens and ones. Write the number.

1. Subtract 13 from 41.

Tens	Ones

____ tens ____ ones

_____

2. Subtract 9 from 48.

Tens	Ones

____ tens ____ ones

_____

3. Subtract 28 from 52.

Tens	Ones

____ tens ____ ones

_____

Name _____

Draw to show the regrouping. Write the difference two ways. Write the tens and ones. Write the number.

4. Subtract 8 from 23.

Tens	Ones

_____ ten _____ ones

_____

5. Subtract 36 from 45.

Tens	Ones

_____ tens_____ ones

_____

6. Subtract 6 from 43.

Tens	Ones

_____ tens _____ ones

_____

7. Subtract 39 from 67.

Tens	Ones

_____ tens _____ ones

_____

8. Subtract 21 from 50.

Tens	Ones

_____ tens_____ ones

_____

9. Subtract 29 from 56.

Tens	Ones

_____ tens _____ ones

_____

10. **GO DEEPER** Draw to find what number was subtracted from 53.

Subtract _____ from 53.

_3_ tens _4_ ones

_34_

Tens	Ones

© Houghton Mifflin Harcourt Publishing Company

Problem Solving • Applications (Real World)   WRITE ▶ Math

Write or draw to explain.

11. **THINK SMARTER** Billy has 18 fewer marbles than Sara. Sara has 34 marbles. How many marbles does Billy have?

_____ marbles

Personal Math Trainer

12. **THINK SMARTER +** There are 67 toy animals in the store. Then the clerk sells 19 toy animals. How many toy animals are in the store now?

Draw to show how to find the answer.

Tens	Ones

_____ toy animals

Describe how you solved the problem.

_____

_____

_____

TAKE HOME ACTIVITY • Ask your child to write a subtraction story and then explain how to solve it.

Model Regrouping for Subtraction

Learning Objective You will model subtraction within 100 with regrouping.

Draw to show the regrouping.
Write the difference two ways.
Write the tens and ones. Write the number.

1. Subtract 9 from 35.

Tens	Ones

_____ tens _____ ones

_____

2. Subtract 14 from 52.

Tens	Ones

_____ tens _____ ones

_____

Problem Solving Real World

Choose a way to solve. Write or draw to explain.

3. Mr. Ortega made 51 cookies. He gave 14 cookies away. How many cookies does he have now?

_____ cookies

4. **WRITE** Math Draw a quick picture for 37. Draw to show how you would subtract 19 from 37. Write to explain what you did.

_____

_____

_____

Lesson Check

1. Subtract 9 from 36. What is the difference?

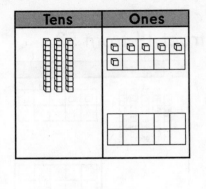

Tens	Ones

_____

2. Subtract 28 from 45. What is the difference?

Tens	Ones

_____

Spiral Review

3. What is the difference?

$$51 - 8 = \text{\_\_\_}$$

40 41 42 43 44 45 46 47 48 49 **50** 51 52 53 54 55 56 57 58 59 **60**

4. What is the sum?

$$38 + 35 = \text{\_\_\_}$$

5. What is the sum?

$$
\begin{array}{r}
63 \\
18 \\
+\ 9 \\
\hline
\end{array}
$$

FOR MORE PRACTICE
GO TO THE
Personal Math Trainer

Name _____

Model and Record 2-Digit Subtraction

Learning Objective You will model and record subtraction within 100.

Essential Question How do you record 2-digit subtraction?

Listen and Draw (Real World) (Hands On)

Use to model the problem.
Draw quick pictures to show your model.

Tens	Ones

FOR THE TEACHER • Read the following problem. Mr. Kelly made 47 muffins. His students ate 23 of the muffins. How many muffins were not eaten?

Math Talk Math Processes and Practices 6

Explain a Method Did you trade blocks in your model? Explain why or why not.

Chapter 5

Model and Draw

Trace over the quick pictures in the steps.

Subtract.   56
            − 19

Step 1 Show 56. Are there enough ones to subtract 9?

Tens	Ones
‖‖‖‖‖	○○○○○○

Tens	Ones
☐	☐
5	6
− 1	9

Step 2 If there are not enough ones, regroup 1 ten as 10 ones.

Tens	Ones
‖‖‖‖‖	○○○○○○

Tens	Ones
4	16
5̸	6̸
− 1	9

Step 3 Subtract the ones.
$16 − 9 = 7$

Tens	Ones
‖‖‖‖	○○○○○

Tens	Ones
4	16
5̸	6̸
− 1	9
	7

Step 4 Subtract the tens.
$4 − 1 = 3$

Tens	Ones
‖‖	○○○○○

Tens	Ones
4	16
5̸	6̸
− 1	9
3	7

Share and Show

Draw a quick picture to solve. Write the difference.

1.

Tens	Ones
☐	☐
4	7
− 1	5

Tens	Ones

2.

Tens	Ones
☐	☐
3	2
− 1	8

Tens	Ones

On Your Own

Draw a quick picture to solve. Write the difference.

3.

Tens	Ones
☐	☐
3	5
− 2	9

Tens	Ones

4.

Tens	Ones
☐	☐
2	8
−	5

Tens	Ones

5.

Tens	Ones
☐	☐
5	3
− 2	6

Tens	Ones

6.

Tens	Ones
☐	☐
3	2
− 1	3

Tens	Ones

7. **GO DEEPER** There are 16 robins in the trees. 24 more fly in. Then 28 robins fly away. How many robins are still in the trees?

_____ robins

Problem Solving • Applications

WRITE Math

8. **THINK SMARTER** Claire's puzzle has 85 pieces. She has used 46 pieces so far. How many puzzle pieces have not been used yet?

_____ puzzle pieces

9. **Math Processes and Practices ①** **Analyze** There were some people at the park. 24 people went home. Then there were 19 people at the park. How many people were at the park before?

_____ people

10. **THINK SMARTER** Mr. Sims has a box of 44 erasers. He gives 28 erasers to his students. How many erasers does Mr. Sims have now?

Show how you solved the problem.

_____ erasers

TAKE HOME ACTIVITY • Write 73 − 28 on a sheet of paper. Ask your child if he or she would regroup to find the difference.

Model and Record 2-Digit Subtraction

Learning Objective You will model and record subtraction within 100.

Draw a quick picture to solve.
Write the difference.

1.

Tens	Ones
□	□
4	3
− 1	7

Tens	Ones

2.

Tens	Ones
□	□
3	8
− 2	9

Tens	Ones

Problem Solving (Real World)

Solve. Write or draw to explain.

3. Kendall has 63 stickers.
Her sister has 57 stickers.
How many more stickers does
Kendall have than her sister?

_____ more stickers

4. **WRITE Math** Draw a quick picture to show the number 24. Then draw a quick picture to show 24 after you have regrouped 1 ten as 10 ones. Explain how both pictures show the same number, 24.

_____

_____

_____

three hundred thirty-nine **339**

Lesson Check

1. What is the difference?

Tens	Ones
4	7
− 1	8

2. What is the difference?

Tens	Ones
3	3
− 2	9

Spiral Review

3. What is the difference?

$$10 - 6 = \underline{\quad}$$

4. What is the sum?

$$16 + 49 = \underline{\quad}$$

5. What is the sum?

$$28 + 8 = \underline{\quad}$$

6. What is the difference?

$$52 - 6 = \underline{\quad}$$

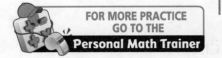

FOR MORE PRACTICE
GO TO THE
Personal Math Trainer

Name _____

2-Digit Subtraction

Essential Question How do you record the steps when subtracting 2-digit numbers?

Learning Objective You will record the steps for subtracting within 100.

Listen and Draw (Real World)

Draw a quick picture to model each problem.

Tens	Ones

Tens	Ones

Math Talk Math Processes and Practices ②

Use Reasoning
Explain why regrouping works.

FOR THE TEACHER • Read the following problem. Devin had 36 toy robots on his shelf. He moved 12 of the robots to his closet. How many robots are on the shelf now? Repeat the activity with this problem: Devin had 54 toy cars. He gave 9 of them to his brother. How many cars does Devin have now?

Subtract. 42
          −15

Step 1 Are there enough ones to subtract 5?

Tens	Ones
4	2
− 1	5

Step 2 Regroup 1 ten as 10 ones.

Tens	Ones
3	12
4̸	2̸
− 1	5

Step 3 Subtract the ones.

$12 − 5 = 7$

Tens	Ones
3	12
4̸	2̸
− 1	5
	7

Step 4 Subtract the tens.

$3 − 1 = 2$

Tens	Ones
3	12
4̸	2̸
− 1	5
2	7

Share and Show MATH BOARD

Regroup if you need to. Write the difference.

1.

Tens	Ones
3	1
− 1	4

☑ 2.

Tens	Ones
5	6
− 2	1

☑ 3.

Tens	Ones
7	2
− 3	5

Name _____

On Your Own

Regroup if you need to. Write the difference.

4.

Tens	Ones
☐	☐
2	3
− 1	4

5.

Tens	Ones
☐	☐
8	7
− 5	7

6.

Tens	Ones
☐	☐
3	4
− 1	8

7.

Tens	Ones
☐	☐
6	1
− 1	3

8.

$$\begin{array}{r} 4\,5 \\ -\ 1\,8 \\ \hline \end{array}$$

9.

$$\begin{array}{r} 5\,2 \\ -\ 3\,6 \\ \hline \end{array}$$

10.

$$\begin{array}{r} 3\,2 \\ -\ 1\,3 \\ \hline \end{array}$$

11.

$$\begin{array}{r} 7\,5 \\ -\ 4\,3 \\ \hline \end{array}$$

12.

$$\begin{array}{r} 5\,6 \\ -\ 2\,7 \\ \hline \end{array}$$

13.

$$\begin{array}{r} 9\,4 \\ -\ 2\,9 \\ \hline \end{array}$$

14.

$$\begin{array}{r} 8\,7 \\ -\ 3\,9 \\ \hline \end{array}$$

15.

$$\begin{array}{r} 8\,3 \\ -\ 4\,6 \\ \hline \end{array}$$

16. **THINK SMARTER** Spencer wrote 5 fewer stories than Katie. Spencer wrote 18 stories. How many stories did Katie write?

_____ stories

Problem Solving • Applications (Real World)   WRITE ▸ Math

17. (Math Processes and Practices 6) **Explain a Method**

Circle the problems below that you could
use mental math to solve.

54 − 10 = _____   63 − 27 = _____   93 − 20 = _____

39 − 2 = _____   41 − 18 = _____   82 − 26 = _____

Explain when to use mental math.

_____

_____

_____

Personal Math Trainer

18. THINK SMARTER ✚   There are 34 chickens
in the barn. If 16 chickens go outside
into the yard, how many chickens
will still be in the barn?

Circle the number from the box to make
the sentence true.

There are | 8
          | 18 | chickens still in the barn.
          | 28

TAKE HOME ACTIVITY • Ask your child to write a 2-digit subtraction
problem with no regrouping needed. Have your child explain why he
or she chose those numbers.

2-Digit Subtraction

Learning Objective You will record
the steps for subtracting within 100.

Regroup if you need to.
Write the difference.

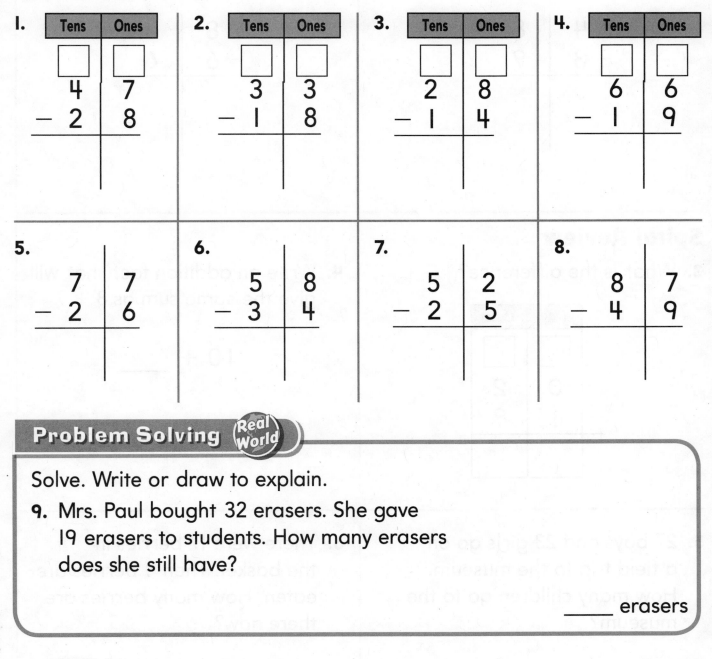

1.

Tens	Ones
□	□
4	7
− 2	8

2.

Tens	Ones
□	□
3	3
− 1	8

3.

Tens	Ones
□	□
2	8
− 1	4

4.

Tens	Ones
□	□
6	6
− 1	9

5.

7	7
− 2	6

6.

5	8
− 3	4

7.

5	2
− 2	5

8.

8	7
− 4	9

Problem Solving *Real World*

Solve. Write or draw to explain.

9. Mrs. Paul bought 32 erasers. She gave
19 erasers to students. How many erasers
does she still have?

_____ erasers

10. **WRITE** Math Write a few sentences about different
ways to show subtraction for a problem like 32 − 15.

_____

_____

Lesson Check

1. What is the difference?

$$
\begin{array}{c|c}
4 & 8 \\
-\,3 & 9 \\
\hline
 & \\
\end{array}
$$

2. What is the difference?

$$
\begin{array}{c|c}
8 & 4 \\
-\,6 & 6 \\
\hline
 & \\
\end{array}
$$

Spiral Review

3. What is the difference?

4. Write an addition fact that will give the same sum as $8 + 7$.

$$10 + \underline{\hspace{2em}}$$

5. 27 boys and 23 girls go on a field trip to the museum. How many children go to the museum?

_____ children

6. There were 17 berries in the basket. Then 9 berries are eaten. How many berries are there now?

_____ berries

FOR MORE PRACTICE
GO TO THE
Personal Math Trainer

Practice 2-Digit Subtraction

Essential Question How do you record the steps when subtracting 2-digit numbers?

Learning Objective You will practice 2-digit subtraction with and without regrouping.

Listen and Draw (Real World)

Choose one way to solve the problem.
Draw or write to show what you did.

Math Talk Math Processes and Practices ①

Describe a different way that you could have solved the problem.

FOR THE TEACHER • Read the following problem and have children choose their own methods for solving it. There are 74 books in Mr. Barron's classroom. 19 of the books are about computers. How many of the books are not about computers?

Chapter 5

Carmen had 50 game cards. Then she gave 16 game cards to Theo. How many game cards does Carmen have now?

Step 1 Look at the ones. There are not enough ones to subtract 6 from 0. So, regroup.

$$
\begin{array}{r}
4\ \ 10 \\
\cancel{5}\ \cancel{0} \\
-\ 1\ \ 6 \\
\hline
\end{array}
$$

Step 2 Subtract the ones.

$10 - 6 = 4$

$$
\begin{array}{r}
4\ \ 10 \\
\cancel{5}\ \cancel{0} \\
-\ 1\ \ 6 \\
\hline
4
\end{array}
$$

Step 3 Subtract the tens.

$4 - 1 = 3$

$$
\begin{array}{r}
4\ \ 10 \\
\cancel{5}\ \cancel{0} \\
-\ 1\ \ 6 \\
\hline
3\ \ 4
\end{array}
$$

Share and Show MATH BOARD

Write the difference.

1.
$$
\begin{array}{r}
3\ 8 \\
-\ 1\ 9 \\
\hline
\end{array}
$$

2.
$$
\begin{array}{r}
6\ 5 \\
-\ 3\ 2 \\
\hline
\end{array}
$$

3.
$$
\begin{array}{r}
5\ 0 \\
-\ 1\ 2 \\
\hline
\end{array}
$$

4.
$$
\begin{array}{r}
2\ 3 \\
-\ \ \ 4 \\
\hline
\end{array}
$$

☑ 5.
$$
\begin{array}{r}
7\ 0 \\
-\ 3\ 8 \\
\hline
\end{array}
$$

☑ 6.
$$
\begin{array}{r}
5\ 2 \\
-\ 1\ 7 \\
\hline
\end{array}
$$

Name _____

On Your Own

Write the difference.

7.
```
  4 1
- 2 4
_____
```

8.
```
  5 8
- 1 6
_____
```

9.
```
  6 0
- 1 3
_____
```

10.
```
  5 2
- 4 7
_____
```

11.
```
  7 2
- 4 6
_____
```

12.
```
  3 7
-   6
_____
```

13.
```
  7 4
- 4 6
_____
```

14.
```
  9 0
- 1 8
_____
```

15. **GO DEEPER** Write the missing numbers in the subtraction problems. The regrouping for each problem is shown.

```
6 15          7 13

-   ___       -   ___
_____       _____
  4  7          2  5
```

16. **THINK SMARTER** Adam takes 38 rocks out of a box. There are 23 rocks left in the box. How many rocks were in the box to start?

_____ rocks

TAKE HOME ACTIVITY • Ask your child to show you one way to find 80 − 34.

Name _____

✓ Mid-Chapter Checkpoint

Personal Math Trainer
Online Assessment and Intervention

Concepts and Skills

Break apart the number you are subtracting. Use the number line to help. Write the difference.

20 21 22 23 24 25 26 27 28 29 **30** 31 32 33 34 35 36 37 38 39 **40** 41 42 43 44 45 46 47 48 49 **50**

1. $34 - 8 =$ _____

2. $45 - 17 =$ _____

Draw a quick picture to solve. Write the difference.

3.

Tens	Ones
☐	☐
4	2
− 2	9

Tens	Ones

4.

Tens	Ones
☐	☐
5	4
− 2	3

Tens	Ones

Write the difference.

5.
```
   7 8
 − 4 3
```

6.
```
   6 0
 − 2 6
```

7.
```
   8 5
 − 3 7
```

8. **THINK SMARTER** Marissa had 51 toy dinosaurs.
She gave 14 toy dinosaurs to her brother.
How many toy dinosaurs does she have now?

_____ toy dinosaurs

Name _____

Practice 2-Digit Subtraction

Learning Objective You will practice 2-digit subtraction with and without regrouping.

Write the difference.

1.

$$\begin{array}{r} 5\ 0 \\ -1\ 8 \\ \hline \end{array}$$

2.

$$\begin{array}{r} 4\ 3 \\ -1\ 7 \\ \hline \end{array}$$

3.

$$\begin{array}{r} 7\ 5 \\ -1\ 8 \\ \hline \end{array}$$

4.

$$\begin{array}{r} 2\ 2 \\ -\ \ 6 \\ \hline \end{array}$$

5.

$$\begin{array}{r} 6\ 0 \\ -3\ 5 \\ \hline \end{array}$$

6.

$$\begin{array}{r} 4\ 2 \\ -3\ 4 \\ \hline \end{array}$$

Problem Solving · Real World

Solve. Write or draw to explain.

7. Julie has 42 sheets of paper. She gives 17 sheets to Kari. How many sheets of paper does Julie have now?

____ sheets of paper

8. WRITE Math Draw and write to explain how these two problems are different: $35 - 15 =$ _____ and $43 - 26 =$ _____.

_____

Lesson Check

1. What is the difference?

$$
\begin{array}{r}
73 \\
-\ 47 \\
\hline
\end{array}
$$

2. What is the difference?

$$
\begin{array}{r}
54 \\
-\ 13 \\
\hline
\end{array}
$$

Spiral Review

3. What is the sum?

$9 + 9 =$ _____

4. What is the difference?

$14 - 7 =$ _____

5. What is the sum?

$36 + 25 =$ _____

6. What is the sum?

$7 + 2 + 3 =$ _____

FOR MORE PRACTICE
GO TO THE
Personal Math Trainer

Name _____

Rewrite 2-Digit Subtraction

Essential Question What are two different ways to write subtraction problems?

Learning Objective You will rewrite subtraction problems within 100 in a different way.

Listen and Draw Real World

Write the numbers for each subtraction problem.

Math Talk Math Processes and Practices 6

Explain why it is important to line up the digits of the numbers in columns.

FOR THE TEACHER • Read the following problem. Have children write the numbers in vertical format. There were 45 children at a party. Then 23 children went home. How many children were still at the party? Repeat for three more problems.

© Houghton Mifflin Harcourt Publishing Company

What is 81 − 36?
Rewrite the subtraction problem.
Then find the difference.

Step 1 For 81, write the tens digit in the tens column.

Write the ones digit in the ones column.

Repeat for 36.

$$
\begin{array}{r}
8\ 1 \\
-\ 3\ 6 \\
\hline
\end{array}
$$

Step 2 Look at the ones. Regroup if you need to.

Subtract the ones.
Subtract the tens.

$$
\begin{array}{r}
\overset{7}{\cancel{8}}\ \overset{11}{\cancel{1}} \\
-\ 3\ \ 6 \\
\hline
\end{array}
$$

Share and Show MATH BOARD

Rewrite the subtraction problem. Then find the difference.

1. 37 − 4 _____

2. 48 − 24 _____

3. 85 − 37 _____

4. 63 − 19 _____

5. 62 − 37 _____

6. 51 − 27 _____

⊘7. 76 − 3 _____

⊘8. 95 − 48 _____

Name _____

Rewrite the subtraction problem. Then find the difference.

9. 49 – 8

10. 85 – 47

11. 63 – 23

12. 51 – 23

_ _____

_ _____

_ _____

_ _____

13. 60 – 15

14. 94 – 58

15. 47 – 20

16. 35 – 9

_ _____

_ _____

_ _____

_ _____

17. 78 – 10

18. 54 – 38

19. 92 – 39

20. 87 – 28

_ _____

_ _____

_ _____

_ _____

21. **THINK SMARTER** For which of the problems above could you find the difference without rewriting it? Explain.

_____

_____

_____

Problem Solving • Applications (Real World) WRITE Math

Read about the class trip. Then answer the questions.

> Pablo's class went to the art museum. They
> saw 26 paintings done by children. They
> saw 53 paintings done by adults. They also
> saw 18 sculptures and 31 photographs.

22. How many more paintings were
done by adults than by children?

_____ more paintings

23. GO DEEPER How many more
paintings than sculptures did
they see?

_____ more paintings

24. THINK SMARTER Tom drew 23 pictures last
year. Beth drew 14 pictures. How many
more pictures did Tom draw than Beth?

Fill in the bubble next to all the ways to
show the problem.

○   23   ○   23   ○ 23 − 14   ○ 23 + 14
    − 14   + 14

_____ more pictures

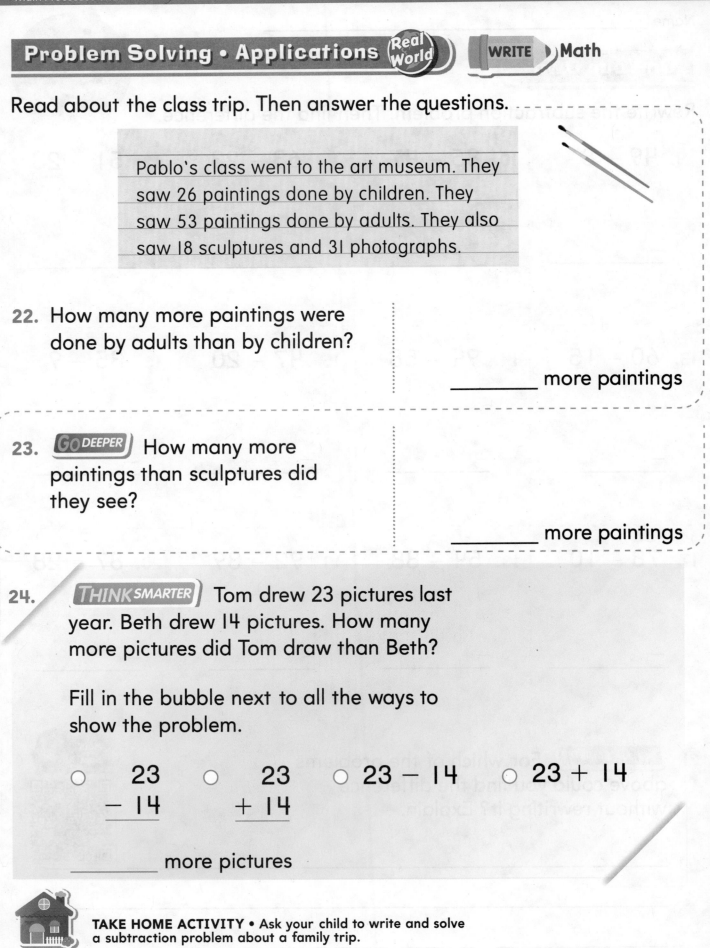

TAKE HOME ACTIVITY • Ask your child to write and solve
a subtraction problem about a family trip.

Rewrite 2-Digit Subtraction

Learning Objective You will rewrite subtraction problems within 100 in a different way.

Rewrite the subtraction problem.
Then find the difference.

1. 35 − 19

2. 47 − 23

3. 55 − 28

Problem Solving Real World

Solve. Write or draw to explain.

4. Jimmy went to the toy store. He saw 23 wooden trains and 41 plastic trains. How many more plastic trains than wooden trains did he see?

_____ more plastic trains

5. **WRITE** Math Is it easier to subtract when the numbers are written above and below each other? Explain your answer.

_____

_____

_____

Lesson Check

1. What is the difference for 43 − 17?

_____

2. What is the difference for 50 − 16?

_____

Spiral Review

3. What is the sum?

29
4
25
+ 16

4. What is the sum of 41 + 19?

_____

5. Write an addition fact that will give the same sum as 5 + 9.

10 + ____

6. What is the difference?

45 − 13 = ____

© Houghton Mifflin Harcourt Publishing Company

FOR MORE PRACTICE
GO TO THE
Personal Math Trainer

Name _____

Add to Find Differences

Essential Question How can you use addition to solve subtraction problems?

Learning Objective You will use addition to solve subtraction problems.

Listen and Draw (Real World)

Draw pictures to show the problem.
Then write a number sentence for your drawing.

_____   _____ markers

Now draw pictures to show the next part of the
problem. Write a number sentence for your drawing.

_____   _____ markers

FOR THE TEACHER • Have children draw
pictures to represent this problem. Sophie had
25 markers. She gave 3 markers to Josh. How
many markers does Sophie have now? Then ask
children: How many markers will Sophie have if
Josh gives the 3 markers back to her?

Math Talk

Math Processes and Practices ①

Describe what happens
when you add back the
number that you had
subtracted.

Count up from the number you are subtracting to find the difference.

$$45 - 38 = \blacksquare$$

Start at 38. Count up to 40.

+2   +5

30 31 32 33 34 35 36 37 38 39 **40** 41 42 43 44 45 46 47 48 49 **50**

Then count up 5 more to 45.

$$2 + 5 = 7$$

So, $45 - 38 =$ _____.

Share and Show MATH BOARD

Use the number line. Count up to find the difference.

1. $36 - 27 =$ _____

20 21 22 23 24 25 26 27 28 29 **30** 31 32 33 34 35 36 37 38 39 **40**

2. $56 - 49 =$ _____

40 41 42 43 44 45 46 47 48 49 **50** 51 52 53 54 55 56 57 58 59 **60**

3. $64 - 58 =$ _____

50 51 52 53 54 55 56 57 58 59 **60** 61 62 63 64 65 66 67 68 69 **70**

On Your Own

Use the number line. Count up to find the difference.

4. 33 − 28 = _____

20 21 22 23 24 25 26 27 28 29 **30** 31 32 33 34 35 36 37 38 39 **40**

5. 45 − 37 = _____

30 31 32 33 34 35 36 37 38 39 **40** 41 42 43 44 45 46 47 48 49 **50**

6. 58 − 49 = _____

40 41 42 43 44 45 46 47 48 49 **50** 51 52 53 54 55 56 57 58 59 **60**

7. **THINK SMARTER** There were 55 books on the table. Sandra picked up some of the books. Now there are 49 books on the table. How many books did Sandra pick up?

40 41 42 43 44 45 46 47 48 49 **50** 51 52 53 54 55 56 57 58 59 **60**

_____ books

Problem Solving • Applications

Solve. You may wish to use the number line to help.

```
←——+——+——+——+——+——+——+——+——+——+——+——+——+——+——+——+——+——+——+——+——→
  30 31 32 33 34 35 36 37 38 39 40 41 42 43 44 45 46 47 48 49 50
```

8. There are **46** game pieces in a box. Adam takes 38 game pieces out of the box. How many game pieces are still in the box?

_____ game pieces

9. **THINK SMARTER** Rachel had 27 craft sticks. Then she gave 19 craft sticks to Theo. How many craft sticks does Rachel have now?

Circle the number from the box to make the sentence true.

Rachel has
| 6 |
| 7 |
| 8 |
craft sticks now.

Explain how you can use addition to solve the problem.

_____

_____

  TAKE HOME ACTIVITY • Have your child describe how he or she used a number line to solve one problem in this lesson.

Add to Find Differences

Learning Objective You will use addition to solve subtraction problems.

Use the number line. Count up to find the difference.

1. $36 - 29 =$ _____

←┼──┼→
 20 21 22 23 24 25 26 27 28 29 **30** 31 32 33 34 35 36 37 38 39 **40**

2. $43 - 38 =$ _____

←┼──┼→
 30 31 32 33 34 35 36 37 38 39 **40** 41 42 43 44 45 46 47 48 49 **50**

Problem Solving · Real World

Solve. You may wish to use the number line.

←┼──┼→
 50 51 52 53 54 55 56 57 58 59 **60** 61 62 63 64 65 66 67 68 69 **70**

3. Jill has 63 index cards. She uses 57 of them for a project. How many index cards does Jill have now?

_____ index cards

4. **WRITE** Math Explain how a number line can be used to find the difference for $34 - 28$.

_____

_____

Lesson Check

Use the number line. Count up to find the difference.

70 71 72 73 74 75 76 77 78 79 80 81 82 83 84 85 86 87 88 89 90

1. $82 - 75 = $ _____

2. $90 - 82 = $ _____

Spiral Review

3. Jordan has 41 toy cars at home. He brings 24 cars to school. How many cars are at home?

_____ cars

4. Pam has 15 fish. 9 are goldfish and the rest are guppies. How many fish are guppies?

_____ guppies

5. What is the sum?

$$
\begin{array}{c|c}
3 & 5 \\
+\ 1 & 9 \\
\hline
\end{array}
$$

6. Each table has 5 pencils. There are 3 tables. How many pencils are there altogether?

_____ pencils

FOR MORE PRACTICE
GO TO THE
Personal Math Trainer

Name _____

Problem Solving • Subtraction

Essential Question How can drawing a diagram help when solving subtraction problems?

Learning Objective You will use the strategy *draw a diagram* by making bar models to solve subtraction problems within 100.

Jane and her mom made 33 puppets for the craft fair. They sold 14 puppets. How many puppets do they still have?

🔑 Unlock the Problem

What do I need to find?

how many puppets

they still have

What information do I need to use?

They made _____ puppets.

They sold _____ puppets.

Show how to solve the problem.

33 – 14 = ■

_____ puppets

HOME CONNECTION • Your child used a bar model and a number sentence to represent the problem. Using a bar model helps show what is known and what is needed to solve the problem.

Try Another Problem

Label the bar model. Write a number sentence with a ■ for the missing number. Solve.

* What do I need to find?
* What information do I need to use?

1. Carlette had a box of 46 craft sticks. She used 28 craft sticks to make a sailboat. How many craft sticks were not used?

_____   _____ craft sticks

2. Rob's class made 31 clay bowls. Sarah's class made 15 clay bowls. How many more clay bowls did Rob's class make than Sarah's class?

_____   _____ more clay bowls

Math Talk Math Processes and Practices ①

Explain how you know that Exercise 1 is a take-away problem.

© Houghton Mifflin Harcourt Publishing Company

Name _____

Label the bar model. Write a number sentence
with a ▢ for the missing number. Solve.

3. Mr. Hayes makes 32 wooden
   frames. He gives away
   15 frames as gifts. How many
   frames does he still have?

_____ frames

_____

4. Wesley has 21 ribbons in a
   box. He has 15 ribbons on
   the wall. How many more
   ribbons does he have in
   the box than on the wall?

_____ more ribbons

_____

5. **THINK SMARTER** Jennifer wrote
   9 poems at school and
   11 poems at home. She wrote
   5 more poems than Nell. How
   many poems did Nell write?

_____ poems

On Your Own WRITE Math

6. GO DEEPER There are 70 children. 28 children are hiking and 16 are at a picnic. The rest of the children are playing soccer. How many children are playing soccer?

Draw a model with bars for the problem. Describe how your drawing shows the problem. Then solve the problem.

_____

_____

_____

7. THINK SMARTER There are 48 crackers in a bag. The children eat 25 crackers. How many crackers are still in the bag?

Circle the bar model that can be used to solve the problem.

25	23
48	

48	25
73	

73	48
25	

Write a number sentence with a ■ for the missing number. Solve.

_____

_____ crackers

TAKE HOME ACTIVITY • Ask your child to explain how he or she solved one of the problems on this page.

Problem Solving • Subtraction

Learning Objective You will use the strategy *draw a diagram* by making bar models to solve subtraction problems within 100.

Label the bar model. Write a number sentence with a ■ for the missing number. Solve.

1. Megan picked 34 flowers. Some of the flowers are yellow and 18 flowers are pink. How many of the flowers are yellow?

_____ yellow flowers

_____

2. Alex had 45 toy cars. He put 26 toy cars in a box. How many toy cars are not in the box?

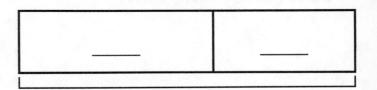

_____ toy cars

_____

3. WRITE Math Explain how a bar model can be used to show a subtraction problem.

_____

_____

_____

_____

Lesson Check

1. There were 39 pumpkins at the store. Then 17 of the pumpkins were sold. How many pumpkins are still at the store?

_____ pumpkins

2. There were 48 ants on a hill. Then 13 of the ants marched away. How many ants are still on the hill?

_____ ants

Spiral Review

3. Ashley had 26 markers. Her friend gave her 17 more markers. How many markers does Ashley have now?

_____ markers

4. What is the sum?

$$\begin{array}{r} 46 \\ + \ 24 \\ \hline \end{array}$$

5. Write a subtraction fact that will give the same difference as 15 − 7.

10 − _____

6. What is the sum?

34 + 5 = _____

FOR MORE PRACTICE
GO TO THE
Personal Math Trainer

Algebra • Write Equations to Represent Subtraction

Essential Question How do you write a number sentence to represent a problem?

Learning Objective You will show a subtraction problem by writing a number sentence with a symbol for the missing number.

Listen and Draw

Draw to show the problem. Write a number sentence. Then solve.

_____

FOR THE TEACHER • Read this problem to children. Franco has 53 crayons. He gives some crayons to Courtney. Now Franco has 38 crayons. How many crayons did Franco give to Courtney?

Math Talk Math Processes and Practices ④

Describe how your drawing shows the problem.

Chapter 5

three hundred seventy-one **371**

You can write a number sentence to show a problem.

Liza has 65 postcards. She gives 24 postcards to Wesley. How many postcards does Liza have now?

$$65 - 24 = \blacksquare$$

THINK:

```
  65 postcards
 -24 postcards
 ─────────────
  41 postcards
```

Liza has _____ postcards now.

Share and Show | MATH BOARD

Write a number sentence for the problem.
Use a ■ for the missing number. Then solve.

✔ 1. There were 32 birds in the trees. Then 18 birds flew away. How many birds are in the trees now?

_____

_____ birds

✔ 2. Carla read 43 pages in her book. Joe read 32 pages in his book. How many more pages did Carla read than Joe?

_____

_____ more pages

Name _____

On Your Own

Write a number sentence for the problem.
Use a ▇ for the missing number. Then solve.

3. There were 40 ants on a rock.
Some ants moved to the
grass. Now there are 26 ants
on the rock. How many ants
moved to the grass?

_____   _____ ants

4. **THINK SMARTER** Keisha had a bag
of ribbons. She took 29 ribbons
out of the bag. Then there
were 17 ribbons still in the bag.
How many ribbons were in the
bag to start?

_____   _____ ribbons

5. **GO DEEPER** There are 50 bees in
a hive. Some bees fly out.
If fewer than 20 bees are still
in the hive, how many bees
could have flown out?

_____ bees

Use subtraction to prove your
answer.

Problem Solving • Applications (Real World)   WRITE ▸ Math

6. Math Processes and Practices **6**   **Make Connections**
Brendan made this number line
to find a difference. What was
he subtracting from 100?
Explain your answer.

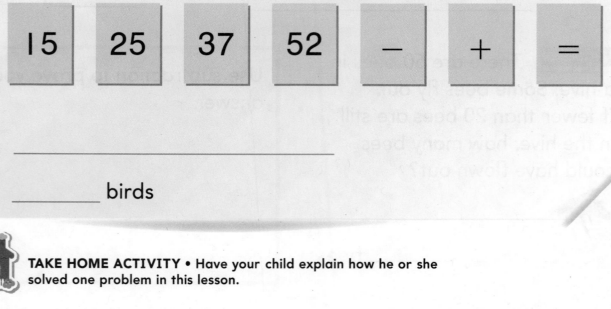

_____

_____

_____

_____

7. **THINK SMARTER**   There are 52 pictures on the wall.
37 are wild cats and the rest are birds.
How many of the pictures are birds?

Use the numbers and symbols on the tiles to write
a number sentence for the problem.

| 15 | 25 | 37 | 52 | − | + | = |

_____

_____ birds

🏠 **TAKE HOME ACTIVITY** • Have your child explain how he or she
solved one problem in this lesson.

Algebra • Write Equations to Represent Subtraction

Learning Objective You will show a subtraction problem by writing a number sentence with a symbol for the missing number.

**Write a number sentence for the problem.
Use a ▪ for the missing number. Then solve.**

I. 29 children rode their bikes to school. After some of the children rode home, there were 8 children with bikes still at school. How many children rode their bikes home?

_____

_____ children

Problem Solving · Real World

Solve. Write or draw to explain.

2. There were 21 children in the library. After 7 children left the library, how many children were still in the library?

_____ children

3. WRITE · Math Describe different ways that you can show a story problem. Use one of the problems in this lesson as your example.

_____

_____

_____

Lesson Check

1. Cindy had 42 beads. She used some beads for a bracelet. She has 14 beads left. How many beads did she use for the bracelet?

_____ beads

2. Jake had 36 baseball cards. He gave 17 cards to his sister. How many baseball cards does Jake have now?

_____ cards

Spiral Review

3. What is the sum?

$6 + 7 =$ _____

4. What is the difference?

$16 - 9 =$ _____

5. What is the difference?

$$\begin{array}{c|c} 4 & 6 \\ -\ 3 & 9 \\ \hline \end{array}$$

6. Write an addition fact that will give the same sum as $6 + 8$.

$10 +$ _____

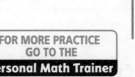

FOR MORE PRACTICE
GO TO THE
Personal Math Trainer

Name _____

Solve Multistep Problems

Essential Question How do you decide what steps to do to solve a problem?

Learning Objective You will decide what steps to do to solve a problem.

Listen and Draw

Label the bar model to show each problem. Then solve.

_____

_____

Math Talk Math Processes and Practices ①

Describe how the two bar models are different.

FOR THE TEACHER • Read this 1st problem for children. Cassie has 32 sheets of paper. She gives Jeff 9 sheets of paper. How many sheets of paper does Cassie have now? After children solve, read this 2nd problem. Cassie draws 18 pictures. Jeff draws 16 pictures. How many pictures do they draw?

Chapter 5

Bar models help you know what to do to solve a problem.

Ali has 27 stamps. Matt has 38 stamps. How many more stamps are needed so they will have 91 stamps?

27	38

_____

They have _____ stamps now.

_____	_____

91

They need _____ more stamps.

> First, find how many stamps they have now.

> Next, find how many more stamps they need.

Complete the bar models for the steps you do to solve the problem.

> **THINK:** What do you need to find first?

1. Jen has 93 beads. Ana has 46 red beads and 29 blue beads. How many more beads does Jen have than Ana?

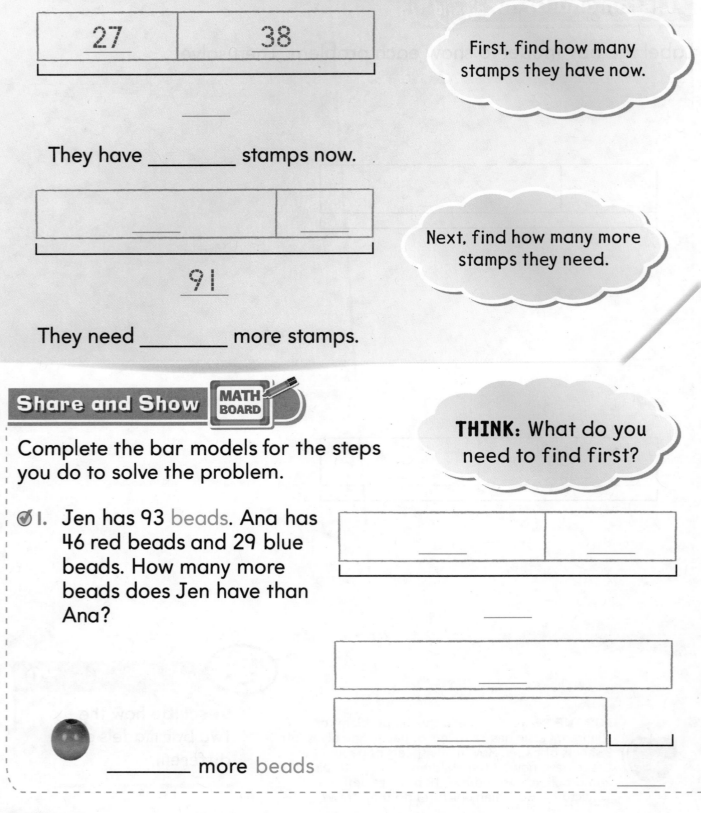

_____ more beads

© Houghton Mifflin Harcourt Publishing Company

On Your Own

Complete the bar models for the steps you do
to solve the problem.

2. Max has 35 trading cards. He
buys 22 more cards. Then he
gives 14 cards to Rudy. How
many cards does Max have
now?

_____ cards

3. Drew has 32 toy cars. He
trades 7 of those cars for
11 other toy cars. How many
toy cars does Drew have now?

_____ toy cars

4. Marta and Debbie each have
17 ribbons. They buy 1 package
with 8 ribbons in it. How many
ribbons do they have now?

_____ ribbons

Problem Solving • Applications (Real World)   WRITE) Math

5. **THINK SMARTER** Shelby had 32 rocks. She finds 33 more rocks at the park and gives 28 rocks to George. How many rocks does she have now?

_____ rocks

6. **GO DEEPER** Benjamin finds 31 pinecones at the park. Together, Jenna and Ellen find the same number of pinecones as Benjamin. How many pinecones could each girl have found?

Jenna: _____ pinecones

Ellen: _____ pinecones

7. **THINK SMARTER** Tanya finds 22 leaves. Maurice finds 5 more leaves than Tanya finds. How many leaves do the children find in all?

Draw or write to show how you solve the problem.

_____ leaves

TAKE HOME ACTIVITY • Have your child explain how he or she would solve Exercise 6 if the number 31 was changed to 42.

Solve Multistep Problems

Complete the bar models for the steps you do to solve the problem.

1. Greg has 60 building blocks. His sister gives him 17 more blocks. He uses 38 blocks to make a tower. How many blocks are not used in the tower?

_____ blocks

_____

Problem Solving Real World

Solve. Write or draw to explain.

2. Ava has 25 books. She gives away 7 books. Then Tom gives her 12 books. How many books does Ava have now?

_____ books

3. WRITE Math Choose one of the problems on this page. Describe how you decided what steps were needed to solve the problem.

_____

_____

_____

_____

Lesson Check

1. Sara has 18 crayons. Max has 19 crayons. How many more crayons do they need to have 50 crayons altogether?

_____ crayons

2. Jon has 12 pennies. Lucy has 17 pennies. How many more pennies do they need to have 75 pennies altogether?

_____ pennies

Spiral Review

3. What is the difference?

$$58 - 13 = \text{\_\_\_}$$

40 41 42 43 44 45 46 47 48 49 **50** 51 52 53 54 55 56 57 58 59 **60**

4. What is the sum?

$$\begin{array}{r} 4\,|\,7 \\ +\ 1\,|\,5 \\ \hline \end{array}$$

5. There are 26 cards in a box. Bryan takes 12 cards. How many cards are still in the box?

_____ cards

FOR MORE PRACTICE
GO TO THE
Personal Math Trainer

✓ Chapter 5 Review/Test

Personal Math Trainer
Online Assessment and Intervention

I. Do you need to regroup to subtract? Choose Yes or No.

65 – 23   ○ Yes   ○ No

50 – 14   ○ Yes   ○ No

37 – 19   ○ Yes   ○ No

77 – 60   ○ Yes   ○ No

2. Use the number line. Count up to find the difference.

52 – 48 = _____

41 42 43 44 45 46 47 48 49 **50** 51 52 53 54 55 56 57 58 59 **60**

3. Ed has 28 blocks. Sue has 34 blocks. Who has more blocks? How many more? Label the bar model. Solve.

Circle the word and number from each box to make the sentence true.

Ed	has	6	more blocks.
Sue		16	
		52	

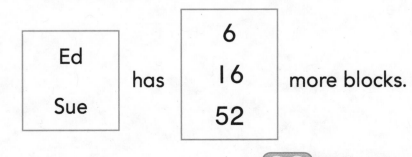

Break apart the number you are subtracting.
Write the difference.

4. 42 − 8 = _____

5. 53 − 16 = _____

6. What is 33 − 19? Use the numbers on the tiles to rewrite the subtraction problem. Then find the difference.

| 14 | 19 | 33 | 52 |

_____

− _____

_____

7. **GO DEEPER** Jacob's puzzle has 84 pieces. Jacob puts together 27 pieces in the morning. He puts together 38 more pieces in the afternoon. How many pieces does Jacob need to put together to finish the puzzle?

Complete the bar models for the steps you do to solve the problem.

_____ more pieces

Regroup if you need to. Write the difference.

8.

Tens	Ones
□	□
5	5
− 2	8

9.

Tens	Ones
□	□
3	2
− 1	2

10. Find the difference.

$$
\begin{array}{r}
90 \\
-\ 62 \\
\hline
\square
\end{array}
$$

Fill in the bubble next to one number from each column to show the difference.

Tens	Ones
○ 2	○ 1
○ 3	○ 2
○ 5	○ 8

11. There are 22 children at the park. 5 children are on the swings. The rest of the children are playing ball. How many children are playing ball?

○ 13   ○ 23   ○ 17   ○ 27

12. **THINK SMARTER +** Subtract 27 from 43. Draw to show the regrouping. Fill in the bubble next to all the ways to write the difference.

   ○ 1 ten 6 ones

   ○ 66

   ○ 6 tens 1 one

   ○ 16

13. Jill collects stamps. Her stamp book has space for 64 stamps. She needs 18 more stamps to fill the book. How many stamps does Jill have now?

   Write a number sentence for the problem.

   Use a ▮ for the missing number. Then solve.

   _____

   Jill has _____ stamps.

14. Draw a quick picture to solve. Write the difference.

Tens	Ones
□	□
6	2
− 2	5

Tens	Ones

   Explain what you did to find the difference.

   _____

   _____

3-Digit Addition and Subtraction

Curious about Math

Monarch butterflies roost together during migration.

If you count 83 butterflies on one tree and 72 on another, how many butterflies have you counted altogether?

✓ Show What You Know

Personal Math Trainer
Online Assessment
and Intervention

Model Subtracting Tens

Write the difference.

1.

5 tens — 3 tens = _____ tens

50 — 30 = _____

2.

7 tens — 2 tens = _____ tens

70 — 20 = _____

2-Digit Addition

Write the sum.

3.
$$54$$
$$+ 25$$

4.
$$35$$
$$+ 18$$

5.
$$82$$
$$+ 67$$

6.
$$29$$
$$+ 81$$

Hundreds, Tens, and Ones

Write the hundreds, tens, and ones shown. Write the number.

7.

Hundreds	Tens	Ones

_____

8.

Hundreds	Tens	Ones

_____

This page checks understanding of important skills needed for success in Chapter 6.

Vocabulary Builder

Visualize It

Fill in the graphic organizer by writing examples of ways to **regroup**.

regroup

name 13 ones as 1 ten 3 ones

Understand Vocabulary

1. Write a number that has a **hundreds** digit that is greater than its tens digit. _____

2. Write an addition sentence that has a **sum** of 20. _____

3. Write a subtraction sentence that has a **difference** of 10. _____

Game 2-Digit Shuffle

Materials

- number cards 10–50
- 15 ● ● 15 ○

Play with a partner.

1 Shuffle the number cards. Place them face down in a pile.

2 Take two cards. Say the sum of the two numbers.

3 Your partner checks your sum.

4 If your sum is correct, place a counter on a button. If you regrouped to solve, place a counter on another button.

5 Take turns. Cover all the buttons. The player with more counters on the board wins.

6 Repeat the game, saying the difference between the two numbers for each turn.

Chapter 6 Vocabulary

addend

sumando

1

column

columna

7

difference

diferencia

14

digit

dígito

15

hundred

centena

31

is equal to (=)

es igual a

33

regroup

reagrupar

56

sum

suma o total

59

column

$$
\begin{array}{r}
3\,3 \\
3\,4 \\
+3\,2 \\
\end{array}
$$

5 + 3 = 8

addends

0, 1, 2, 3, 4, 5, 6, 7, 8, and 9 are digits.

5 − 3 = 2

difference

2   plus   1   is equal to   3

2   +   1   =   3

There are 10 tens in 1 **hundred**.

4   +   2   =   6

sum

Tens	Ones

You can trade 10 ones for 1 ten to **regroup**.

© Houghton Mifflin Harcourt Publishing Company

Picture It

For 3 to 4 players

Materials
- timer
- sketch pad

How to Play
1. Take turns to play.
2. Choose a math word from the Word Box. Do not say the word.
3. Set the timer for 1 minute.
4. Draw pictures and numbers to give clues about the math word.
5. The first player to guess the word gets 1 point. If he or she uses the word in a sentence, they get 1 more point. That player gets the next turn.
6. The first player to score 5 points wins.

Word Box
addends
column
difference
digit
hundred
is equal to
regroup
sum

The Write Way

Reflect

Choose one idea. Write about it on the lines below.

- Tell how to solve this problem.

$$42 - 25 = \underline{\qquad}$$

- Write a paragraph that uses at least **three** of these words.

  addends   digit   sum   hundred   regroup

- Explain something you know about regrouping.

_____

_____

_____

_____

_____

_____

_____

Draw to Represent 3-Digit Addition

Essential Question How do you draw quick pictures to show adding 3-digit numbers?

Learning Objective You will draw quick pictures to show addition within 1,000.

Listen and Draw (Real World)

Draw quick pictures to model the problem. Then solve.

Tens	Ones

_____ pages

Math Talk Math Processes and Practices 5

Use Tools Explain how your quick pictures show the problem.

FOR THE TEACHER • Read this problem to children. Manuel read 45 pages in a book. Then he read 31 more pages. How many pages did Manuel read? Have children draw quick pictures to solve the problem.

Model and Draw

Add 234 and 141.

Hundreds	Tens	Ones

___3___ hundreds ___7___ tens ___5___ ones

___375___

Share and Show MATH BOARD

Draw quick pictures. Write how many hundreds, tens, and ones in all. Write the number.

1. Add 125 and 344.

Hundreds	Tens	Ones

_____ hundreds _____ tens _____ ones

_____

2. Add 307 and 251.

Hundreds	Tens	Ones

_____ hundreds _____ tens _____ ones

_____

Name _____

On Your Own

Draw quick pictures. Write how many hundreds, tens, and ones in all. Write the number.

3. Add 231 and 218.

Hundreds	Tens	Ones

_____ hundreds _____ tens _____ ones

_____

4. Add 232 and 150.

Hundreds	Tens	Ones

_____ hundreds _____ tens _____ ones

_____

5. **THINK SMARTER** Use the quick pictures to find the two numbers being added. Then write how many hundreds, tens, and ones in all. Write the number.

Hundreds	Tens	Ones

Add _____ and _____.

_____ hundreds _____ tens _____ ones

_____

Problem Solving • Applications

6. **Math Processes and Practices 2** **Represent a Problem**
There are 125 poems in Carrie's book and 143 poems in Angie's book. How many poems are in these two books?

Draw a quick picture to solve.

_____ poems

Personal Math Trainer

7. **THINK SMARTER +** Rhys wants to add 456 and 131.

Help Rhys solve this problem. Draw quick pictures. Write how many hundreds, tens, and ones in all. Write the number.

Hundreds	Tens	Ones

_____ hundreds _____ tens _____ ones

_____

  TAKE HOME ACTIVITY • Write 145 + 122. Have your child explain how he or she can draw quick pictures to find the sum.

Name _____

Draw to Represent 3-Digit Addition

Learning Objective You will draw quick pictures to show addition within 1,000.

Draw quick pictures. Write how many hundreds, tens, and ones in all. Write the number.

1. Add 142 and 215.

Hundreds	Tens	Ones

_____ hundreds _____ tens _____ ones

_____

Problem Solving (Real World)

Solve. Write or draw to explain.

2. A farmer sold 324 lemons and 255 limes. How many pieces of fruit did the farmer sell altogether?

_____ pieces of fruit

3. WRITE Math Draw quick pictures and write to tell how you would add 342 and 416.

_____

_____

_____

Lesson Check

1. Ms. Carol sold 346 child tickets and 253 adult tickets. How many tickets did Ms. Carol sell?

_____ tickets

2. Mr. Harris counted 227 gray pebbles and 341 white pebbles. How many pebbles did Mr. Harris count?

_____ pebbles

Spiral Review

3. Pat has 3 rows of shells. There are 4 shells in each row. How many shells does Pat have?

_____ shells

4. Kara counted 32 red pens, 25 blue pens, 7 black pens, and 24 green pens. How many pens did Kara count?

_____ pens

5. Kai had 46 blocks. He gave 39 blocks to his sister. How many blocks does Kai have left?

$46 - 39 =$ _____ blocks

6. A shop has 55 posters for sale. 34 posters show sports. The rest of the posters show animals. How many posters show animals?

_____ posters

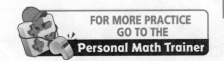

FOR MORE PRACTICE
GO TO THE
Personal Math Trainer

Break Apart 3-Digit Addends

Essential Question How do you break apart addends to add hundreds, tens, and then ones?

Learning Objective You will break apart addends to find sums within 1,000.

Listen and Draw

Write the number. Draw a quick picture for the number. Then write the number in different ways.

_____

____ hundreds ____ tens ____ ones

_____ + _____ + _____

_____

____ hundreds ____ tens ____ ones

_____ + _____ + _____

Math Talk

Math Processes and Practices ⑥

Make Connections
What number can be written as 400 + 20 + 9?

FOR THE TEACHER • Have children write 258 on the blank in the left corner of the first box. Have children draw a quick picture for this number and then complete the other two forms for the number. Repeat the activity for 325.

Break apart the addends into hundreds, tens, and ones. Add the hundreds, the tens, and the ones. Then find the total sum.

538 $\longrightarrow$ 500 + 30 + 8

+216 $\longrightarrow$ 200 + 10 + 6

700 + ___ + ___ = _____

Share and Show MATH BOARD

Break apart the addends to find the sum.

1.   321 $\longrightarrow$ _____ + _____ + _____

+457 $\longrightarrow$ _____ + _____ + _____

_____ + _____ + _____ = _____

2.   744 $\longrightarrow$ _____ + _____ + _____

+162 $\longrightarrow$ _____ + _____ + _____

_____ + _____ + _____ = _____

3.   254 $\longrightarrow$ _____ + _____ + _____

+536 $\longrightarrow$ _____ + _____ + _____

_____ + _____ + _____ = _____

Name _____

On Your Own

Break apart the addends to find the sum.

4. 374 ⟶ _____ + _____ + _____

    +518 ⟶ _____ + _____ + _____

    _____ + _____ + _____ = _____

5. 425 ⟶ _____ + _____ + _____

    +232 ⟶ _____ + _____ + _____

    _____ + _____ + _____ = _____

6. 849 ⟶ _____ + _____ + _____

    +123 ⟶ _____ + _____ + _____

    _____ + _____ + _____ = _____

7. **THINK SMARTER** Mr. Jones has many sheets of paper. He has 158 sheets of blue paper, 100 sheets of red paper, and 231 sheets of green paper. How many sheets of paper does he have?

    _____ sheets of paper

Problem Solving • Applications (Real World)   WRITE ▸ Math

8. **GO DEEPER** Wesley added in a different way.

$$327$$
$$+ 468$$

700	7 hundreds
80	8 tens
+ 15	15 ones
795	

Use Wesley's way to find the sum.

$$539$$
$$+ 247$$

9. **THINK SMARTER** There are 376 children at one school.
There are 316 children at another school.
How many children are at the two schools?

$$376 \longrightarrow 300 + 70 + 6$$
$$+ 316 \longrightarrow 300 + 10 + 6$$

Select one number from each column to solve the problem.

Hundreds	Tens	Ones
○ 2	○ 4	○ 2
○ 4	○ 8	○ 3
○ 6	○ 9	○ 6

TAKE HOME ACTIVITY • Write 347 + 215. Have your child break apart the numbers and then find the sum.

Break Apart 3-Digit Addends

Learning Objective You will break apart addends to find sums within 1,000.

Break apart the addends to find the sum.

1.   518 ⟶ _____ + _____ + _____

   + 221 ⟶ _____ + _____ + _____

   _____ + _____ + _____ = _____

_____

2.   438 ⟶ _____ + _____ + _____

   + 142 ⟶ _____ + _____ + _____

   _____ + _____ + _____ = _____

Problem Solving (Real World)

Solve. Write or draw to explain.

3. There are 126 crayons in a bucket.
   A teacher puts 144 more crayons
   in the bucket. How many crayons
   are in the bucket now?

   _____ crayons

4. **WRITE Math** Draw quick pictures
   and write to explain how to
   break apart addends to find
   the sum of 324 + 231.

_____

Lesson Check

1. What is the sum?

$$\begin{array}{r} 218 \\ + \ 145 \\ \hline \end{array}$$

2. What is the sum?

$$\begin{array}{r} 664 \\ + \ 223 \\ \hline \end{array}$$

Spiral Review

3. Ang found 19 berries and Barry found 21 berries. How many berries did they find altogether?

$19 + 21 =$ _____ berries

4. Write a subtraction fact related to $9 + 6 =$

_____

5. There are 25 goldfish and 33 betta fish. How many fish are there?

$25 + 33 =$ _____ fish

6. Subtract 16 from 41. Draw to show the regrouping. What is the difference?

Tens	Ones

_____

FOR MORE PRACTICE
GO TO THE
Personal Math Trainer

Name _____

3-Digit Addition: Regroup Ones

Learning Objective You will regroup ones to add within 1,000.

Essential Question When do you regroup ones in addition?

Use [ ] [ ] to model the problem.
Draw quick pictures to show what you did.

Hundreds	Tens	Ones

FOR THE TEACHER • Read the following problem and have children model it with blocks. There were 213 people at the show on Friday and 156 people at the show on Saturday. How many people were at the show on the two nights? Have children draw quick pictures to show how they solved the problem.

Math Talk Math Processes and Practices ⑥

Describe how you modeled the problem.

Model and Draw

Add the ones.
$6 + 7 = 13$

Regroup 13 ones as 1 ten 3 ones.

Hundreds	Tens	Ones
	1	
2	4	6
+ 1	1	7
		3

Hundreds	Tens	Ones

Add the tens.
$1 + 4 + 1 = 6$

Hundreds	Tens	Ones
	1	
2	4	6
+ 1	1	7
	6	3

Hundreds	Tens	Ones

Add the hundreds.
$2 + 1 = 3$

Hundreds	Tens	Ones
	1	
2	4	6
+ 1	1	7
3	6	3

Hundreds	Tens	Ones

Share and Show MATH BOARD

Write the sum.

1.

Hundreds	Tens	Ones
	☐	
3	2	8
+ 1	3	4

2.

Hundreds	Tens	Ones
	☐	
4	4	5
+	2	3

Name _____

On Your Own

Write the sum.

3.

Hundreds	Tens	Ones
	☐	
5	2	6
+ 1	0	3

4.

Hundreds	Tens	Ones
	☐	
3	4	8
+ 1	1	9

5.

Hundreds	Tens	Ones
	☐	
6	2	8
+ 3	4	7

6.

Hundreds	Tens	Ones
	☐	
2	3	5
+ 2	5	7

7.

Hundreds	Tens	Ones
	☐	
5	6	2
+ 3	2	9

8.

Hundreds	Tens	Ones
	☐	
1	4	7
+ 1	2	5

9. THINK SMARTER On Thursday, there were 326 visitors at the zoo. There were 200 more visitors at the zoo on Friday than on Thursday. How many visitors were at the zoo on both days?

Math on the Spot

_____ visitors

Problem Solving • Applications (Real World) WRITE ▶ Math

Solve. Write or draw to explain.

10. **Model with Mathematics** The gift shop is 140 steps away from the zoo entrance. The train stop is 235 steps away from the gift shop. How many total steps is this?

_____ steps

11. **THINK SMARTER** Katina's class used 249 noodles to decorate their bulletin board. Gunter's class used 318 noodles. How many noodles did the two classes use?

_____ noodles

Did you have to regroup to solve? Explain.

 TAKE HOME ACTIVITY • Ask your child to explain why he or she regrouped in only some of the problems in this lesson.

3-Digit Addition: Regroup Ones

Learning Objective You will regroup ones to add within 1,000.

Write the sum.

1.

Hundreds	Tens	Ones
	☐	
1	4	8
+ 2	3	4

2.

Hundreds	Tens	Ones
	☐	
3	2	1
+ 3	1	8

3.

Hundreds	Tens	Ones
	☐	
4	1	4
+ 1	7	9

4.

Hundreds	Tens	Ones
	☐	
6	0	2
+ 2	5	8

Problem Solving · Real World

Solve. Write or draw to explain.

5. In the garden, there are 258 yellow daisies and 135 white daisies. How many daisies are in the garden altogether?

_____ daisies

6. **WRITE Math** Find the sum of 136 + 212. Explain why you did or did not regroup.

_____

Lesson Check

1. What is the sum?

Hundreds	Tens	Ones
	☐	
4	3	5
+ 1	4	6

2. What is the sum?

Hundreds	Tens	Ones
	☐	
4	3	6
+ 3	0	6

Spiral Review

3. What is the difference?

$$9 - 4 = \underline{\qquad}$$

4. What is the sum?

$$\begin{array}{r} 82 \\ + 59 \\ \hline \end{array}$$

5. What is the sum?

$$26 + 7 = \underline{\qquad}$$

6. Add 243 and 132. How many hundreds, tens, and ones are there in all?

_____ hundreds _____ tens

_____ ones

FOR MORE PRACTICE
GO TO THE
Personal Math Trainer

Name _____

3-Digit Addition: Regroup Tens

Essential Question When do you regroup tens in addition?

Learning Objective You will regroup tens to add within 1,000.

Listen and Draw Real World   Hands On

Use to model the problem.
Draw quick pictures to show what you did.

Hundreds	Tens	Ones

Math Talk Math Processes and Practices 6

FOR THE TEACHER • Read the following problem and have children model it with blocks. On Monday, 253 children visited the zoo. On Tuesday, 324 children visited the zoo. How many children visited the zoo those two days? Have children draw quick pictures to show how they solved the problem.

Explain how your quick pictures show what happened in the problem.

Model and Draw

Add the ones.

$2 + 5 = 7$

Hundreds	Tens	Ones
☐	☐	
1	4	2
+ 2	8	5
		7

Add the tens.

$4 + 8 = 12$

Regroup 12 tens as 1 hundred 2 tens.

Hundreds	Tens	Ones
1	☐	
1	4	2
+ 2	8	5
	2	7

Add the hundreds.

$1 + 1 + 2 = 4$

Hundreds	Tens	Ones
1	☐	
1	4	2
+ 2	8	5
4	2	7

Share and Show MATH BOARD

Write the sum.

1.
Hundreds	Tens	Ones
☐	☐	
3	4	7
+ 2	9	1

2.
Hundreds	Tens	Ones
☐	☐	
1	6	5
+ 3	5	4

3.
Hundreds	Tens	Ones
☐	☐	
5	3	8
+ 1	4	0

On Your Own

Write the sum.

4.

Hundreds	Tens	Ones
☐	☐	
1	5	6
+	4	2

5.

Hundreds	Tens	Ones
☐	☐	
7	6	4
+ 1	5	3

6.

Hundreds	Tens	Ones
☐	☐	
3	7	2
+ 1	8	5

7.

2	2	4
+ 1	5	7

8.

3	1	4
+ 4	3	5

9.

7	5	3
+ 1	5	2

10. **GO DEEPER** In a bowling game, Jack scored
116 points and 124 points. Hal scored 128 points
and 134 points. Who scored more points? How
many more points were scored?

_____ _____ more points

Math Processes and Practices 6 **Attend to Precision**
Rewrite the numbers. Then add.

11. $760 + 178$

+ _____
_____

12. $216 + 346$

+ _____
_____

13. $423 + 285$

+ _____
_____

Problem Solving • Applications Real World   WRITE ▸ Math

14. **THINK SMARTER** These lists show the pieces of fruit sold. How many pieces of fruit did Mr. Olson sell?

Mr. Olson	**Mr. Lee**
257 apples	314 pears
281 plums	229 peaches

_____ pieces of fruit

15. **GO DEEPER** Who sold more pieces of fruit?

_____

How many more?

_____ more pieces of fruit

16. **THINK SMARTER** At the city park theater, 152 people watched the morning play. Another 167 watched the afternoon play.

How many people watched the two plays?   _____ people

Fill in the bubble next to each true sentence about how to solve the problem.

○ You need to regroup the tens as 1 ten and 9 ones.

○ You need to regroup the tens as 1 hundred and 1 ten.

○ You need to add 2 ones + 7 ones.

○ You need to add 1 hundred + 1 hundred + 1 hundred.

TAKE HOME ACTIVITY • Have your child choose a new combination of two fruits on this page and find the total number of pieces of the two types of fruit.

3-Digit Addition: Regroup Tens

Learning Objective You will regroup tens to add within 1,000.

Write the sum.

1.

Hundreds	Tens	Ones
□	□	
1	8	7
+ 2	3	2

2.

Hundreds	Tens	Ones
□	□	
3	2	2
+ 3	5	6

3.

Hundreds	Tens	Ones
□	□	
2	8	5
+ 5	3	1

4.

4	4	5
+	3	4

5.

6	2	0
+ 2	8	8

6.

5	5	7
+ 1	8	0

Problem Solving Real World

Solve. Write or draw to explain.

7. There are 142 blue toy cars and 293 red toy cars at the toy store. How many toy cars are there?

_____ toy cars

8. **WRITE** Math Find the sum of 362 + 265. Explain why you did or did not regroup.

_____

_____

Lesson Check

1. What is the sum?

$$472 + 255$$

2. Annika has 144 pennies and Yahola has 284 pennies. How many do they have altogether?

$$144 + 284$$

Spiral Review

3. What is the sum?

$$56 + 38$$

4. What is the sum?

$$326 + 139$$

5. Francis had 8 toy cars, then his brother gave him 9 more. How many toy cars does Francis have now?

$$8 + 9 = \underline{\qquad} \text{ cars}$$

6. What is the difference?

$$82 - 34$$

FOR MORE PRACTICE
GO TO THE
Personal Math Trainer

Name _____

Addition: Regroup Ones and Tens

Essential Question How do you know when to regroup in addition?

Learning Objective You will regroup ones and tens to add within 1,000.

Listen and Draw (Real World)

Use mental math. Write the sum for each problem.

$$\begin{array}{r} 40 \\ + 20 \\ \hline \end{array} \qquad \begin{array}{r} 200 \\ + 700 \\ \hline \end{array} \qquad \begin{array}{r} 70 \\ + 30 \\ \hline \end{array} \qquad \begin{array}{r} 500 \\ + 300 \\ \hline \end{array}$$

$10 + 30 + 40 =$ _____

$100 + 400 + 200 =$ _____

$10 + 50 + 40 =$ _____

$600 + 300 =$ _____

Math Talk Math Processes and Practices ①

Analyze Were some problems easier to solve than other problems? Explain.

FOR THE TEACHER • Encourage children to do these addition problems quickly. You may wish to first discuss the problems with children, noting that each problem is limited to just adding tens or just adding hundreds.

Sometimes you will regroup more than once in addition problems.

```
  | |
  2 5 9
+ 4 7 6
───────
  7 3 5
```

| 9 ones + 6 ones = 15 ones, or 1 ten 5 ones |

| 1 ten + 5 tens + 7 tens = 13 tens, or 1 hundred 3 tens |

| 1 hundred + 2 hundreds + 4 hundreds = 7 hundreds |

THINK:
Are there 10 or more ones?
Are there 10 or more tens?

Share and Show MATH BOARD

Write the sum.

1.
```
  1 8 4
+ 3 2 9
───────
```

2.
```
  5 4 6
+ 2 7 8
───────
```

3.
```
  3 2 7
+ 3 5 3
───────
```

4.
```
  2 3 4
+ 1 5 2
───────
```

☑ 5.
```
  3 7 5
+ 2 7 2
───────
```

☑ 6.
```
  1 8 9
+ 6 2 3
───────
```

On Your Own

Write the sum.

7.
```
  5 7 4
+ 2 8 1
———————
```

8.
```
  4 1 6
+ 4 8 3
———————
```

9.
```
  3 4 6
+ 5 9 7
———————
```

10.
```
  3 6 5
+ 2 8 3
———————
```

11.
```
  6 4 7
+ 1 0 9
———————
```

12.
```
  5 4 6
+ 3 5 6
———————
```

13.
```
  3 4 8
+ 6 3 1
———————
```

14.
```
  4 5 5
+ 1 3 9
———————
```

15.
```
  5 6 3
+ 2 4 5
———————
```

16. THINK SMARTER Miko wrote these problems.
What are the missing digits?

```
  ▢ ▢ 6
+ 4 5 ▢
———————
  6 9 0
```

```
  6 ▢ 7
+ 2 3 ▢
———————
  ▢ 6 2
```

TAKE HOME ACTIVITY • Have your child explain how to solve 236 + 484.

✓ **Mid-Chapter Checkpoint**

Personal Math Trainer
Online Assessment
and Intervention

Concepts and Skills

Break apart the addends to find the sum.

1.   567 ⟶   _____ + _____ + _____

   +324 ⟶   _____ + _____ + _____

   _____ + _____ + _____ = _____

Write the sum.

2.

      2 4 8
   + 3 4 6
   _____

3.

      6 3 7
   + 2 6 4
   _____

4.

      3 9 1
   + 5 3 7
   _____

5. **THINK SMARTER** There are 148 small sand dollars
and 119 large sand dollars on the beach.
How many sand dollars are on the
beach?

_____ sand dollars

© Houghton Mifflin Harcourt Publishing Company • Image Credits: (b) Siede Preis/PhotoDisc/Getty Images

Addition: Regroup Ones and Tens

Learning Objective You will regroup ones and tens to add within 1,000.

Write the sum.

I.

$$\begin{array}{r} 5\ 4\ 7 \\ +\ 4\ 3\ 5 \\ \hline \end{array}$$

2.

$$\begin{array}{r} 3\ 6\ 7 \\ +\ 2\ 8\ 4 \\ \hline \end{array}$$

3.

$$\begin{array}{r} 4\ 8\ 5 \\ +\ 4\ 5\ 6 \\ \hline \end{array}$$

4.

$$\begin{array}{r} 1\ 8\ 7 \\ +\ 3\ 0\ 6 \\ \hline \end{array}$$

5.

$$\begin{array}{r} 6\ 4\ 7 \\ +\ 1\ 2\ 8 \\ \hline \end{array}$$

6.

$$\begin{array}{r} 5\ 2\ 3 \\ +\ 1\ 7\ 4 \\ \hline \end{array}$$

Problem Solving Real World

Solve. Write or draw to explain.

7. Saul and Luisa each scored 167 points on a computer game. How many points did they score together?

_____ points

8. **WRITE** Math Write the addition problem for 275 plus 249 and find the sum. Then draw quick pictures to check your work.

_____

Lesson Check

1. What is the sum?

$$348$$
$$+ \ 272$$

2. What is the sum?

$$123$$
$$+ \ 217$$

Spiral Review

3. Write an addition fact that has the same sum as $9 + 4$.

$$10 + \underline{\hspace{1cm}}$$

4. What is the sum?

$$32$$
$$15$$
$$+ \ 46$$

5. Add 29 and 35. Draw to show the regrouping. What is the sum?

Tens	Ones

$$\underline{\hspace{1.5cm}}$$

6. Tom had 25 pretzels. He gave away 12 pretzels. How many pretzels does Tom have left?

$$25 - 12 = \underline{\hspace{1cm}} \text{ pretzels}$$

FOR MORE PRACTICE GO TO THE Personal Math Trainer

Name _____

Problem Solving • 3-Digit Subtraction

Essential Question How can making a model help when solving subtraction problems?

Learning Objective You will use blocks and the strategy *make a model* to solve subtraction problems within 1,000.

There were 436 people at the art show. 219 people went home. How many people stayed at the art show?

⚷ Unlock the Problem Real World   Hands On

What do I need to find?

how many people
_____
stayed at the art show

What information do I need to use?

_____ people were at the art show.

Then, _____ people went home.

Show how to solve the problem.

Make a model. Then draw a quick picture of your model.

_____ people

🏠 **HOME CONNECTION** • Your child used a model and a quick picture to represent and solve a subtraction problem.

Make a model to solve. Then draw a quick picture of your model.

- What do I need to find?
- What information do I need to use?

1. There are 532 pieces of art at the show. 319 pieces of art are paintings. How many pieces of art are not paintings?

_____ pieces of art

2. 245 children go to the face-painting event. 114 of the children are boys. How many of the children are girls?

_____ girls

Math Talk

Math Processes and Practices 6

Explain how you solved the first problem on this page.

Name _____

Make a model to solve. Then draw a quick picture of your model.

3. There were 237 books on the table. Miss Jackson took 126 books off the table. How many books were still on the table?

_____ books

4. There were 232 postcards on the table. The children used 118 postcards. How many postcards were not used?

_____ postcards

5. **THINK SMARTER** 164 children and 31 adults saw the movie in the morning. 125 children saw the movie in the afternoon. How many fewer children saw the movie in the afternoon than in the morning?

_____ fewer children

On Your Own

Math Processes and Practices ①   Make Sense of Problems

6. There were some grapes in a bowl. Clancy's friends ate 24 of the grapes. Then there were 175 grapes in the bowl. How many grapes were in the bowl before?

_____ grapes

7. **THINK SMARTER**   At Gregory's school, there are 547 boys and girls. There are 246 boys. How many girls are there?

Draw a quick picture to solve.

Circle the number that makes the sentence true.

There are
| 201 |
| 301 | girls.
| 793 |

TAKE HOME ACTIVITY • Ask your child to choose one of the problems in this lesson and solve it in a different way.

Problem Solving • 3-Digit Subtraction

Learning Objective You will use blocks and the strategy *make a model* to solve subtraction problems within 1,000.

Make a model to solve. Then draw a quick picture of your model.

1. On Saturday, 770 people went to the snack shop. On Sunday, 628 people went. How many more people went to the snack shop on Saturday than on Sunday?

_____ more people

2. There were 395 lemon ice cups at the snack shop. People bought 177 lemon ice cups. How many lemon ice cups are still at the snack shop?

_____ cups

3. There were 576 bottles of water at the snack shop. People bought 469 bottles of water. How many bottles of water are at the snack shop now?

_____ bottles

4. **WRITE** Math Draw quick pictures to show how to subtract 314 from 546.

Lesson Check

1. There are 278 math and science books. 128 of them are math books. How many science books are there?

_____ books

2. A book has 176 pages. Mr. Roberts has read 119 pages. How many pages does he have left to read?

_____ pages

Spiral Review

3. What is the sum?

$$1 + 6 + 2 = \underline{\qquad}$$

4. What is the difference?

$$54 - 8 = \underline{\qquad}$$

5. What is the sum?

$$
\begin{array}{r}
356 \\
+\ 174 \\
\hline
\end{array}
$$

6. What is the sum?

$$
\begin{array}{r}
22 \\
+\ 16 \\
\hline
\end{array}
$$

FOR MORE PRACTICE
GO TO THE
Personal Math Trainer

3-Digit Subtraction: Regroup Tens

Essential Question When do you regroup tens in subtraction?

Learning Objective You will regroup tens to subtract within 1,000.

Use _____ . to model the problem.
Draw a quick picture to show what you did.

Hundreds	Tens	Ones

Math Talk Math Processes and Practices ①

Describe what to do when there are not enough ones to subtract from.

FOR THE TEACHER • Read the following problem and have children model it with blocks. 473 people went to the football game. 146 people were still there at the end of the game. How many people left before the end of the game? Have children draw quick pictures of their models.

354 − 137 = ?

Are there enough ones to subtract 7?

yes (no)

Regroup 1 ten as 10 ones.

Hundreds	Tens	Ones
	4	14
3	5̶	4̶
− 1	3	7

Hundreds	Tens	Ones

Now there are enough ones.

Subtract the ones.

14 − 7 = 7

Hundreds	Tens	Ones
	4	14
3	5̶	4̶
− 1	3	7
		7

Hundreds	Tens	Ones

Subtract the tens.

4 − 3 = 1

Subtract the hundreds.

3 − 1 = 2

Hundreds	Tens	Ones
	4	14
3	5̶	4̶
− 1	3	7
2	1	7

Hundreds	Tens	Ones

Share and Show   MATH BOARD

Solve. Write the difference.

✓ 1.

Hundreds	Tens	Ones
□	□	
4	3	1
− 3	2	6

✓ 2.

Hundreds	Tens	Ones
□	□	
6	5	8
− 2	3	7

Name _____

Solve. Write the difference.

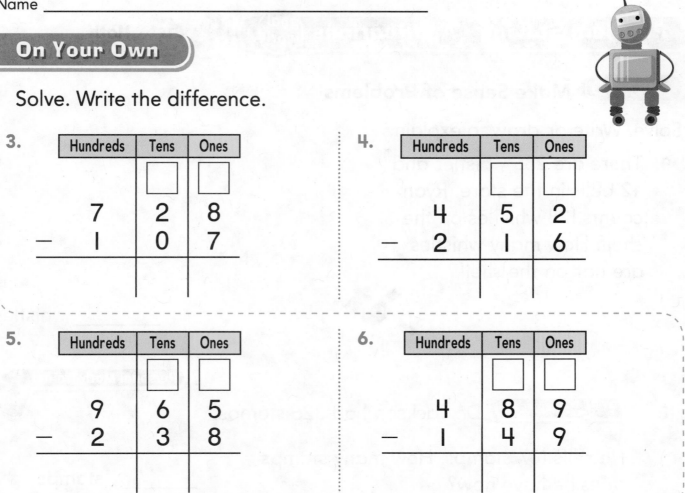

3.

Hundreds	Tens	Ones
	☐	☐
7	2	8
− 1	0	7

4.

Hundreds	Tens	Ones
	☐	☐
4	5	2
− 2	1	6

5.

Hundreds	Tens	Ones
	☐	☐
9	6	5
− 2	3	8

6.

Hundreds	Tens	Ones
	☐	☐
4	8	9
− 1	4	9

7. **GO DEEPER** A bookstore has 148 books about people and 136 books about places. Some books were sold. Now there are 137 books left. How many books were sold?

_____ books

8. **THINK SMARTER** There were 287 music books and 134 science books in the store. After some books were sold, there are 159 books left. How many books were sold?

_____ books

Problem Solving • Applications   WRITE Math

Math Processes and Practices ① Make Sense of Problems

Solve. Write or draw to explain.

9. There are 235 whistles and 42 bells in the store. Ryan counts 128 whistles on the shelf. How many whistles are not on the shelf?

_____ whistles

Personal Math Trainer

10. **THINK SMARTER +** Dr. Jackson had 326 stamps.

He sells 107 stamps. How many stamps does he have now?

_____ stamps

Would you do these things to solve the problem?
Choose Yes or No.

Subtract 107 from 326.	○ Yes	○ No
Regroup 1 ten as 10 ones.	○ Yes	○ No
Regroup the hundreds.	○ Yes	○ No
Subtract 7 ones from 16 ones.	○ Yes	○ No
Add 26 + 10.	○ Yes	○ No

 TAKE HOME ACTIVITY • Ask your child to explain why he or she regrouped in only some of the problems in this lesson.

3-Digit Subtraction: Regroup Tens

Learning Objective You will regroup tens to subtract within 1,000.

Solve. Write the difference.

1.

Hundreds	Tens	Ones
	☐	☐
7	7	4
− 2	3	6

2.

Hundreds	Tens	Ones
	☐	☐
5	5	1
− 1	1	3

3.

Hundreds	Tens	Ones
	☐	☐
4	8	9
− 2	7	3

4.

Hundreds	Tens	Ones
	☐	☐
7	7	2
− 2	5	4

Problem Solving (Real World)

Solve. Write or draw to explain.

5. There were 985 pencils. Some pencils were sold. Then there were 559 pencils left. How many pencils were sold?

_____ pencils

6. **WRITE** Math Choose one exercise from above. Draw quick pictures to check your work.

Lesson Check

1. What is the difference?

$$\begin{array}{r} 346 \\ -\ 127 \\ \hline \end{array}$$

2. What is the difference?

$$\begin{array}{r} 568 \\ -\ 226 \\ \hline \end{array}$$

Spiral Review

3. What is the difference?

$$45 - 7 = \underline{\hspace{1cm}}$$

4. Leroy has 11 cubes. Jane has 15 cubes. How many cubes do they have altogether?

_____ cubes

5. Mina puts 5 flowers in each vase. How many flowers will she put in 3 vases?

_____ flowers

6. Mr. Hill had 471 pencils. He gave away 164 pencils. How many pencils did he keep?

_____ pencils

FOR MORE PRACTICE
GO TO THE
Personal Math Trainer

3-Digit Subtraction: Regroup Hundreds

Learning Objective You will regroup hundreds to subtract within 1,000.

Essential Question When do you regroup hundreds in subtraction?

Listen and Draw *Real World*

Draw quick pictures to show the problem.

Hundreds	Tens	Ones

Math Talk Math Processes and Practices ①

Describe what to do when there are not enough tens to subtract from.

FOR THE TEACHER • Read the following problem and have children model it with quick pictures. The Reading Club has 349 books. 173 of the books are about animals. How many books are not about animals?

428 − 153 = ?

Subtract the ones.

8 − 3 = 5

Hundreds	Tens	Ones
4	2	8
− 1	5	3
		5

There are not enough tens to subtract from.

Regroup 1 hundred. 4 hundreds 2 tens is now 3 hundreds 12 tens.

Hundreds	Tens	Ones
3	12	
4	2	8
− 1	5	3
		5

Subtract the tens.

12 − 5 = 7

Subtract the hundreds.

3 − 1 = 2

Hundreds	Tens	Ones
3	12	
4	2	8
− 1	5	3
2	7	5

Share and Show MATH BOARD

Solve. Write the difference.

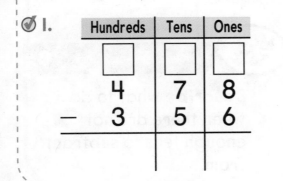

1.

Hundreds	Tens	Ones
4	7	8
− 3	5	6

2.

Hundreds	Tens	Ones
8	1	4
− 2	6	3

Name _____

Solve. Write the difference.

3.

Hundreds	Tens	Ones
☐	☐	☐
6	2	9
− 4	8	2

4.

Hundreds	Tens	Ones
☐	☐	☐
9	3	6
− 1	7	3

5.

```
    4 | 3 | 5
  − 1 | 9 | 2
```

6.

```
    3 | 8 | 7
  −   | 4 | 7
```

7.

```
    5 8 8
  − 4 5 0
```

8.

```
    3 4 5
  − 2 6 3
```

Math Processes and Practices **3**   **Make Arguments**

9. Choose one exercise above. Describe the subtraction that you did. Be sure to tell about the values of the digits in the numbers.

_____

_____

_____

_____

Problem Solving • Applications
WRITE Math

10. **THINK SMARTER** Sam made two towers. He used 139 blocks for the first tower. He used 276 blocks in all. For which tower did he use more blocks? _____

Explain how you solved the problem.

_____

_____

11. **THINK SMARTER** This is how many points each class scored in a math game.

Mrs. Rose
444 points

Mr. Chang
429 points

Mr. Pagano
293 points

How many more points did Mr. Chang's class score than Mr. Pagano's class? Draw a picture and explain how you found your answer.

_____ more points

 TAKE HOME ACTIVITY • Have your child explain how to find the difference for 745 – 341.

3-Digit Subtraction: Regroup Hundreds

Learning Objective You will regroup hundreds to subtract within 1,000.

Solve. Write the difference.

1.

Hundreds	Tens	Ones
☐	☐	☐
7	2	7
− 2	5	6

2.

Hundreds	Tens	Ones
☐	☐	☐
9	6	7
− 1	5	3

3.

6	3	9
− 4	7	2

4.

4	4	8
− 3	6	3

Problem Solving (Real World)

Solve. Write or draw to explain.

5. There were 537 people in the parade. 254 of these people were playing an instrument. How many people were not playing an instrument?

_____ people

6. WRITE Math Write the subtraction problem for 838 − 462 and find the difference. Then draw quick pictures to check your difference.

_____

Lesson Check

1. What is the difference?

$$\begin{array}{r} 5\;3\;8 \\ -\;1\;3\;5 \\ \hline \end{array}$$

2. What is the difference?

$$\begin{array}{r} 2\;1\;8 \\ -\;1\;2\;6 \\ \hline \end{array}$$

Spiral Review

3. What is the difference?

$$52 - 15 = \underline{\hspace{1cm}}$$

4. Wallace has 8 crayons and Alma has 7. How many do the have together?

$$8 + 7 = \underline{\hspace{1cm}} \text{ crayons}$$

5. What is the sum?

$$\begin{array}{r} 4\;7 \\ +\;2\;6 \\ \hline \end{array}$$

6. Mrs. Lin's class read 392 books in February. Mr. Hook's class read 173 books. How many more books did Mrs. Lin's class read?

$$\begin{array}{r} 3\;9\;2 \\ -\;1\;7\;3 \\ \hline \end{array}$$

_____ books

FOR MORE PRACTICE
GO TO THE
Personal Math Trainer

Subtraction: Regroup Hundreds and Tens

Learning Objective You will regroup hundreds and tens to subtract within 1,000.

Essential Question How do you know when to regroup in subtraction?

Listen and Draw Real World

Use mental math. Write the difference for each problem.

$$
\begin{array}{r} 50 \\ -\ 20 \\ \hline \end{array}
\qquad
\begin{array}{r} 600 \\ -\ 400 \\ \hline \end{array}
\qquad
\begin{array}{r} 80 \\ -\ 30 \\ \hline \end{array}
\qquad
\begin{array}{r} 900 \\ -\ 300 \\ \hline \end{array}
$$

$90 - 40 =$ _____

$700 - 500 =$ _____

$70 - 60 =$ _____

$800 - 300 =$ _____

FOR THE TEACHER • Encourage children to do these subtraction problems quickly. You may wish to first discuss the problems with children, noting that each problem is limited to just subtracting tens or just subtracting hundreds.

Math Talk Math Processes and Practices 6

Were some problems easier to solve than other problems? **Explain.**

Model and Draw

Sometimes you will regroup more than once in subtraction problems.

$$
\begin{array}{r}
\overset{6}{\cancel{7}}\ \overset{11}{\cancel{2}}\ \overset{15}{\cancel{5}} \\
-\ 3\ 4\ 9 \\
\hline
3\ 7\ 6
\end{array}
$$

Regroup 2 tens 5 ones as I ten 15 ones. Subtract the ones.

Regroup 7 hundreds I ten as 6 hundreds II tens. Subtract the tens.

Subtract the hundreds.

Share and Show   MATH BOARD

Solve. Write the difference.

1.
$$
\begin{array}{r}
4\ 2\ 1 \\
-\ 1\ 3\ 8 \\
\hline
\end{array}
$$

2.
$$
\begin{array}{r}
2\ 7\ 4 \\
-\ 1\ 8\ 2 \\
\hline
\end{array}
$$

3.
$$
\begin{array}{r}
5\ 4\ 6 \\
-\ 2\ 6\ 7 \\
\hline
\end{array}
$$

4.
$$
\begin{array}{r}
8\ 5\ 9 \\
-\ \ \ 5\ 7 \\
\hline
\end{array}
$$

5.
$$
\begin{array}{r}
7\ 4\ 7 \\
-\ 1\ 5\ 9 \\
\hline
\end{array}
$$

6.
$$
\begin{array}{r}
9\ 3\ 8 \\
-\ 3\ 7\ 0 \\
\hline
\end{array}
$$

On Your Own

Solve. Write the difference.

7.
```
  3 4 2
- 1 3 8
-------
```

8.
```
  4 6 3
- 2 8 1
-------
```

9.
```
  8 5 5
- 4 9 7
-------
```

10.
```
  6 5 7
- 3 8 4
-------
```

11.
```
  5 2 1
- 1 4 6
-------
```

12.
```
  7 5 8
- 5 3 7
-------
```

13.
```
  5 4 2
- 1 6 8
-------
```

14.
```
  8 2 3
- 6 7 3
-------
```

15.
```
  9 4 7
- 5 7 9
-------
```

16. THINK SMARTER Alex wrote these problems.
What are the missing digits?

```
      4  15
  9  ▢   ▢
-    6 2 8
----------
     3 2 7
```

```
      7  13
  ▢  ▢   7
-    1 5 ▢
----------
     6 8 1
```

Problem Solving • Applications (Real World)   WRITE Math

17. GO DEEPER This is how Walter found the difference for 617 — 350.

Find the difference for 843 — 270 using Walter's way.

350 ⟩ + 50
400
600 ⟩ + 200
617 ⟩ + 17

267

18. Math Processes and Practices ❶ **Analyze** There are 471 children at Caleb's school. 256 children ride buses to get to school.

How many children do not ride buses to get to school?

_____ children

19. THINK SMARTER Mrs. Herrell had 427 pinecones. She gave 249 pinecones to her children.

How many pinecones does she still have?

_____ pinecones

TAKE HOME ACTIVITY • Ask your child to find the difference when subtracting 182 from 477.

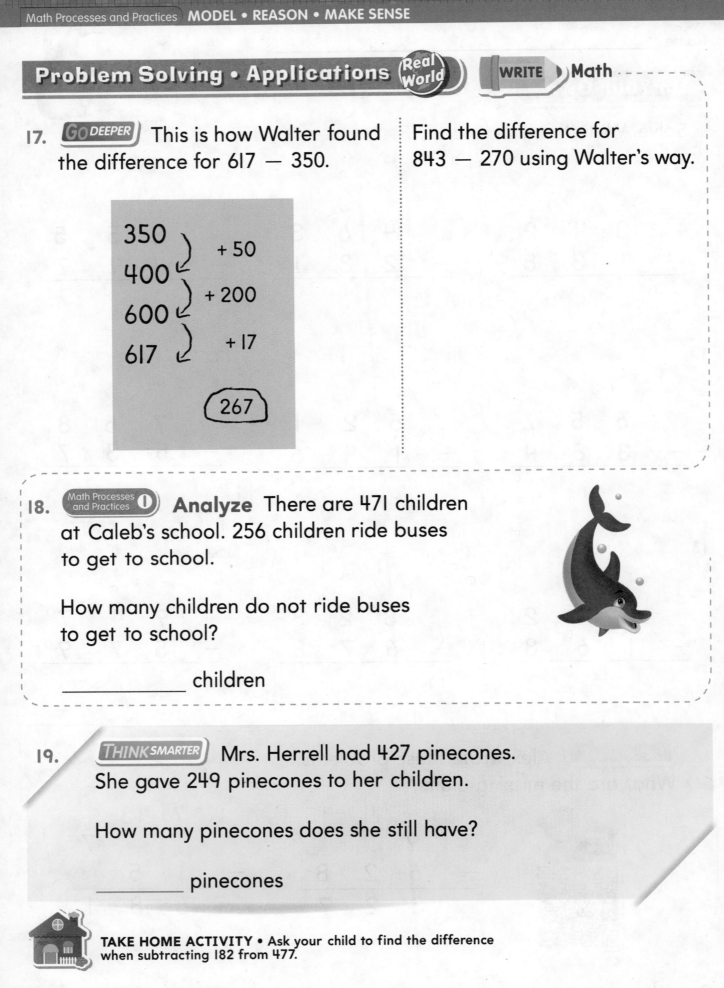

Subtraction: Regroup Hundreds and Tens

Learning Objective You will regroup hundreds and tens to subtract within 1,000.

Solve. Write the difference.

1.
```
   8  1  6
 - 3  4  5
 ─────────
```

2.
```
   9  3  2
 - 1  6  3
 ─────────
```

3.
```
   7  9  6
 - 4  6  8
 ─────────
```

Problem Solving Real World

Solve.

4. Mia's coloring book has 432 pages. She has already colored 178 pages. How many pages in the book are left to color?

_____ pages

5. **WRITE** Math Draw quick pictures to show how to subtract 546 from 735.

Lesson Check

1. What is the difference?

$$\begin{array}{r} 349 \\ -\ 187 \\ \hline \end{array}$$

2. What is the difference?

$$\begin{array}{r} 336 \\ -\ 178 \\ \hline \end{array}$$

Spiral Review

3. What is the sum?

$$\begin{array}{r} 246 \\ +\ 533 \\ \hline \end{array}$$

4. What is the difference?

$$\begin{array}{r} 38 \\ -\ 14 \\ \hline \end{array}$$

5. What is the difference?

$$17 - 9 = \underline{\qquad}$$

6. Lisa had 15 daisies.
She gave away 7 daisies.
Then she found 3 more daisies.
How many daisies does Lisa have now?

_____ daisies

FOR MORE PRACTICE
GO TO THE
Personal Math Trainer

Name _____

Regrouping with Zeros

Essential Question How do you regroup when there are zeros in the number you start with?

Learning Objective You will find the difference of 3-digit numbers when there are zeros in the number you start with.

Listen and Draw

Draw or write to show how you solved the problem.

FOR THE TEACHER • Read the following problem and have children solve. Mr. Sanchez made 403 cookies. He sold 159 cookies. How many cookies does Mr. Sanchez have now? Encourage children to discuss and show different ways to solve the problem.

Math Talk Math Processes and Practices ①

Describe another way that you could solve the problem.

Chapter 6

Ms. Dean has a book with 504 pages in it. She has read 178 pages so far. How many more pages does she still have to read?

$$\begin{array}{r} 5\ 0\ 4 \\ -\ 1\ 7\ 8 \\ \hline \end{array}$$

Step 1 There are not enough ones to subtract from.

Since there are 0 tens, regroup 5 hundreds as 4 hundreds 10 tens.

$$\begin{array}{r} {}^{4}\ {}^{10} \\ \cancel{5}\ \cancel{0}\ 4 \\ -\ 1\ 7\ 8 \\ \hline \end{array}$$

Step 2 Next, regroup 10 tens 4 ones as 9 tens 14 ones.

Now there are enough ones to subtract from.

$14 - 8 = 6$

$$\begin{array}{r} {}^{4}\ {}^{9}\!\!\!\cancel{10}\ {}^{14} \\ \cancel{5}\ \cancel{0}\ \cancel{4} \\ -\ 1\ 7\ 8 \\ \hline 6 \end{array}$$

Step 3 Subtract the tens.

$9 - 7 = 2$

Subtract the hundreds.

$4 - 1 = 3$

$$\begin{array}{r} {}^{4}\ {}^{9}\!\!\!\cancel{10}\ {}^{14} \\ \cancel{5}\ \cancel{0}\ \cancel{4} \\ -\ 1\ 7\ 8 \\ \hline 3\ 2\ 6 \end{array}$$

Share and Show MATH BOARD

Solve. Write the difference.

1.

$$\begin{array}{r} 3\ 0\ 8 \\ -\ 2\ 5\ 9 \\ \hline \end{array}$$

2.

$$\begin{array}{r} 7\ 5\ 5 \\ -\ 4\ 3\ 8 \\ \hline \end{array}$$

3.

$$\begin{array}{r} 8\ 0\ 1 \\ -\ 3\ 7\ 5 \\ \hline \end{array}$$

Name _____

Solve. Write the difference.

4.
$$\begin{array}{r} 5\ 6\ 3 \\ -\ 1\ 8\ 2 \\ \hline \end{array}$$

5.
$$\begin{array}{r} 9\ 0\ 4 \\ -\ 5\ 6\ 8 \\ \hline \end{array}$$

6.
$$\begin{array}{r} 7\ 0\ 5 \\ -\ 2\ 3\ 1 \\ \hline \end{array}$$

7.
$$\begin{array}{r} 6\ 0\ 3 \\ -\ 3\ 2\ 8 \\ \hline \end{array}$$

8.
$$\begin{array}{r} 4\ 4\ 2 \\ -\ 2\ 3\ 8 \\ \hline \end{array}$$

9.
$$\begin{array}{r} 9\ 0\ 1 \\ -\ 6\ 7\ 5 \\ \hline \end{array}$$

10.
$$\begin{array}{r} 7\ 0\ 2 \\ -\ 4\ 2\ 6 \\ \hline \end{array}$$

11.
$$\begin{array}{r} 6\ 8\ 4 \\ -\ 2\ 1\ 9 \\ \hline \end{array}$$

12.
$$\begin{array}{r} 4\ 7\ 9 \\ -\ 1\ 3\ 7 \\ \hline \end{array}$$

13. **THINK SMARTER** Miguel has 125 more baseball cards than Chad. Miguel has 405 baseball cards. How many baseball cards does Chad have?

_____ baseball cards

Problem Solving • Applications (Real World)   WRITE Math

14. **Math Processes and Practices ①** **Analyze** Claire has 250 pennies. Some are in a box and some are in her bank. There are more than 100 pennies in each place. How many pennies could be in each place?

_____ pennies in a box

_____ pennies in her bank

Explain how you solved the problem.

_____

_____

_____

_____

15. **THINK SMARTER** There are 404 people at the baseball game. 273 people are fans of the blue team. The rest are fans of the red team. How many people are fans of the red team?

Does the sentence describe how to find the answer? Choose Yes or No.

Regroup 1 ten as 14 ones.	○ Yes	○ No
Regroup 1 hundred as 10 tens.	○ Yes	○ No
Subtract 3 ones from 4 ones.	○ Yes	○ No
Subtract 2 hundreds from 4 hundreds.	○ Yes	○ No

There are _____ fans of the red team.

TAKE HOME ACTIVITY • Ask your child to explain how he or she solved one of the problems in this lesson.

Regrouping with Zeros

Name _____

Learning Objective You will find the difference of 3-digit numbers when there are zeros in the number you start with.

Solve. Write the difference.

1.
$$\begin{array}{r} 8\;0\;6 \\ -\;3\;4\;5 \\ \hline \end{array}$$

2.
$$\begin{array}{r} 9\;0\;2 \\ -\;7\;8\;3 \\ \hline \end{array}$$

3.
$$\begin{array}{r} 7\;9\;4 \\ -\;2\;6\;8 \\ \hline \end{array}$$

4.
$$\begin{array}{r} 6\;8\;7 \\ -\;1\;4\;4 \\ \hline \end{array}$$

5.
$$\begin{array}{r} 5\;0\;5 \\ -\;1\;6\;7 \\ \hline \end{array}$$

6.
$$\begin{array}{r} 3\;0\;7 \\ -\;1\;5\;4 \\ \hline \end{array}$$

Problem Solving · Real World

Solve.

7. There are 303 students.
   There are 147 girls.
   How many boys are there?

   _____ boys

8. **WRITE Math** Write the subtraction problem 604 − 357. Describe how you will subtract to find the difference.

   _____

   _____

Lesson Check

1. What is the difference?

$$301 - 187$$

2. What is the difference?

$$406 - 268$$

Spiral Review

3. What is the sum?

$$35 + 79$$

4. There are 555 students at Roosevelt Elementary School and 282 students at Jefferson Elementary. How many students are at the two schools altogether?

$$555 + 282$$

_____ students

5. What is the difference?

$$10 - 2 = \underline{\hspace{1cm}}$$

6. Gabriel's goal is to read 43 books this year. So far he has read 11 books. How many books does he have left to meet his goal?

$$43 - 11$$

_____ books

FOR MORE PRACTICE
GO TO THE
Personal Math Trainer

✓ Chapter 6 Review/Test

Personal Math Trainer
Online Assessment and Intervention

1. Mr. Kent had 948 craft sticks. His art class used 356 craft sticks. How many craft sticks does Mr. Kent have now?

   _____ craft sticks

2. At the library, there are 668 books and magazines. There are 565 books at the library. How many magazines are there?

   Circle the number that makes the sentence true.

   There are | 13
   103
   1,233 | magazines.

3. There are 176 girls and 241 boys at school. How many children are at school?

   176 ⟶ 100 + 70 + 6
   + 241 ⟶ 200 + 40 + 1

   Select one number from each column to solve the problem.

Hundreds	Tens	Ones
○ 2	○ 1	○ 3
○ 3	○ 3	○ 5
○ 4	○ 4	○ 7

4. **THINK SMARTER +** Anna wants to add 246 and 132.

Help Anna solve this problem. Draw quick pictures. Write how many hundreds, tens, and ones in all. Write the number.

Hundreds	Tens	Ones

_____ hundreds _____ tens _____ ones

_____

5. Mrs. Preston had 513 leaves. She gave 274 leaves to her students. How many leaves does she still have? Draw to show how you found your answer.

_____ leaves

6. A farmer has 112 pecan trees and 97 walnut trees. How many more pecan trees does the farmer have than walnut trees?

Fill in the bubble next to all the sentences that describe what you would do.

○ I would regroup the hundreds.

○ I would add 12 + 97.

○ I would subtract 7 ones from 12 ones.

○ I would regroup the tens.

7. Amy has 408 beads. She gives 322 beads to her sister. How many beads does Amy have now?

Does the sentence describe how to find the answer? Choose Yes or No.

Regroup 1 ten as 18 ones.	○ Yes	○ No
Regroup 1 hundred as 10 tens.	○ Yes	○ No
Subtract 2 tens from 10 tens.	○ Yes	○ No

Amy has _____ beads.

---

8. **GO DEEPER** Raul used this method to find the sum 427 + 316.

```
  427
+ 316
  700
   30
+  13
  743
```

Use Raul's method to find this sum.

```
  229
+ 313
```

Describe how Raul solves addition problems.

_____

_____

9. Sally scores 381 points in a game. Ty scores 262 points. How many more points does Sally score than Ty?

○ 121   ○ 643   ○ 129   ○ 119

---

10. Use the numbers on the tiles to solve the problem.

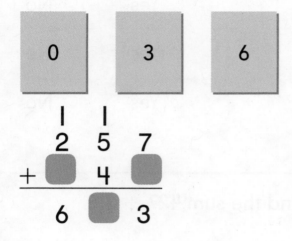

Describe how you solved the problem.

_____

_____

_____

_____

Picture Glossary

addend sumando

$$5 + 8 = 13$$
addends

a.m. a.m.

Times after midnight and before noon are written with **a.m.**

11:00 a.m. is in the morning.

angle ángulo

bar graph gráfica de barras

cent sign símbolo de centavo

53¢
cent sign

centimeter centímetro

column columna

column

$$
\begin{array}{r}
3\,|3\\
3\,|4\\
+3\,|2\\
\hline
\end{array}
$$

compare comparar

Use these symbols when you **compare**: $>$, $<$, $=$.

$$241 > 234$$

$$123 < 128$$

$$247 = 247$$

compare comparar

Compare the lengths of the pencil and the crayon.

The pencil is longer than the crayon.

The crayon is shorter than the pencil.

cone cono

cube cubo

cylinder cilindro

data datos

Favorite Lunch	
Lunch	Tally
pizza	IIII
sandwich	⊬⊬⊬ I
salad	III
pasta	⊬⊬⊬

The information in this chart is called **data**.

decimal point punto decimal

$1.00
↑
decimal point

---

difference diferencia

9 − 2 = 7
↑
difference

---

digit dígito

0, 1, 2, 3, 4, 5, 6, 7, 8, and 9 are **digits**.

---

dime moneda de 10¢

A **dime** has a value of 10 cents.

dollar dólar

One **dollar** is worth 100 cents.

---

dollar sign símbolo de dólar

$1.00
↑
dollar sign

---

doubles dobles

2   +   2   =   4

---

edge arista

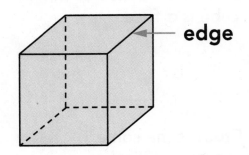

edge

An **edge** is formed where two faces of a three-dimensional shape meet.

estimate estimación

An **estimate** is an amount that tells about how many.

even par

2, 4, 6, 8, 10, . . .

even numbers

face cara

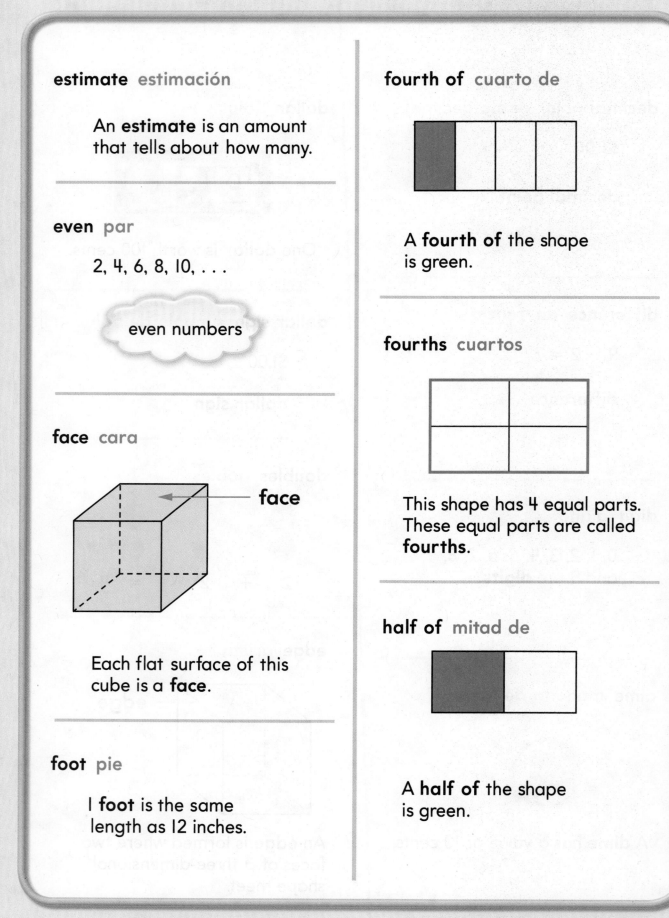

face

Each flat surface of this cube is a **face**.

foot pie

I **foot** is the same length as 12 inches.

fourth of cuarto de

A **fourth of** the shape is green.

fourths cuartos

This shape has 4 equal parts. These equal parts are called **fourths**.

half of mitad de

A **half of** the shape is green.

halves mitades

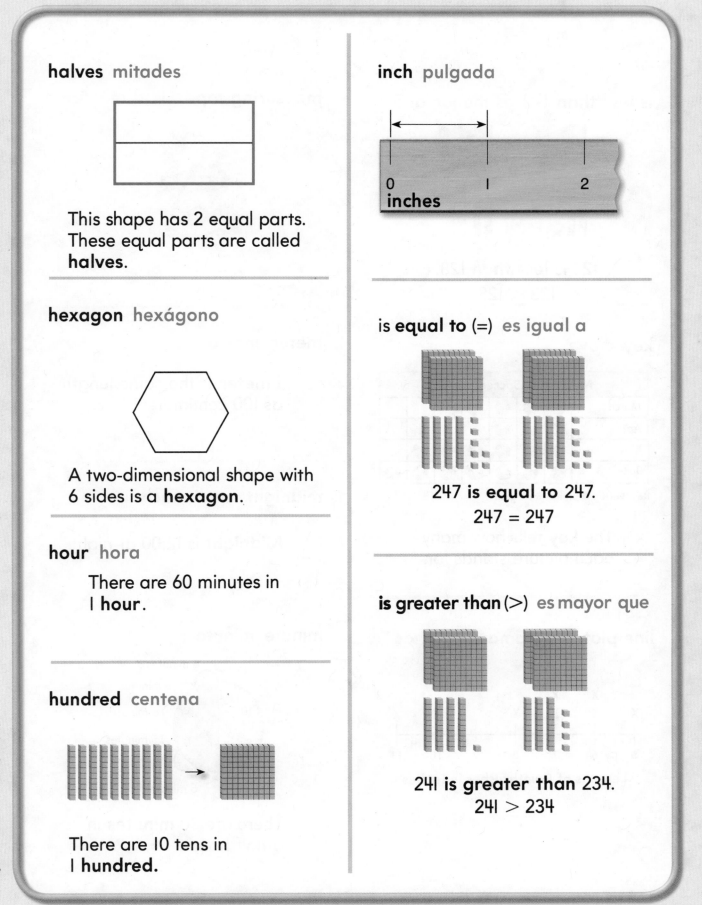

This shape has 2 equal parts.
These equal parts are called
halves.

hexagon hexágono

A two-dimensional shape with
6 sides is a **hexagon**.

hour hora

There are 60 minutes in
1 **hour**.

hundred centena

There are 10 tens in
1 **hundred**.

inch pulgada

0 1 2
inches

is equal to (=) es igual a

247 **is equal to** 247.
247 = 247

is greater than (>) es mayor que

241 **is greater than** 234.
241 > 234

is less than (<) es menor que

123 **is less than** 128.
123 < 128

---

key clave

Number of Soccer Games							
March	⚽	⚽	⚽	⚽			
April	⚽	⚽	⚽				
May	⚽	⚽	⚽	⚽	⚽	⚽	
June	⚽	⚽	⚽	⚽	⚽	⚽	⚽

Key: Each ⚽ stands for 1 game.

The **key** tells how many each picture stands for.

---

line plot diagrama de puntos

Lengths of Paintbrushes in Inches

---

measuring tape cinta métrica

---

meter metro

1 **meter** is the same length as 100 centimeters.

---

midnight medianoche

Midnight is 12:00 at night.

---

minute minuto

There are 30 **minutes** in a half hour.

H6

nickel moneda de 5¢

A **nickel** has a value of 5 cents.

---

noon mediodía

Noon is 12:00 in the daytime.

---

odd impar

1, 3, 5, 7, 9, 11, . . .

odd numbers

---

ones unidades

10 ones = 1 ten

penny moneda de 1¢

A **penny** has a value of 1 cent.

---

pentagon pentágono

A two-dimensional shape with 5 sides is a **pentagon**.

---

picture graph gráfica con dibujos

Number of Soccer Games						
March	⚽	⚽	⚽	⚽		
April	⚽	⚽	⚽			
May	⚽	⚽	⚽	⚽	⚽	
June	⚽	⚽	⚽	⚽	⚽	⚽	⚽

Key: Each ⚽ stands for 1 game.

plus (+) más

2	plus	1	is equal to	3
2	+	1	=	3

p.m. p.m.

Times after noon and before midnight are written with **p.m.**

11:00 p.m. is in the evening.

quadrilateral cuadrilátero

A two-dimensional shape with 4 sides is a **quadrilateral.**

quarter moneda de 25¢

A **quarter** has a value of 25 cents.

quarter of cuarta parte de

A **quarter of** the shape is green.

quarter past y cuarto

8:15

15 minutes after 8
quarter past 8

rectangular prism prisma rectangular

regroup reagrupar

You can trade 10 ones for
1 ten to **regroup**.

side lado

side

This shape has 4 **sides**.

sphere esfera

sum suma o total

$$9 + 6 = 15$$

sum

survey encuesta

Favorite Lunch	
Lunch	Tally
pizza	IIII
sandwich	Ⱨ‖ I
salad	III
pasta	Ⱨ‖

A **survey** is a collection
of data from answers to
a question.

ten decena

10 ones = 1 ten

third of tercio de

A **third of** the shape
is green.

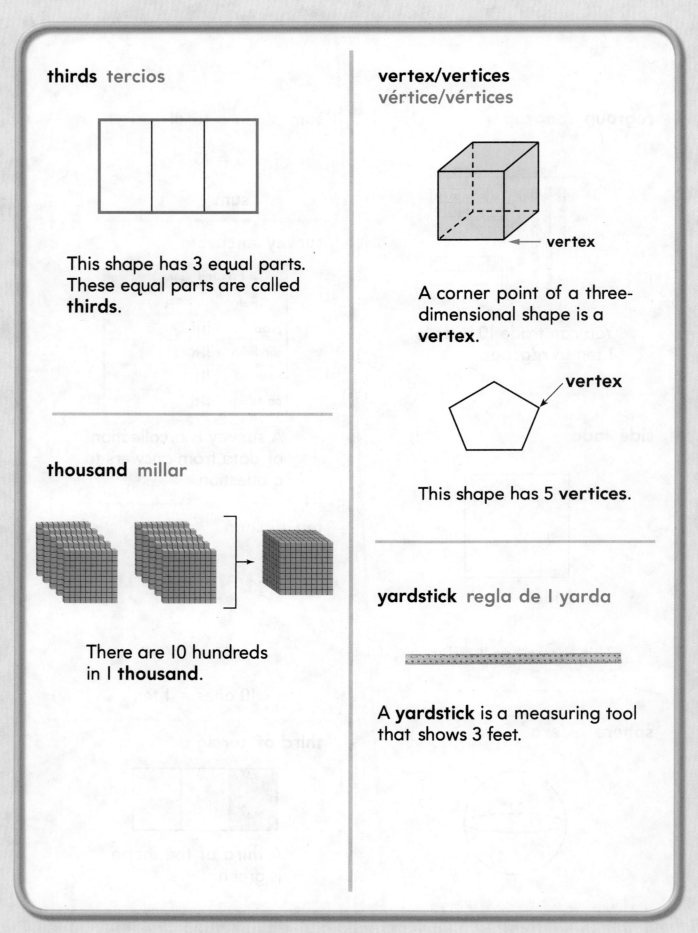

thirds tercios

This shape has 3 equal parts. These equal parts are called **thirds**.

thousand millar

There are 10 hundreds in 1 **thousand**.

vertex/vertices vértice/vértices

← **vertex**

A corner point of a three-dimensional shape is a **vertex**.

vertex →

This shape has 5 **vertices**.

yardstick regla de 1 yarda

A **yardstick** is a measuring tool that shows 3 feet.

Index

A

Act It Out strategy, 217–220, 503–506

Activities

Games. See Games

Hands On Activities: 13, 19, 31, 43, 87,
237, 255, 329, 335, 403, 409, 427,
467, 473, 479, 485, 541, 547, 553,
571, 583, 589, 603, 609, 615, 627,
639, 653, 665, 671, 723, 729, 735,
741, 747

Take Home Activity, 16, 22, 28, 34, 39,
46, 52, 58, 64, 78, 84, 90, 96, 102,
108, 113, 120, 126, 132, 138, 144,
166, 172, 178, 184, 190, 195, 202,
208, 214, 220, 226, 240, 246, 252,
258, 264, 270, 275, 282, 288, 294,
300, 306, 320, 326, 332, 338, 344,
349, 356, 362, 368, 374, 380, 394,
400, 406, 412, 417, 424, 430, 436,
442, 448, 470, 476, 482, 488, 493,
500, 506, 512, 518, 524, 530, 544,
550, 556, 562, 567, 574, 592, 606,
612, 618, 630, 636, 642, 656, 662,
667, 674, 680, 686, 708, 714, 720,
726, 732, 738, 743, 750, 756, 762,
768

Addends

adding 3 one-digit, 181–184

adding 3 two-digit, 297–300

adding 4 two-digit, 303–306

breaking apart to add, 176–177,
237–240, 249–252, 397–400

defined, 170

missing, See Addends, unknown

order of, 169–172, 181–184, 297–300,
303–306

unknown, 183, 194, 212–214, 232,
285–287, 292–293, 300, 305, 309,
371–373, 622–623, 648

Addition

adding three 1-digit addends,
181–184

basic facts, 163–166, 169–172,
175–178, 181–184, 187–190,
211–214

basic fact strategies

doubles and near doubles facts,
163–166

make a ten, 175–178, 182–184

use related facts, 187–190

breaking apart addends to add,
176–177, 237–240, 249–252,
397–400

of equal groups, 217–220, 223–226

regrouping in, 255–258,
261–264, 267–270, 273–275,
280–282, 297–300, 303–306,
403–406, 409–412, 415–417

relate to subtraction, 187–190,
359–362

represented with bar models,
187–188, 205–208, 285–288,
377–380

three-digit numbers, 391–394,
397–400, 403–406, 409–412,
415–417

breaking apart to add, 397–400

regrouping, 403–406, 409–412,
415–417

to find differences, 187–189, 359–362

two-digit numbers, 237–240, 243–246,
249–252, 255–258, 261–264,
267–270, 273–275, 279–282,
285–288, 291–294, 297–300,
303–306

breaking apart addends to add,
237–240, 249–252

finding sums of 3 two-digit
numbers, 297–300

finding sums of 4 two-digit
numbers, 303–306

using compensation, 243–246

using models and quick pictures,
237–238, 243, 255–258, 261–264,
267, 329, 335–338, 341, 391–394,
397, 403, 409, 419, 421, 427

write equations to represent problems, 205–208, 211–214, 285–288, 291–294

Algorithms
    alternative, 237–240, 243–246, 249–252, 317–320, 323–326, 397–400
    standard, 261–264, 267–270, 273–275, 279–282, 335–338, 341–344, 347–349, 353–356, 403–406, 409–412, 415–417, 421–424, 427–430, 433–436

a.m., 527–530

Analog clocks, 509–512, 515–518, 521–524, 527–530

Analyze, 319, 326, 338, 448, 470, 719

Angles
    defined, 730
    in two-dimensional shapes, 729–732, 735–738

Apply, 586, 655

Assessment
    Show What You Know, 10, 72, 160, 234, 314, 388, 464, 538, 600, 650, 702
    Mid-Chapter Checkpoint, 40, 114, 196, 276, 350, 418, 494, 568, 624, 668, 744
    Chapter Review/Test, 67–70, 147–150, 229–232, 309–312, 383–386, 451–454, 533–536, 595–598, 645–648, 689–692, 771–774

Attend to Precision, 411

B

Bar graphs,
    defined, 672
    making, 677–680, 683–686
    reading, 671–674
    using to solve problems, 671–674, 677–680, 683–686

Bar models
    addition problems, 187–188, 205–208, 285–288, 291, 377–380
    multistep problems, 377–380

subtraction problems, 205–208, 365–368, 377–380

Basic Facts, 163–166, 169–172, 175–178, 181–184, 187–190, 193–195, 199–202, 205–208, 211–214

Break Apart strategy
    addition, 176–177, 237–240, 249–252, 397–400
    subtraction, 317–320, 323–326

C

Centimeters, 603–606, 609–612, 615–618, 621–624, 627–630

Cent sign, 468–470, 473–476, 479–482, 485–488, 491, 497

Chapter Review/Test, 67–70, 147–150, 229–232, 309–312, 383–386, 451–454, 533–536, 595–598, 645–648, 689–692, 771–774

Circles, 705, 711

Clocks, 509–512, 515–518, 521–524, 527–530

Coins
    cent sign, 468–470, 473–476, 479–482, 485–488, 491, 497
    counting collections, 467–470, 479–482, 485–488
    dimes, 467–470, 473–476, 479–482, 485–488, 491–493, 497–498, 503–506
    nickels, 467–470, 473–476, 479–482, 485–488, 491–493, 497–500, 503–506
    pennies, 467–470, 473–476, 479–482, 485–488, 491–493, 497–500, 503–506
    quarters, 473–476, 479–482, 485–488, 492–493, 497–500

Communicate math ideas. See Math Talk

Compare
    defined, 142
    numbers, 135–138, 141–144
    numbers using symbols 141–144

F

Faces
  defined, 712
  of three-dimensional shapes, 711–714

Facts. See Basic Facts

Family Involvement
  Take Home Activity, 16, 22, 28, 34, 39,
    46, 52, 58, 64, 78, 84, 90, 96, 102,
    108, 113, 120, 126, 132, 138, 144,
    166, 172, 178, 184, 190, 195, 202,
    208, 214, 220, 226, 240, 246, 252,
    258, 264, 270, 275, 282, 288, 294,
    300, 306, 320, 326, 332, 338, 344,
    349, 356, 362, 368, 374, 380, 394,
    400, 406, 412, 417, 304, 424, 430,
    436, 442, 448, 328, 470, 476, 482,
    488, 493, 500, 506, 512, 518, 524,
    530, 392, 544, 550, 556, 562, 574,
    580, 586, 592, 606, 612, 618, 630,
    636, 642, 656, 662, 667, 674, 680,
    686, 708, 714, 720, 726, 732, 738,
    743, 750, 756, 762, 768

Feet, 571–574, 577–580

Find a Pattern strategy, 49–52

Fluency
  addition and subtraction within 20,
    163–166, 169–172, 175–178,
    181–184, 187–190, 193–195,
    199–202, 205–208, 211–214
  addition and subtraction within 100,
    237–240, 243–246, 249–252,
    255–258, 261–264, 267–270,
    273–275, 279–282, 297–300,
    303–306, 317–320, 323–326,
    329–332, 335–338, 341–344,
    347–349, 353–356, 359–362

For the Teacher
  In most Student Edition lessons. Some
    examples are: 13, 37, 359, 409,
    633, 705

Fourths, 747–750, 753–756, 759–762,
  765–768

Fractions, foundation for,
  equal parts of a whole, 747–750,
    753–756, 759–762, 765–768

G

Games
  5 and 10 Count, 466
  Caterpillar Chase, 162
  Count the Sides, 704
  2-Digit Shuffle, 390
  Estimating Length, 602
  Fish for Digits, 74
  Longer or Shorter?, 540
  Making Tens, 652
  Subtraction Search, 316
  Three in a Row, 12
  What is the Sum?, 236

Glossary, H1–H10

Go Deeper, 46, 96, 101, 126, 132, 166,
  172, 178, 202, 207, 214, 226, 240, 270,
  288, 306, 325, 331, 349, 356, 368, 373,
  380, 400, 412, 442, 482, 500, 530, 629,
  655, 662, 667, 673, 680, 686, 713, 714,
  720, 725, 756, 768

Graphic Organizers, 11, 73, 161, 235,
  315, 389, 465, 539, 601, 651, 703

Graphs and charts
  bar graphs
    defined, 672
    making, 677–680, 683–686
    reading, 671–674
    using to solve problems, 671–674,
      677–680, 683–686
  line plots, 589–592
  picture graphs
    defined, 660
    making, 665–667
    reading, 659–662
    using to solve problems, 659–662,
      665–667, 671
  tally charts, 653–656, 659, 666–667

H

Halves, 747–750, 753–756, 759–762,
  765–768

Hands On activities. See Activities